To Mike
Best Wishes
Pete

About the Author

Born in Castle Cary, Somerset, Pete Strickland joined the Royal Navy aged fifteen at the boys' training establishment, HMS *Ganges*. Most of his service life was spent in the Far East, the Mediterranean and fishery protection in the Arctic during the "Cod War" with Iceland. After twelve years' service he settled in Bristol where he worked as a timber salesman. He soon became bored with civilian life, and his feet were itching to move on again, so he jumped at the chance to get away from the mundane 9-5 routine and answer Sweaty Betty's call.

After nearly three years away he returned to Bristol, working in the amusement machine business. He has a son, a daughter and four grandchildren.

He was a member of the HSF (Home Service Force) and the RNXS (Royal Naval Auxiliary Service). At present he is a bosun on the Pride of Bristol (an ex-Royal Navy Fleet Tender) which is a charity for taking out youngsters training for and experiencing life at sea. He is also a member of the MVS (Maritime Volunteer Service).

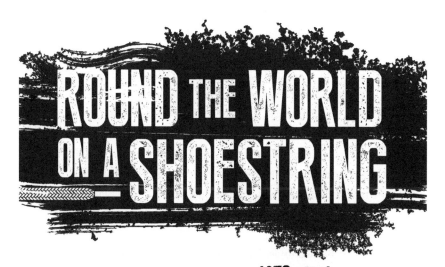

A journey made in the 1970s that
would be impossible today

Pete Strickland

BROWN
DOG
BOOKS

Published under licence by Brown Dog Books and
The Self-Publishing Partnership, 7 Green Park Station, Bath BA1 1JB

www.selfpublishingpartnership.co.uk

ISBN printed book: 978-1-78545-164-5
ISBN e-book: 978-1-78545-165-2

Cover design by Kevin Rylands
Internal design by Tim Jollands

Front cover photo: Main road through Syria

Printed and bound by CPI Group (UK) Ltd, Croydon CR0 4YY

To
Daniel and Victoria
who never thought I'd get into print.
And to my gorgeous granddaughters, Darcy,
Piper and India, and grandson Finn.

Contents

Preface

This is a true story of a journey made in the 1970s that would be very difficult if not practically impossible to attempt in today's political climate. A time not so long ago when the world was a totally different place. The 60s were over, the summers of 'free love' and 'grass' were just a distant memory, flower power had withered to the stem, music was changing and inflation setting in. For the 'hippies' alternative waypoints were beckoning, Afghanistan, India, Thailand and Australia were all places where you could live the chilled-out lifestyle, but there were no budget airlines so you had to travel overland on a shoestring.

The story takes you around the world and recounts the adventures and escapades of four naïve young men who travelled in a dilapidated vehicle over land and sea on a shoestring budget. Travelling across Europe in the middle of winter and on through the Middle East, Far East and thence on to Australia, working in the outback before returning to the UK via New Zealand, Fiji, Mexico and America.

Imagine setting off on a journey to Australia in a 21-year-old Series 1 short wheelbase Land Rover (Sweaty Betty) rescued from a pig farm in Somerset. A journey in an era before mobile phones, social media, sat nav, internet or credit cards, and with minimal insurance or breakdown cover and having virtually no way of having any contact with home. Although we carried knives, more as a comfort blanket than as an offensive weapon, they did come in useful for obtaining turnips and other vegetables from fields close to the road. Nowadays you couldn't get past a supermarket checkout with a knife, let alone over 50 customs and border posts, sea- and airports, plus numerous police and Army checkpoints. The only other items we were armed with were *Daily Telegraph* maps of Europe, the Middle East and the Far East, plus a *Daily Express* world map.

Mix into the melting pot four individuals of diverse backgrounds and you have a recipe for an epic adventure. Living rough through Europe and in such diverse places as Aleppo, Raqqa, Baghdad, Tehran, Helmand Province, Kandahar, Kabul, Peshawar and Sri Lanka, and hitch-hiking through Malaysia, and being met with nothing but friendship and warm-hearted hospitality.

Introduction

Sweaty Betty was bored with retirement. She had been a loyal workhorse helping out on a pig farm in deepest Somerset during her 21 years since she had rolled off the Land Rover production line at Solihull. She had been trustworthy and reliable, but her bones were creaking somewhat and her bodywork had many wrinkles; she was showing her age. Her canvas roof was fading and her green paint was showing signs of flaking. Alas, her seats were worn and no longer comfortable, she was draughty and had no heater, her gaiters had perished and her hood leaked; not only that, her windscreen wipers were sluggish and her handling hard and acceleration slow, and there were many other parts of her that no longer functioned. Regardless of all that, her 1600cc heart was strong and even at her age she was still up for an adventure, although in her retirement she was probably thinking more of a leisurely jaunt towing a caravan around Devon and Cornwall: since her owners had bought a younger version to replace the Series 1 Land Rover, she had been relegated to the ignominy of a far corner of an old barn, with only a pile of straw bales to keep her company.

One day the sun hit her as the barn door opened and she heard her owner talking to a stranger. "Will she take me across Europe and beyond?" she heard the young man say. "Of course, she has never let me down," was her owner's reply. "I'll take her," the stranger replied, and she saw £160 change hands. Sweaty Betty would have blown a gasket if she only knew what lay ahead of her.

The young man sat on her worn, dusty seat, twiddled with her knobs and played with her levers in his keenness to get acquainted with her. Regardless, she fired up first time and left the safety of the barn. Soon she was heading for the city of Bristol where she was taken to a garage and stripped of her green paint and painted bright blue. A roof rack was welded to her and her canvas hood was repaired;

a new clutch was fitted and her old agricultural oils were replaced with high-grade lubricants and modern additives. She felt reborn: her excitement mounted as she felt an adventure coming on.

If she could have spoken she would have asked the young men who were working on her, "Where am I taking you?" The answer would have been, "You are taking us through the snow-capped mountains of Europe to Turkey, Syria, Iraq, Iran, Afghanistan and beyond." Are you ready for an adventure? Then (if she had had any) fasten your seat belts. This is the young man's and Sweaty Betty's story.

CHAPTER 1

Preparation

July 1971

Very rarely did I read the small ads in the local paper. Perhaps fate steered my eyes through the columns to that insignificant couple of lines sandwiched between frustrated spinsters' pleas for a partner and an Alcoholics Anonymous contribution: "Persons interested in an overland trip to Australia contact…"

I'd recently completed twelve years in the Royal Navy, and still with a lust for travel this ad aroused my curiosity, having recently had a double-decker bus adventure through Europe aborted and only a short safari to Morocco to whet my appetite since leaving the forces. Little did I realise that the letter I wrote to Dennis Young in reply to his advert would be the start of an adventure that would take me around the world.

The awaited reply came, along with an invitation to meet Dennis in his local at Frome. The meeting in the congenial atmosphere of his local soon put aside any misgivings I might have had. It was not long before we had taken over the lounge bar, with maps and screeds of literature that Dennis had already gleaned from the various motoring organisations, embassies and travel agents. What Dennis lacked in stature he certainly made up for in enthusiasm. I agreed to accompany him there and then: I believed we were already in Australia before we had even left the pub.

Our immediate task was to get together a well-balanced team. Dennis had been in touch with Tim Evans, an engineer from Dursley in Gloucestershire. Tim had already gathered much information, having been involved in a previous venture that failed to get off the ground.

My next appointment was to meet Tim. Along with Dennis, we rendezvoused at the Cross Hands Hotel at Old Sodbury, South Gloucestershire. This was to be our weekly meeting place right up to our departure.

Tim, who towered above Dennis and me, soon made his presence felt in his flamboyant way. He was to be our mechanic, and a first-class one he turned out to be.

Our main task now was to complete the team, and obtain a suitable vehicle. Among people keen to come were two Bristol nurses who were eventually discouraged by the possible expense of the venture, and another interested person to reply to the ad was a sixty-year-old widow. Keen as she was, we had to kindly inform her that the rigours of such a trip would probably prove too much for her. We finally got our fourth and final member of the team, Dick Williams, son of a garage owner in Bristol. Dick was intent on seeing as much of the world as possible before business commitments would forestall any future possibilities.

By now, Dennis had managed to obtain a vehicle, a twenty-one-year-old short wheelbase Series 1 Land Rover, complete with canvas hood. Even though we were somewhat perturbed by the age of the vehicle, we were soon assured that she was as good as new. Well, as new as a twenty-one-year-old Land Rover can possibly be.

It was now time to really get down to some planning. A provisional date of November the first was agreed. Pending no unforeseen hitches, this date should enable us to be out of Europe before winter really set in. Consideration also had to be given to avoid being in India during the monsoon season. Planning an expedition can be exciting and rewarding in itself, but it can also be a very frustrating and worrying time with many setbacks. One of our first disappointments was our inability to obtain permission to travel through Burma. Our alternative was to travel by sea from India to Penang. With regard to planning a route, although we had worked out a rough itinerary, we decided to leave a reasonable amount of flexibility to our plans. We did, however, arrange rough dates to arrive at major cities, thus allowing the forwarding of any mail or messages.

Attempts were made at the possibility of sponsorship. Letters were sent to various companies, tyre firms etc. Although we didn't succeed in getting any firm offers, we did at least receive many well-wishes. It appeared that we were just another one of "those overlanders" out to try and get something for nothing. We did, however, through Dick's garage contacts, manage to obtain a good supply of fuel and engine additives and also many other useful items such as instant snow chain, waterproofing etc. An ample supply of oil was also forthcoming. In return for these items we prominently displayed the company logos on the Land Rover.

A series of visits to the local health clinic for the certificates of vaccination against smallpox, Yellow fever, typhus and cholera left us feeling like walking germs. Still, better safe than sorry. Apart from the precautionary side, these certificates are necessary for entry into certain countries.

With barely a month to go before our intended departure, we came up against an unexpected obstacle which looked like foiling our plans.

Prior to one of our weekly meetings at the Cross Hands Hotel, I phoned Dennis, only to be told: "Sorry, the trip will have to be called off, Peter! Have just been informed by the AA that we have to put up a surety of over £2,000 for the issue of a Carnet, and we cannot possibly get that amount together in time." True, it did seem a large amount to have available, especially on top of all the other expenses that we were incurring.

Disappointed, but nevertheless undeterred, I drove on up to the Cross Hands to meet Dick and Tim. They had already heard the news, but I was delighted to find that they were not as pessimistic as Dennis. They were still intent on going, come what may, Carnet or no Carnet.

Calculating how much we could each afford, we found we were still about £1,000 short. After much chasing around we eventually came to an arrangement with an insurance company who, at a price, agreed to put up the remainder of the money for us.

The Carnet de Passages is the document required to take a vehicle into and out of certain countries, mainly Middle and Far Eastern countries. Briefly, it is a guarantee that once a vehicle is taken into a country it will in fact be taken out, and not sold or disposed of without having paid the import duty on it. Failure to take the vehicle out of the country, unless of course you have paid the duty, would mean the forfeiture of the surety on the Carnet to the country where the vehicle was disposed of.

We discovered later that we could have got a similar document from a German motoring organisation for a fraction of the cost involved in England. Ah well, as the saying goes, "He who learns after the event is at least a little wiser".

With less than three weeks to go before our intended departure date, we received a further serious setback, this time in the form of a note from Dennis, stating that due to unforeseen circumstances, he would be unable to accompany us on the trip.

This was a great disappointment to us: not only had Dennis been one of the originators, but had put in much time and work in getting the venture off the ground. Apart from that, where were we going to get a replacement necessary to share the burden of costs at such short notice? The course of inoculations alone takes over six weeks.

As luck would have it, I knew of someone who was extremely interested when I first spoke of the trip a few months ago. He had in fact recently returned from a holiday in America, so was already up to date with his inoculations and passport. When I approached him he had no hesitation in agreeing to make up the fourth member of our party. So enter Ron Harvey, a Bristol bus driver with an enthusiasm for politics, having already entered the local political scene. I had known Ron for some time, as he was living in the flat above me, so it was not as if we were taking on a complete stranger. To give Ron a chance to prepare himself, we decided to delay our departure date by one week to November 7th.

As if the previous setback was not enough, along came another, this time in the form of the clutch going in the Land Rover. We were lucky in having all the facilities of Dick's garage at our disposal. Along with Tim's expert mechanical knowledge, a new clutch was assembled in record time.

Whilst at the garage, the Land Rover was given a thorough overhaul and service. Later performances of the vehicle reflected well on all those who worked on her. Much work was done on the bodywork, spare petrol and water can racks, and spare tyre racks were welded on. Tim did an excellent job of fixing a very sturdy roof rack above the canvas roof. The majority of the rear space of the Land Rover was taken up by a wooden lockable compartment in which we were to store most of our food and personal gear. Being a short wheelbase vehicle, we were left with little room for any extras. Apart from the bare essentials, all personal gear was kept to a minimum. We did manage to find enough room to squeeze a fairly comfortable seat in the rear. The whole of the inside of the Land Rover was covered with underfelt to minimise noise.

With only two weeks to go before our intended departure date, the escalation of preparations necessitated me finishing work as a timber salesman. A very hectic couple of days were spent in London visiting the various embassies obtaining our visas. Due to Dennis's withdrawal we had to get the ownership of the vehicle changed over to Tim.

Just before our departure we had a few anxious days whilst we waited on the return of our vehicle insurance cover, which had to be sent away to have the necessary names changed. Luckily it arrived back the day prior to our departure. Apart from the vehicle's insurance, we all arranged to have our own personal insurance cover.

Preparations were now almost complete. All that was left, more or less, was just our own personal needs, such as travellers' cheques, International Driving Licences etc. Over £30 worth of canned food was purchased at the Cash and Carry. Also a good assortment of spares for the Land Rover were acquired. It certainly looked as if it was going to be a problem finding storage space for it all. Somehow we managed.

Final checks on the vehicle were made and we also put in a few practice sessions on erecting the tent. The last few days prior to departure were spent in packing our personal gear and tying up loose ends. Also the round of farewells to relatives and friends. We had, of course, the inevitable farewell parties, and the resultant thick heads. I well remember one particular party I had in my 'local'. To this day I still swear that I was walking on the ceiling (needless to say, that is the last I remember). I must have thought I was already down under. Early the following morning, a guy came to buy my car, I threw the keys at him, and that was the last I saw of my dear old Mini. Sunday November 7th, 'D' Day.

It seemed very much an anticlimax, that after five months of planning, along with the upsets and doubts that the trip would ever materialise, we were actually going that day. I felt very much how a bridegroom must feel on the morning of his wedding, not really knowing what the coming night has in store for him.

We intended leaving on the late-night ferry from Southampton, so there was no early morning rush. Apart from the final packing, much of the day was spent in having a last look around.

As I was at my home near Castle Cary, I was to be the last to be picked up. Tim did the final gear stowing of the Land Rover at Dursley then proceeded down to Bristol to collect Dick and Ron. Whilst at Bristol the opportunity was taken to fill up the vehicle and spare cans with petrol, with the compliments of Williams Automobiles. They eventually arrived at Castle Cary in the late afternoon just in time for tea. After loading on my gear we began to wonder just where we were going to put ourselves. Apart from the seats there was not an inch of space left. It was practically impossible to see out of the rear window. What with a full roof rack, the tent strung on the front bumper, and full spare petrol cans plus the spare tyres, we were well and truly overloaded.

Our final farewells made and a send-off from the whole street, we were at long last on our way. It was 7 pm.

True to English form, it was a miserable night: cold, wet and windy. Most of the journey down to Southampton was in comparative silence: we all appeared to be lost in our own private thoughts.

Owing to overloading, the handling of the vehicle on the journey to Southampton was well below par. It soon became apparent that one of our priorities was to repack the vehicle at the first opportunity.

In pouring rain we arrived at Southampton just after 8.30 pm. After a check on ferry times at the docks, we went to the nearest dockyard pub for our last pint of beer on English soil.

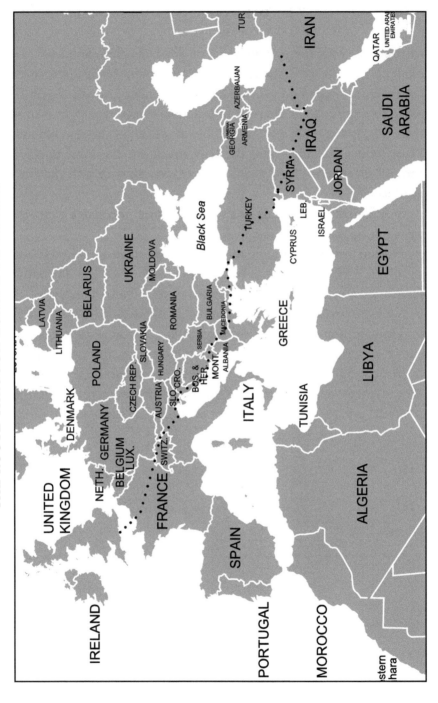

CHAPTER 2

Into France and Europe

Proceeding back to the docks, we purchased our tickets and waited for our call to embark the ferry.

At 9.30 pm we drove onto the *Viking*. On completion of having the Land Rover chained to the deck, we made our way to the saloon, which was to be our first 'bed' of the trip. The splashes as the hawsers were thrown off the jetty bollards and the hoots of the ship's siren heralded the start of our long-awaited venture. Leaning over the ship's rails I watched the lights of Southampton diminishing. Passing the flaming stacks of the Fawley oil refinery we steamed slowly down the Solent. With only the soothing rush of water to disturb my thoughts I was wondering just how long it would be before I saw the shores of England again. Somewhat bemused by the magnitude of what I had let myself in for, I slowly retired to the practically deserted saloon for a rather restless sleep.

Dawn was breaking as I awoke from my intermittent night's 'kip'. Looking out of the *Viking*'s window, I could see the French coastline ahead. The boat stirred into life as the few passengers lethargically began gathering their luggage and refreshing themselves into activity. It was 6 am as we slid silently towards the ferry terminus at Le Havre. We made our way down to the holds to await the lowering of the ramps. At long last we drove unceremoniously onto foreign soil.

On completion of a brief police check we drove on through Le Havre, which was witnessing the start of another Monday morning 'rat race'. A feeling of self-satisfaction that at least that was one part of the 'humdrum' daily life that I was leaving behind for the time being.

Leaving the rather uninteresting seaport of Le Havre, we headed out through the French countryside towards Paris. We were now having to get used to driving on the 'wrong' side of the road, though it was soon to become second nature to us. As we were all qualified drivers, we were to take it in turns on the wheel, usually 2-3-hour stretches depending on road conditions.

Apart from a few insignificant villages, the road to Paris is mainly through forest land. It was late autumn, the rusty leaves were falling as if tired of hanging on all summer. Bypassing Rouen, we made good progress along the excellent French motorway, though the overloading was having an adverse effect on the Land Rover's handling.

Arriving at Paris we soon discovered just why the French capital has earned itself the reputation as a motorists' nightmare. Our first objective was to find ourselves a campsite. This we did with comparative ease, an ideal site on the banks of the Seine. Being off season, the site was fairly empty, allowing us plenty of room to spread out.

Having erected the tent we repacked the Land Rover. Any item that we could possibly do without was discarded. Ron, after some good-natured prompting, agreed to get rid of some of his 'overstock'. He left the campsite with a large bundle of clothing, intending to give them away. He returned a couple of hours later having discarded his surplus gear in a dustbin. I don't think he could find anyone big enough to fit his clothes. Although we ribbed Ron about his outsize wellington boots, there were going to be times later when we all could have done with a pair.

We had decided to name the Land Rover "Sweaty Betty". I was commissioned to sign write the name, along with other motifs, on the side of the vehicle.

With regard to finance, we budgeted ourselves to a limit of £1.50 per day. This was to cover food, fuel, camping and any other expenses that occurred.

Our meal that day of tinned beans and hot dogs gave a taste of things to come. Dick had been assigned the job of chef. His skill at opening cans was soon to become legendary. The remainder of our first day in Paris was spent in sorting ourselves out and generally acclimatising ourselves to the nomadic life. In the evening I took a stroll along the bank of the Seine, which looked very impressive with a backcloth of Paris lights.

It was extremely cold as I made my way back to the campsite, not relishing the thought of sleeping on the frost-covered ground in a sleeping bag. Whether it was fatigue from the rush of the last few days or the lullaby of Ron's snoring, but I had a surprisingly comfortable first night under the stars.

Whilst in Paris we took the opportunity to see the sights. Tim was really in his element, charging through the Paris traffic. We were only too pleased to leave the city driving to him. Approaching the Notre-Dame we were puzzled as to why we should be honoured with a police escort. We discovered that we were in the wake of President Pompidou's cortège on their way to the cathedral for an armistice service.

On completion of our couple of days reorganising and restowing the Land Rover, we proceeded eastwards through flat and mundane countryside to Troyes.

Whilst driving through France we took advantage of the exceedingly good and cheap wines. Our meal usually consisted of an outsize French roll washed down with a bottle of wine.

After Troyes the terrain became noticeably hillier and fairly well forested.

It was dusk as we arrived at Chaumont. Unable to find a campsite there, we moved on about six miles before finding a forest clearing about a hundred yards off the track. It was a really desolate spot with no sign of habitation. We soon had a roaring log fire going, by the light of which we managed to pitch the tent. Tim, Dick and I, leaving Ron guarding the tent, went to the nearest village (Villiers) which was about three miles away. We came across what looked like

Thumbs up from Dick prior to loading Sweaty Betty.

Being held up by President Pompidou and police escort at the Notre Dame Cathedral.

Swiss village in Alps.

a bar. Whether it was a bar or someone's house I don't know, but we managed to get a glass of brandy, along with some strange looks.

Leaving the stillness of the forest at dawn, we continued in pouring rain, passing the very imposing walled city of Langres. Stopping to do some shopping at Belfort, we were greeted with a procession of brass bands (our fame was spreading).

We were now getting into more scenic country, much more mountainous with twisting roads leading up to the Swiss border. The border into Switzerland was crossed at Basle which is the crossroads of France, Switzerland and Germany.

The excellent Swiss motorway to Zurich starts at Basle, which enabled us to make good progress. Although the advantages of a good motorway system greatly outweigh the disadvantages, there is a tendency to pass through a country too quickly. There is also the difficulty in side-tracking off the motorway once on it, thus missing many of the sights. Even taking into account the speed we were now travelling at, we did see some spectacular scenery. The motorway is interrupted by numerous tunnels, on the emergence of which we beheld a kaleidoscope of ever-changing scenery. We were now in mountainous country and it was not long before we saw our first snow of the trip.

Still about sixty miles from Zurich as dusk approached, we took the first opportunity we could to get off the motorway. Near to the small town of Muhen we branched off along a small mountain road which wound its way steeply towards a pine forest. In a small clearing we set up camp for the night. Having cleansed ourselves from a nearby mountain stream we set off to sample Muhen's nightlife.

Leaving Muhen we rejoined the Zurich motorway. A novel idea on the Swiss motorways is the areas set aside for exercise along with a varied assortment of equipment such as stretch bars, barbells etc.

Arriving at Zurich we found time to have a good look around. Zurich is a very attractive city, bordering a large lake, not very industrialised, banking being its main claim to fame. I was intrigued by the female traffic controllers who appear to control the traffic and numerous trams with gay abandonment.

Once outside Zurich we were soon back amongst the snow-capped mountains. Although we were now off the motorway, the road was still very good, plenty of tunnels and frequent minor mountain passes. A wooden bridge announced our arrival in Liechtenstein, a cute little country with an area of only 62 mountainous square miles and a population of around 20,000, many of whom live in the principality's capital, Vaduz. The country survives on its agriculture, market and cotton industries, plus a useful income from stamps and tourism.

After a short stop to stock up with a few provisions, we proceeded to the Austrian border at Feldkirch, an ancient old world-type of town and the site of the 10th-century Schattenburg Castle. From Feldkirch the road goes through some really great country, including the 5,880-feet Alberg Pass which is just before the ski resort of St. Anton.

Near Langen we found a small forest track leading to the base of a mountain. Well off the road and right alongside a mountain river, completely hidden by fir trees, we made our camp for the night.

We soon had our tent up and a roaring fire going, whilst Dick 'slaved' over the Primus stove cooking our day's meal.

Our location that night really looked like the scene from a Dracula movie, quite eerie. Perhaps it was with that in mind that we all readily agreed to see if we could find some sort of civilisation to pass the evening away.

Driving about five miles we came across a small village. The noise coming from one of the buildings soon told us where the local inn was. Stepping through the doors we were confronted with a three-piece, Bavarian-type band and a room full of drunks. You could have heard a pin drop as we walked cagily through the room towards the bar. After being given the once-over and being certified as quite harmless, the band struck up again and the room was back to its original uproar. Never did find out what all the celebrations were about; nevertheless, we had a very enjoyable evening, most of which was spent in trying to keep out of arguments with the drunken locals.

Leaving the 'friendly' atmosphere of the inn we made our way back to our 'pad' (complete with running water). Keeping the fire going (they say it keeps the wolves at bay!) we settled down for the night. Lying in your sleeping bag in a place like that you could easily let your imagination run amok. Was that wolves howling or Ron snoring?! It was an eerie sensation: in the blackness of the night we could see what looked like a caterpillar of lights about 1,000 feet above us slowly crossing the sky coupled with intermittent screeching. In the morning we discovered that it was a railway winding its way around the mountain.

Not knowing when our next chance would be, we decided to spend the morning in servicing the Land Rover (Tim's perk) and catching up on odd jobs. Chipping away the ice, we even managed to have a stripped wash in the river.

The weather was gradually deteriorating: that morning the snow line had crept down the mountain and was now only a few feet above us.

Odd jobs completed, we left our scenic (or was it satanic?) spot and made our way back onto the main road. The scenery now was really something, just like those winter holiday adverts, deep mountain valleys and high passes. Alpine houses, gaily painted with artistically drawn decorative graffiti depicting local folklore. Beneath the eaves of these houses were piles of neatly stacked logs collected in preparation for the winter. The snow deepened as we ascended towards the Alberg Pass, the most spectacular to date. From the top, the view looking down through the valley is really fantastic.

The snow was now about two feet deep, though continual ploughing kept the road open. Gradually we descended to the skiing resort of Innsbruck, the majority of which was shrouded in a thick mist. As it was the 'off season', we had no difficulty in finding an empty campsite for the night, practically in the centre of the town.

Innsbruck appears to be in two parts, the old and the new. The old is centred around a very large church, and consists of a maze of narrow streets. The city is set in a bowl, surrounded by mountains, famous for their ski slopes. Over 700 years old, Innsbruck is reputed to be the most beautiful city in Austria, competing with Salzburg for the title.

We had now been on the road for a week and getting quite accustomed to the nomadic life, having already put 1,100 miles between us and the UK.

Leaving a mist-enshrouded Innsbruck, we progressed along the '182' which climbs steeply past the ski slopes out of the city, joining the autobahn which brings us to the spectacular Europa Bridge, once the highest bridge in Europe, being 624 feet above the Sill River and 2,500 feet long. The bridge forms part of the Brenner Pass highway through the Austrian Alps.

Considering the amount of snow about, we negotiated the Brenner Pass into Italy with comparative ease. Surrounded by snow and temperatures near freezing we proceeded non-stop across the Dolomites, through the lovely Isarco Valley to Fortezza. From Fortezza the road slowly climbs through the lush valley of the Pusteria River to Dabbiaco where the mountain scenery is amazing.

At the ski resort of Cortina we stopped for a break. Tim was keen to camp here but was outvoted, Dick, Ron and myself preferring to carry on southwards to warmer climes.

The road continues through the Dolomites, gradually descending via a continual series of hairpins to the valley of the Piave River near Perarolo. It was on one of those bends that I nearly got my first Italian motorcyclist.

Once out of the mountains the weather improved considerably. We emerged onto the open plain surrounded by fields of grapevines

Austrian mountains near Innsbruck.

Just before Brenner Pass, Austria, Europa Bridge.

Italian Alps near Brenner Pass.

Italy, Dolomite Mountains outside Cortina, the author taking a rest.

which told us we were now in the wine-growing area of Italy. It's a pity to see the Italian countryside disfigured by frequent unsightly advertising hoardings.

Hunger forced us to stop at the picturesque medieval town of Treviso where we replenished with a pizza.

It was dark by the time we reached the coast town of Cavallino, a holiday resort near Venice. We spent a fruitless hour searching for an open campsite. Eventually we came across one right on the beach, and although closed, we were allowed to stay by the congenial owners. Having just travelled almost non-stop for nearly 300 miles, we were only too pleased to collapse in our sleeping bags.

It was a perfect campsite, right on the beach and with near-perfect weather, a great change from the snow we had just left. Taking advantage of the site and the weather, we spent three very relaxing days there.

A day was spent on exploring Cavallino and the nearby resort of Jesolo, both of which, being in the holiday off season, were virtually ghost towns.

Our sunbathing session on the beach was interrupted by an 'invasion' of Italian military amphibious vehicles which suddenly spewed forth from a flotilla of ships which arrived in the bay. We thought that this was rather an 'overkill' just to kick us off their beach. Nevertheless, after parading past, they noisily went along the beach and returned to their ships.

Being so near, we could not move on without having a good look around Venice.

Making an early start, we caught the ferry from Cavallino, crossing the narrow strait to Venice.

To me, Venice appeared very much as expected, though the canals appear much dirtier than they do on the postcards, but for all that it must still be the finest constellation of beauty in all Europe. The city is built on a lagoon two and a half miles from the mainland and has road connections spread over 118 tiny islands. It has more than 160 canals.

With the whole day to explore, we left few stones unturned in our quest to see as much as possible.

It was a real pleasure to stroll through a city completely void of traffic. The graceful gondolas plying to and fro and the chugging of the numerous barges were a relaxing substitute for the toxic rush of traffic. Venice is well endowed with historical buildings and fine churches, the most beautiful of which being the Cathedral of San Marco with its huge forecourt as popular with the pigeons as with the visitors. Not all of Venice is a masterpiece. There is the prison garrison from which Casanova escaped, a building of truly medieval horribleness. The city explodes into life in the evening, the narrow streets suddenly becoming alive with people and jammed solid with stalls.

Having been accustomed to drinking coffee out of a pint mug, I was somewhat taken aback by the 'famous' Italian coffee, it was like drinking out of an egg cup; mine had almost evaporated before I had time to drink it.

Our three-day rest over, we continued on our way through flat, uninteresting vine-growing countryside towards the heavily industrialised port of Trieste.

Once through Trieste it was only a short hop before we were at the Yugoslav border.

CHAPTER 3

Into Yugoslavia, Greece and Turkey

A complete change of scenery heralded our introduction to Yugoslavia, much more hilly and quite barren. Following the coast road, we passed through the shipbuilding port of Rijeka.

The road south of Rijeka is very poor, badly surfaced and with an abundance of hairpin bends. The road is also littered with rocks fallen from the craggy, volcanic mountains which rise majestically from the shoreline. The majority of the Yugoslav coast is hewn out from these mountains, resulting in sheer drops into the sea. At times looking down these deep chasms I had the impression of flying rather than driving: it seems so improbable that anyone could build a road on these crags. We came across numerous wreaths on the roadside, presumably the result of drivers who went too close to the edge.

There was a notable absence of traffic on these roads, more peasants with their oxen and carts than motor transport, the majority of which were commercial vehicles whose drivers seemed hell-bent on committing suicide.

Approaching the port of Zadar, the countryside gradually flattens out and takes on a more arid look. Zadar is a fascinating town, being almost completely surrounded by a high defensive wall. Strolling around the town in the evening was quite an experience. The streets were packed with young people, who appeared to spend their time in groups meandering up and down. We were to discover that Zadar was no exception: the custom of socialising in the streets during the evenings is quite common throughout Yugoslavia.

Our drive down the Dalmatian Coast was almost continuously within sight of the sea. Although still very rocky and volcanic, the land was now becoming more fertile with ample signs of cultivation, evidence of which we saw in the numerous donkeys laden with produce, presumably off to the local market.

Much evidence of Yugoslavia's awakening to the tourist revolution is shown by the number of hotels and amenities that are mushrooming along the Dalmatian coastline.

Split, the next large town on our route, was no exception: numerous hotels were in the process of being built in preparation for the expected tourist boom.

Whilst in Split we visited the local market to barter for some fresh vegetables to supplement our 'canned' diet. We had by now become accustomed to bartering for every item purchased. The very sight of a foreigner usually boosted the price threefold. We got wise to hanging back and seeing what the locals paid first.

Finding campsites in Yugoslavia was quite a problem: all the known ones marked in the AA camping guide, being the tourist off season, were locked up. So we had to rely on our luck in finding a patch before it got dark.

We were now back in mountain country as we started crossing the Dinaric Alps which sweep down to the coast.

Nearing Makarska we came across a heavily wooded campsite which, although deserted, had the luxury of a toilet and fresh water.

Having just finished pitching the tent, we were joined by a group of four Canadians, travelling in a Dormobile, whom we had already bumped into twice before since leaving Paris.

Later on in the evening we had even more company by the way of two inquisitive Yugoslavs who, although unable to speak a word of English, could reel off the names of the complete English soccer team. That evening we managed to polish off a bottle of local brandy to the accompaniment of Dick and his banjo.

The following morning we awoke to find our 'lilos' afloat and the tent waterlogged. Swimming out of the tent I discovered we were in the middle of a raging blizzard and the tent in danger of collapsing.

After hurriedly gathering rocks in an attempt to hold the tent down, we made an effort to clear and bale out the tent. It was like trying to do a 'King Canute', so we left it in the hope that the blizzard would ease off. In fact it was now snowing harder than ever and we had difficulty standing up in the wind.

The party of Canadians had already packed up and left in the hope of better weather in the south.

Leaving the tent held down with rocks, we jumped in the Land Rover and headed for Makarska, about six miles to the south, in the hope of finding some shelter. We spent most of that day in a café drinking coffee and wine in an effort to warm ourselves up.

Makarska is a very picturesque town with a palm-fringed seafront and the snow-clad mountains reaching right down to the edge of the town, making a striking contrast. In the afternoon I went with Tim back to the campsite to check on the tent, only to find it had just about collapsed. Hastily dismantling the tent, we drove back to Makarska to rejoin Dick and Ron.

The journey back was, to say the least, hazardous. Blinding snow and hurricane-force winds made it practically impossible to keep to one side of the road, and we had a 200-foot sheer drop to the sea on the other side. At one point as we crossed a bridge over a creek, and the Land Rover was literally blown sideways across the road.

Sighing with relief, we eventually 'touched down' at Makarska. To pass away the evening in a place somewhere warm, we decided to go to the cinema; this turned out to be quite amusing, an Italian western, spoken in pidgin English with Serbo-Croatian subtitles. Even the poor quality of the film did not restrain the locals from jumping up and down in their seats and shouting enthusiastically.

On completion of the show, we decided to run the gauntlet and return to the campsite. On arrival we found that the weather was still too bad to even attempt to erect the tent. Being dark and having nowhere else to go, we prepared to rough it for the night. Dick and

Ron slept in the Land Rover whilst Tim and I slept on the floor of the camp toilets, one cubicle each (such luxury – although not quite Hilton standard). At least it was almost windproof. Surprisingly enough, I had a good night's sleep.

Although it had now stopped snowing, the wind was still gale force and we had to spend over an hour retrieving gear that had been blown over a wide area. (I have still got a pair of underpants somewhere in Yugoslavia!)

Proceeding south, we encountered many obstructions: large boulders, fallen trees in the road coupled with patches of black ice made driving hazardous. Once out of the mountains the weather improved considerably.

Shortly before reaching Dubrovnik we stopped at a very pleasant fishing village in a vain attempt to catch our supper.

Reaching Dubrovnik, where we had intentions of staying for a couple of days, we had difficulty in finding an open campsite, which necessitated us camping in a public park. As it happened, right outside a nunnery. Just our luck, it was Sunday: I do not think the bells stopped ringing all day.

Although inclement weather dampened our stay in the ancient fortress part of Dubrovnik, it was, for all that, well worth the stay. The city is surrounded by tall, medieval ramparts and a series of majestic towers, whilst the seaward walls rise sheer from cliffs. Modern suburbs overflow on either side along the coast, leaving the interior to the historians. Old buildings, churches matured by the ordinance of years, and narrow, cobbled streets lined with shops displaying works of art, local crafts, filigree and reputably the very best of wines from the Dalmatian vineyards.

Whilst in Dubrovnik we visited a community social centre for a drink. These are typical Yugoslav meeting places, their answer to the English pub, though much more drab and bare.

With regard to the people, we found the majority of the Slavs inquisitive but quite friendly, especially along the coast. The younger generation appear very Westernised compared to the rather dull and dreary elder set.

Having soaked up the sights of Dubrovnik we drove on along the final stretch of Yugoslav coastline as far as Kamenari where we caught a ferry across to Lepetane, saving us a twenty-mile detour around the inlet. Thus we had our last sight of the Yugoslav coast as we moved inland, passing close to the Albanian border. Very narrow, twisting mountainous roads kept our speed down to 15 mph as we travelled through barren countryside towards Titograd.

My impressions of Titograd were of a typical community town, very drab and lifeless. The approaches were heavily industrialised whilst the centre consisted of half-stocked, uninteresting shops. Perhaps I am not being fair and that it probably looked worse because of the filthy weather.

On the outskirts of the town we came across our first open campsite since Paris, which unfortunately meant we had to pay. Being a state site, we were given an interrogation before being allowed to stay.

Just after pitching our tent we were hit by a violent thunderstorm, resulting in the complete blackout of the town. Lightning flashed as if some mischievous god were switching on and off a brilliant blue electric light which revealed every detail of our surroundings, whilst the thunder growled continuously like a pack of lions.

Regardless of the blackout, we managed to grope our way through the town. Even managing to get a beer in a café lit by candlelight. At least it lent the place some atmosphere. It was three hours before they managed to get any lighting back, giving me the impression that they had no secondary power. Blindly we made our way back to the campsite, only to be welcomed by yet another waterlogged tent. To top it all, my airbed chose that night to spring a leak. I was woken at regular intervals as I slowly sank into the soggy ground, to be temporarily relieved once reflated.

Malaska, Yugoslavia along the Dalmatian coast. Camped in woods nearby, blizzard blew our tent down, slept in local loo!

Dalmatian coast, Yugoslavia,
the author.

Dick lost!
Trying to convince us he knows
how to read a map.

Bad weather continued to plague us as we left Titograd. Once back in the mountains the rain turned to snow, which worsened as the altitude increased, eventually becoming a full-scale blizzard.

It was impossible to proceed more than a hundred yards at a time without stopping to clear the windscreen of frozen snow. The wiper motor was slowly burning itself out. It would have been impossible to carry on but for four-wheel drive. In fact we appeared to be the only vehicle still able to move. Many had skidded off the road or had become bogged down in the snow. The road was littered with abandoned vehicles, but Sweaty Betty still slowly ploughed her way through. At the time I could not think of a more inappropriate name for our vehicle.

Driving continuously in these conditions was becoming quite a strain on all of us. As only to be expected, tempers were apt to get frayed. I think we were all having doubts on the wisdom of the lateness of our departure from England.

The snow eased off once we had traversed the first range of mountains which was followed by a series of passes and gigantic gorges. The grandeur of which helped to compensate for the preceding frustrations.

Following the Piva River valley we encountered a number of spectacular waterfalls which dropped dramatically down the gorges. Some were close enough to the road to soak us as we passed.

Within seconds of stopping at the 'one-horse' town of Ivangrad we were surrounded by inquisitive locals. The way they stared and pointed at us one would think we had just landed from another planet. By now we were getting accustomed to this sort of treatment, which was just as well as we were to have plenty more to come.

From Ivangrad we took a side road, in fact it was nothing more than a cart track. According to our map this was a short cut over the mountains to Skopje, as opposed to the longer route around the mountains via Kos. The drawback to the shorter route was the heavy snow that could be expected in the mountains and the notorious Cakor Pass. Having confidence in our four-wheel drive, we decided to chance it.

A twenty-mile drive along the potholed track brought us to the base of the mountain. Starting to climb we were approached by a small party of people who were waving us down: we ignored their gesticulations, having heard adverse reports of Albanian bandits who frequent those border areas. A few miles further on we passed a man who kept pointing to the mountains and shaking his head: we were beginning to have our doubts. These doubts were confirmed a few minutes later when a couple of lads informed us by signs and pidgin English that the Cakor Pass was blocked by over six feet of snow and was impassable. We discovered later that the pass is impassable for the majority of the winter. Deciding that it would be useless to attempt it, we about-turned and with our tail between our legs we slunk back down the track. A wasted sixty miles. Driving back we sheepishly passed the group who had tried to stop us earlier on: they just stood and grinned at us as if to say, "We told you so."

Back in Ivangrad we rejoined the recently opened road which winds its way around the mountains to Kos. From there on it's an excellent main road right through to Skopje. Although eighty miles longer than the short route, it's certainly the recommended route during the winter.

It was nearly midnight by the time we reached Skopje (the scene of the severe earthquake in 1963). As luck would have it we had no difficulty in finding an open campsite on the outskirts of the city.

The next day the weather turned up trumps so we decided to stay for a day and take the opportunity to have a good dry-out and catch up on outstanding jobs such as patching the tent and servicing the Land Rover.

Skopje has a very modern appearance, ironically due mainly to the rebuilding that has taken place since the earthquake disaster when

75% of the buildings disappeared in just a few seconds. The hands on the station clock still remain at 5.16, the time when the quake struck.

Driving through the streets in the evening was practically impossible, as they were packed solid with people. We had to literally barge our way through, the Land Rover attracting more than casual glances. The loss of a spotlight taught us not to leave the vehicle unattended in a situation like this.

I shall always remember Skopje as the place where I was charged one dinar to urinate in a bar toilet. Disbelieving Ron, who came out complaining of being charged, I had to go and see for myself. Sure enough, on coming out of the door, there was this ancient gentleman standing in front of me with an extended hand. I pleaded ignorance and not being able to understand him. With this he went through all the motions of what I was being charged for. This proved quite comical and soon gathered quite a crowd. Needless to say he got his dinar: his 'exhibition' was worth it.

Departing from Skopje at 4 am (the things one does to get out of a night's camping fee!) we proceeded in darkness and pouring rain towards the Greek border.

Perhaps Sweaty Betty did not like such an early start, but that morning we had our first spot of vehicle trouble since leaving England. The engine kept cutting out, finally packing up right in the middle of a long tunnel. After much searching and head-scratching, plus a few swear words thrown in for good measure, we discovered that it was nothing more serious than a blocked hole in the petrol filler cap. Much relieved, we drove on through a wide river valley to the Greek border. There is always the feeling of excitement on arriving at a border post. Maybe it's the thought of being on the threshold of a different country or perhaps the expectation of meeting fellow-travellers and the customary exchange of news. At the border post, we once again met up with the Canadian group whom we had last seen at our campsite in Makarska.

An amusing sight at the border was the changing of the Greek guards in full national rig-out, complete with skirts and outsize pompons on their shoes.

Through flat, uninteresting countryside we headed on towards Thessaloniki, stopping only to cut some bamboos to make a fishing line and a rack for Dick's banjo.

My first minor scrape was on the outskirts of Thessaloniki. A crazy Greek in a battered van overtook us and cut in too soon, scraping down our front offside wing. Getting out of the Land Rover we were met by what I can only presume was Greek abuse. Tim's mention of getting the police soon quietened him down as he got back in his van and sped off.

Ten miles outside Thessaloniki we came across a government campsite where we met up with many other overlanders, amongst which was a party of three attractive Canadian girls travelling through Europe in a hired car. A very pleasant evening was spent with them playing cards, plus Ron doing his fortune-telling party piece and Dick supplying the background noise with his banjo.

Taking advantage of the rare fine weather and the excellent camp facilities, we had another good dry-out and clean-up.

The recent foul weather seemed far away as I sat outside a bar on Thessaloniki's seafront enjoying the rare luxury of a beer whilst soaking up the sun.

I was very impressed with Thessaloniki, its clean, modern buildings and long, wide streets, plus a liberal sprinkling of parks giving a very pleasing and fresh appearance. Thessaloniki, capital of Macedonia and Greece's second city. Founded in 315 BC on the site of another city – Thermi. Even with such a long history there are very few ruins to see owing to the great fire of 1917 which destroyed much of the city centre.

Back at the campsite we visited some of the other campers. A few were doing much the same trip as us, whilst others were travelling in the opposite direction. From these we were able to gather much information and advice on what was ahead of us. Many of the people at the campsite were 'hippie' types, intent on spending the winter in the warmer climate of Crete.

Bidding farewell to our fellow-travellers we continued on our way eastwards. The initial twenty miles that day were over a very poor corrugated road, causing a series of undulations, necessitating constantly stopping the Land Rover to prevent it from shaking apart. Once joining up with the main road we made good progress through hilly and barren terrain to the coastal garrison town of Kavala.

Finding campsites in Greece posed no problem, as the government have an excellent chain of sites throughout the country, most of which are open all the year round. The one in Kavala was right on the beach, no doubt a popular spot in the summer. Being well into winter, our only company was a couple driving to India, two Dutchmen cycling to Australia on a tandem, and a Royal Navy commander and his wife on their way to take up a diplomatic post in Turkey. We had in fact met the commander before at previous campsites. A very pleasant evening was spent with the commander and his wife in their caravan, swapping yarns and drinking his Bacardi. Having spent many years in the Navy myself, I knew many of the commander's friends, though in a slightly different capacity.

Whilst at Kavala we took the opportunity to do some musselling, in which we had more success than previous fishing expeditions. Although after washing, boiling and then having to break your way into them, I began to wonder whether they were worth all the trouble: still, it was a meal. For his efforts Tim spent the following morning removing thorns from his foot, the result of paddling barefoot to get at the mussels.

Ron surprised us all that day by stripping off and going for a swim: credit where it's due, he did manage a couple of strokes before turning blue and beating a hasty retreat.

Walking into Kavala we were greeted by a very picturesque town with quaint, old-fashioned streets. The main street ran parallel to the seafront which was full of fishing boats tugging relentlessly at their moorings.

Dominating Kavala is the garrison fortress standing high and mighty on the surrounding hills which enclose the town.

Whether we had mislaid the tin opener or whether it was for a break from Dick's cooking, I cannot remember, but whilst in Kavala we decided to treat ourselves to the extravagance of a restaurant, where for a few pence we got an excellent fish meal. After stocking up with fresh vegetables and provisions at the local market we left Kavala.

By now we had eaten through much of the bulky tinned food that we had brought with us, thus giving us much-needed elbow room. Our plan of eating the tinned food whilst travelling through the more expensive countries of Europe, supplementing our diet with local fruit and vegetables, was working out well. We kept a good supply of mixed canned foods aside in case of later emergencies. Having one meal in the evening supplemented by local fruit or soup at midday was, we found, quite sufficient.

A short journey from Kavala, through flat, arid countryside, brought us to Xanthi which is the centre of the Greek tobacco industry, and hosts many Byzantine churches and picturesque squares.

A common sight whilst travelling through Greece was the roadside shrines with their encased Madonna figurines surrounded by flickering candles. We passed through small, rural villages where old women sat in doorways dressed in their usual black shrouds quite happy to let the modern world pass them by.

Arriving at Porto Lago we consulted our map, according to which we should be at the site of some historical ruins. We made a fruitless search for signs of these ruins, the only ruins we could see being the habitations of the local populace. A story we did hear was that local fishermen, whilst fishing on a nearby lake, had seen ruins at the bottom of the lake. More likely than not, the fishermen had had too much ouzo (which is the local firewater). Whether the story was true or not I do not know: we were not that keen to go out onto the lake to find out.

Abandoning our search for the ruins of Porto Lago, we drove on to the small town of Komotini.

Once through Komotini the preceding barren terrain gives way to a more vegetated and hilly outlook. The road winds its way laboriously through the hills before descending sharply towards Alexandroupoli.

Having such a romantic-sounding name, I had expected better things of Alexandroupoli. Instead it turned out to be a very ordinary, medium-sized Greek garrison town. The Greeks are a superstitious people. Many carry little blue stones to guard them against evil. Girls discreetly pin the stones to their bras, though God only knows which evil eye they are trying to divert.

I should think there must be plenty of work for dentists in Greece, judging by the number of cake and sweet shops we saw. We had quite some trouble dragging Ron away from drooling over all the delicious-looking fancies. In fact we did succumb whilst in Alexandroupoli. Being the last town before the border we gathered all our loose drachmas and had a gastronomic orgy of cakes.

Troops appeared to be everywhere, though being fairly close to the Turkish border and relations between Greece and Turkey very rarely more than lukewarm, this could be expected.

Our campsite at Alexandroupoli was again another perfect site, right on the beach. Being the sole occupiers we had the run of the place.

An early start from Alexandroupoli soon brought us to the Turkish border post guarded by numerous lookout towers with their armoured inmates pacing restlessly like caged animals. Looking for what? A Greek invasion? Or maybe penniless overlanders. On being asked at the border if we liked Turkish cigarettes, smoked hash or wanted a nice Turkish girl, all to which we replied in the negative, the jovial customs official replied, "What the hell do you want to come to Turkey for?" Such was our introduction to Turkey. A quick look through the Land Rover by the official and we were once again speeding on our way.

Whether to create a good first impression or not, I do not know, but we found, as common with many other countries we had been through, that the initial ten miles or so leading from the border post, were over excellent road surfaces, after which it gradually deteriorated into inferior-surfaced road.

The Turkish countryside is quite attractive in its bleak sort of way, not unlike Dartmoor, and noticeably greener than Greece. We were continually being stopped by the military, who appeared to be stationed at every major crossroads. A show of passports and satisfactory answers to their whys and wherefores soon had us on our way again. Evidently Turkey was under martial law at the time.

Our first insight into the real Turkey was at the town of Tekirdağ. Walking through Tekirdağ one felt as if the clocks had been turned back a hundred years. The steep, crowded, narrow streets were cluttered with human and animal offal. It all looked very medieval, even the people look archaic dressed in their baggy pantaloons. The houses, built precariously on the side of a hill, looked as if the slightest disturbance would bring them crashing down. Our intrusion caused many stares but we were used to that by now.

We had travelled 3,000 miles, taking almost a month, as we approached the final bastion of Europe, Istanbul, with its skyline of minarets rising above several hills.

As we intended staying in Istanbul for a few days, we went out of our way to find ourselves a decent campsite. This we found on the outskirts of the city, a pleasant spot, spoilt only by the close proximity of the airport along with its accompanying noises. The campsite even had such luxuries as cooking facilities and a restroom. At least we would be able to give our overworked Primus stove a rest.

Among the other travellers at the site was a group in a Land Rover doing an identical trip to us. Thus enter Bo, Peggy, Mike and Tony with whom we were to have many encounters before arriving in Australia. Also on the site were two girls from Jersey, Penny and Sheila, who were hitch-hiking through Europe, intending to spend the winter in Southern Greece.

With a few days on our hands we had plenty of time to see the sights of Istanbul. From our campsite it was only a short drive to the imposing city walls – the gateway to the mysterious East.

Driving in Istanbul is a harrowing experience, a case of every man for himself. Not only have you the vehicles and suicidal Turks to contend with, but a myriad of horses and carts who jog along in their frustrating way, oblivious to the surrounding traffic.

Our first visit to Istanbul was to the British Embassy to collect our mail, our first since leaving home. Whilst at the Embassy, we visited the Embassy's Christmas bazaar. Penny bought a small Christmas pudding which cost her 80p. Seeing prices such as OXO cubes at 10p each soon had us making a quick exit. No doubt the Ambassador and his staff could afford such prices, but they were not for the likes of us. Our place was in the backstreet stalls haggling for our wares.

Although this being my fourth visit to Istanbul, I could never grow tired of the place, as there is always something different to see. The bazaars are a must. There is the spice bazaar (Mısır Çarşısı), the covered bazaar (Kapalı Çarşı), which is one of the world's greatest markets, and the grand bazaar. Dozens of streets and stalls, each street being devoted to a particular trade. Miles of enclosed, narrow, bustling streets. Each shopkeeper, stallholder and pedlar shouting his wares in the attempt to outdo his neighbour.

Walking through the bazaar we were shoved, pushed and jostled in efforts to get us to make a purchase. Each shop owner with his claim to having the best and cheapest going to great lengths to tell us how crooked all the other shopkeepers were. We had great fun in spending hours haggling over the price of an article, eventually getting it down to a really good price, then walking out of the shop having had no intention of making a purchase. The names we must have been called: luckily we did not speak Turkish.

Leather goods seemed about the best bargain in the bazaars, good quality and very cheap, providing you haggle for a good price and do not get taken for a ride. Antiques are also in abundance: in fact we saw many of these being made in the backstreets.

Coming out of the bazaars we meandered through the maze of back alleys where men sat cross-legged in their cubby holes hammering out brasses, pots and pans, pottery etc. in a way that probably has not changed since biblical times. One could wander for hours, never losing interest in the animated and constantly changing scene.

An amusing incident whilst driving back to the campsite was a tubby policeman directing traffic from his island bollard, who suddenly stopped all the traffic whilst he got out his lunch box and commenced eating his lunch. The excitement reached a crescendo when he triumphantly unzipped his banana, apparently enjoying every bit of attention he was getting.

That night back at the camp we practically got flooded out during a heavy storm. Penny and Sheila were not so lucky. Their bivouac got waterlogged and they ended up sleeping on the floor of the washroom. The following day we all went into the city for a final tour of the sights.

Parking the Land Rover in a back alley near Solomon's Mosque, we were affronted by an insistent Turk who wanted us all to go to his café which was across the road. Not wanting to offend the chap, especially as he had promised to look after the Land Rover during our absence, we agreed to visit his café for a free tea which was brought to us in little glass cups on a brass tray resembling a judge's scales. I think all he wanted was an English lesson, he was not even interested in buying Penny or Sheila off us, which was out of character for a Turk.

Leaving the Land Rover with the café owner, we went for a look around the magnificent Solomon's Mosque, the splendour of which was dwarfed by the nearby Blue Mosque, which is probably the most famous of Istanbul's numerous mosques (there are over 500 of them). Taking our shoes off before entering the mosque, we strolled around the interior which is lavishly decorated in pale blue tiles. Concluding our tour of Istanbul with a visit to the Palace, we returned to the Land Rover which had been in the safe keeping of the hospitable café owner. Surprisingly the vehicle was still in one piece.

For our final night in Istanbul we had a slap-up meal, cooked with the compliments of Penny and Sheila, and washed down with some local wine.

Bidding a farewell to Penny and Sheila, we made an early start in pouring rain, after one of our most enjoyable stops to date. We made our way through early morning traffic to the Golden Horn waterfront where we had to wait our turn in the queue to get on the ferry for the short journey across the Bosphorus. A thirty-minute wait and we were on the ferry, leaving Europe behind us. We gazed back across the Golden Horn to the old city. Its panorama is intriguing – great mosques within their attendant minarets, the Sultan Palace to the fore, whilst steamers and boats zigzagged around us on their way to the Black Sea.

CHAPTER 4

Turkey into Asia

"Look out, Asia, here we come!" shouted Ron as the ferry's ramps were lowered and we trundled into the Asian side of Istanbul. We drove on into Üsküdar which, although regarded as a suburb of Istanbul, is now a city in its own right. The mosques here are interesting but can scarcely compare with those of its mighty neighbour. Many of the old Turkish houses in this area are made of wood, with the first storey overhanging the ground floor. Florence Nightingale worked here in Üsküdar and there is an English cemetery housing the bones of British soldiers killed in the Crimean War.

Between Istanbul and İzmit we were stopped three times by the Army. Passing through İzmit we left the flat, rocky terrain and commenced climbing to more mountainous countryside. Once in the mountains the rain turned to snow and atrocious driving conditions.

It was still snowing heavily as we arrived at a roadside motel near Bolu. Getting permission from the motel manager, we pitched our tent in the motel grounds. Talk about 'mad dogs and Englishmen', here we are, at an ultramodern motel with luxurious centrally heated bedrooms, and us camping outside in below-freezing temperatures and six inches of mud and snow. The looks we got from the motel inmates! Still, at least it was free.

Because of the intense cold, we spent the evening in the motel by a roaring log fire; we even treated ourselves to a beer. After all, there is not much pleasure in sitting cross-legged in six inches of snow.

It was whilst sitting by the roaring log fire in the motel, with our maps spread out over the table, that we made the decision to alter our route. Owing to the possibility of severe weather and adverse road conditions on our intended northern route through Turkey, we decided to take the southern route via Syria and Iraq, in the hope of warmer climes and better conditions.

It was still snowing hard and bitterly cold as we crawled out of our tent the following morning. We had quite a job stowing away the tent as it had frozen solid.

Following snowploughs we made our way down the mountains. Coming out of the mountains, the snow gradually cleared away until we were once again back on flat ground. A vast contrast in scenery as we were now in a large, fertile plain surrounded by snow-covered mountains.

The snowploughs gave way to horse and cart and oxen, the latter still used for ploughing and general farm work.

We arrived at the Turkish capital of Ankara in the early afternoon. Ankara is as modern as Istanbul is ancient. Wide, open streets and tall office blocks, in fact very much like any Westernised city. The city lies amid steep lands at an elevation of some 3,000 feet, ensuring a cold winter. It is comparatively clean and pleasantly green, lively and prosperous. Ankara is an ancient Hittite centre and took over as Turkey's capital from Istanbul in 1923.

A campsite was set up about five miles from the city on a rather muddy lay-by outside a motel garage.

We were compelled to stop in Ankara for a couple of days as, owing to the alteration of our route, we had to arrange for visas to enter Syria and Iraq.

A whole day was spent chasing round embassies and having photographs taken for our visas. We were rather sceptical as to what sort of reception we would get at the Iraq Embassy, as they had recently broken off diplomatic relations with Britain. Apart from making us wait a day for the issue of a visa we had little trouble, though Ron did 'fly off the handle' at the Iraqi Consul for the lackadaisical attitude whilst we sweated in the background.

The extra day in Ankara was not wasted as we had minor repairs to the Land Rover that needed doing. Tim made a good temporary job of the exhaust which was just about disintegrating. Little wonder the Army kept stopping us: we sounded like a tank.

Taking advantage of the extra day in Ankara, we visited the British Embassy to try and find out the latest position of the India/Pakistan war which was beginning to cause us some concern. The news we received was not good: all borders closed. We were still five weeks away from Pakistan, so it looked as if we were going to have to sweat it out and hope that by the time we reached Pakistan the war would be over.

Whilst strolling through Ankara's main street I stopped to purchase a pair of shoelaces from a street hawker. Putting my hand in my pocket for some money to pay him, as I did so he picked up his tray and ran for his life, leaving me standing holding a free pair of laces. My only conclusion was that he was some illegal hawker and thought either I was or he had spotted someone of authority, hence his hasty exodus. Having collected our visas from the Iraqi Embassy, the Syrian Embassy informing us that we could obtain visas at the border post, we left Ankara. Heading south we passed the hillside and hut village of old Ankara, much of which had been taken over by squatters. With barely any roads amongst the shacks it is not easy to see how some could be reached.

Most of the villages south of Ankara are composed of mud and wattle houses and are flat-roofed. The road now is virtually featureless, mostly flat plateau and more than 3,000 feet above sea level.

Our first stop was at a motel near the caravanserai town of Aksaray: here we were entertained by a Turkish band whose music, to say the least, was different. It must have been good as all the locals were in raptures and the men were clapping and dancing with each other.

Refreshed after our short rest we continued, intending to make a mad, all-night dash across the Taurus Mountains with the prospect of better weather on the southern side.

Passing the salt lakes of Tuz Gölü we started climbing the Taurus Mountains where once again we encountered snow. At about 5,000 feet we really hit bad weather, deep snow and black ice. We passed many lorries that had lost their battle against the elements, some of which had overturned. Because of the bad weather we had little option but to press on through the mountains, even though the driving conditions were atrocious.

By the early hours of the morning fatigue was catching up with us, so we decided to look out for somewhere to stop to enable us to 'snatch' a few hours' sleep. Driving through a vast mountain gorge we came across a lay-by. Not knowing what lay ahead, we decided to make the best of a bad job and pull in at the lay-by until dawn.

Dick and Ron settled down in the Land Rover whilst Tim and I (I must have been mad) tried to make ourselves as comfortable as possible wrapped up in a groundsheet on the pavement. It was bitterly cold, well below freezing, and an icy wind howled down through the gorge.

Tim attempted to erect a windbreak with some spare canvas but with little success. I lay down on that cold, damp, concrete pavement attempting to get some sleep. It was hopeless: I was as cold as I have ever been, and with the sound of Tim's teeth chattering! I finally gave up trying to sleep and resigned myself to a night on the 'tiles'. Getting up from my 'recipe for instant pneumonia', I started feeble attempts to get my blood circulating once more. Luckily there was a full moon, though even that cast sinister shadows down through the gorge.

It was an awe-inspiring sight, sheer cliffs either side of me separated only by the road and a wide mountain river, River Cakit. The cliffs appeared to be alive with the sparkling reflection of ice crystals on the snow. Shimmering and glittering from the moon's reflection dancing down the river, they contributed to make the whole situation rather unreal.

Up and down, up and down, I walked, ran and jumped back and

forth through the gorge in an attempt to pass the night away and keep warm. Oh for the dawn! Thoughts of that warm bed I left behind. Was this a nightmare? Pinch, no, I actually was in the middle of a Turkish mountain, freezing cold at 3 o'clock in the morning. How many times I walked up and down that gorge I do not know but eventually I got fed up with doing that. A stroll along the river, hell, even that is half frozen over. What is this? A hole in the ground, looks like the old home of a tree, perhaps it will be warmer in there. Crouched down in the hole it certainly was a bit warmer, but it was far from being comfortable. Up again back on the road, up and down, up and down, will dawn ever come? A peep in the Land Rover, Dick and Ron fast asleep. (Any room for me in there? No. You must go on a diet, Ron!) Tim looks like a corpse wrapped up in the groundsheet lying on the pavement: perhaps he has passed away, shall I wake him up and see? No, I will carry on talking to myself. Back up the road, bark, bark, what is that? Do they have wolves around here? Goodness, I must be getting jumpy. Looking up at the mountains, is it my imagination? Is it the moon or is it actually getting lighter? Yes, I do believe dawn is upon us.

Returning to the Land Rover I jumped up and down in a silent demonstration to wake the others.

Tim's stirring, at last someone to talk to. "Hello, Pete, you're up early!" Confucius he says, "The early bird him catches the worm." I have just learnt a better one: "Him who walks up and down a gorge all night feels shattered in the morning".

Soon sanity returns. Ron is up, followed by Dick, who says, "That is the best sleep I have had since we left England." Even Tim claims to actually have slept, though I have a sneaking suspicion that it was more a show of bravado than anything else.

It is now almost daylight, the gorge looking much friendlier now. Great to be back on the road again after such a long night.

A short drive brought us to a ramshackle transport café near

Pozantı. The heat hit us as we walked through the door and we were soon huddled around the primitive stove in the centre of the room along with a handful of ragged, baggy-trousered Turks. A breakfast of soup and black tea went some way in thawing ourselves out.

Somewhat refreshed, we carried on through the mountains, passing through the Cilician Gates, an imposing rocky gorge (penetrated by Alexander the Great when he burst into the southern plain) that is a pass through the Taurus Mountains.

We were soon leaving the inclement weather behind us as we descended through scenic countryside to the flat plains of Southern Turkey. Being as we were so close, we made a short detour to Tarsus, reputed to be the birthplace of Saint Paul. His home had been identified but has long since disappeared. His birthplace was in the street of the tent makers, a short thoroughfare without distinction. The well which served his house still survives. If Paul came back today I doubt whether he would find much change in his home town apart from the occasional vehicle. Oxen and carts, heavily laden donkeys, ragged, baggy-trousered men, veiled women carrying their wares on their heads, mud-built houses, together with a strong smell of herbs, spices and animal excrement. Tarsus was formally connected to the sea but the course of the river has been diverted, and the lake between Tarsus and the sea has since dried up. This was Tarsus, the real Turkey.

Leaving Tarsus we rejoined our original route, passing through Adana, once the centre of the Turkish cotton industry and an important agricultural centre. Adana was founded in about the 14th century BC by the Hittites.

The weather had by now improved immensely and we were driving in pleasant sunny conditions, a great change from the recent atrocious conditions. Occasional hills dotted the plain, many crowned by a castle, often in ruins.

A short drive from Adana we could see in the distance to our right an impressive-looking castle standing like a sentinel on a hillock.

Taurus Mountains between Ankara and Adana, Turkey, the author.

The Yilankale Castle (Snake Castle) near Adana, Turkey.

Unfortunately the staff were all at prayer so we let ourselves into Syria. No brownie points for that as we found out when we were relieved of our passports!

According to our maps and guidebooks, this castle did not exist, unless this was Yılankale (Snake Castle), a 13th-century Armenian castle which, legend has it, was inhabited by snakes. With no signs to confirm this, it did look imposing enough to warrant a visit.

Taking a dirt track that headed in the general direction of the castle, we bounced our way to the base of the hillock. We drove as far as possible up the hill before abandoning the vehicle and continuing on foot toward the castle. The only sign of any life was a lone shepherd boy tending his flock, who stared inquisitively at us as if we were intruding on his territory, which no doubt we were.

Negotiating the steep climb we could see mountain goats peering at us from behind boulders, nimbly stalking our every movement. A half-hour climb brought us to the base of the ramparts. Scrambling over boulders, up walls and through crannies, we found ourselves on the inside of the castle, parts of which looked as if the occupants had only departed yesterday. Dungeons, banqueting hall and even communal 'loos' (at least that is what I presumed they were) were still intact. No evidence of any tourist invasion here, no cigarette packets, sweet wrappers, souvenir hawkers or guides. Just us and a medieval castle all to ourselves. From the top of the battlements we had a superb view of the surrounding countryside. It was rather like standing in the centre of a vast landscape painting with the Tarsus Mountains providing the picture frame.

A calm sea of treeless fields rolled out to meet the distant mountains and streams. In the foreground we could see oxen plying to and fro, relentlessly towing their archaic wooden ploughs. A couple of hours were spent admiring the view from our commanding position and exploring and rummaging through the rubble, in which we did find some interesting pieces of pottery.

Stumbling out of our fortress we made our way through a gauntlet of goats back down to the Land Rover.

Back on the road again we made good progress and were soon travelling along the Mediterranean Coast.

It was dusk as we arrived at the Turkish naval port of İskenderun exactly one month and 4,000 miles since leaving England. For a change our luck was in: a few enquiries led us to a campsite where the owner very kindly allowed us to use an outhouse. It was by no means a mansion, but to us it was a roof over our heads, our first since we had left home. About 4 yards square and furnished with a table, chair, broken camp bed and a dozen sacks of cement.

An invasion by thousands of ants necessitated us partaking in a fumigation session. They were everywhere: in our sleeping bags, up the walls, and over the floors. I think they resented us disturbing their hibernation. A few pots of boiling water, to which we found they have an allergy, went some way in diminishing their numbers; even so, I still spent most of the evening scratching myself.

Ron, returning from an evening stroll, informed us that he had got into some trouble with the local police: evidently they objected to him gesticulating at one of their statues. Knowing Ron's enjoyment at a good political argument, he had no doubt added fuel to the fire.

Taking advantage of the fine weather we spent the following day servicing the Land Rover, changing a tyre and having a good clean-up.

With our chores completed we went for a tour of İskenderun. A typical naval port, rough-looking bars, nightclubs, plus all the usual 'wares', human and otherwise, for sale. Gari horses (decorated horse cart taxis) were in abundance; we were obvious targets and they followed us everywhere, pimping us for just about every sexual delight going: nice girl, very cheap, very clean. What willpower! Get behind me, Satan: we are trying to do this trip on a limited budget!

Before leaving İskenderun we took advantage of the cheapness of foodstuffs in Turkey to stock up with vegetables and 'rakı', it being the last big town before the Syrian border.

Refreshed and replenished after our short stay we proceeded eastwards via the Amanus mountain range through fairly cultivated terrain. There was ever-increasing evidence of Arab influence with the gradual change of the passing countryside. Baggy trousers were giving way to long, flowing Arab dresses. Houses changing to 'Kur' tents and mud hut settlements, with old ladies in doorways with faces akin to walnut shells crouching in a cowering position as if about to give birth.

There was little traffic on the road: what little we did see was mainly donkey power, though we did pass our first camel train. Once again we were stopped by the police, though the offer of a biscuit, which he readily accepted, soon had us speeding on our way again.

A ramshackle collection of brick buildings heralded the Turkish border post which necessitated a 30-minute session of farcical form-filling. I felt like a tennis ball after being herded back and forth from one petty official to another. Eventually we were allowed on our way and drove on through the five-mile stretch of desert, rolled barbed wire-scarred countryside which is the no man's land between the Turkish and Syrian border.

CHAPTER 5

Into Syria

Nobody appeared interested in us as we waited patiently at the Syrian border barricade. Impatience getting the better of me, I got out of the Land Rover and opened the gate myself to allow us to drive through.

A fatal mistake: no sooner had we driven through than we were accosted by Syrian Army officers who gesticulated in a rather unfriendly way. I think they must have thought I was going to put them out of a job. Anyway, they were upset enough to warrant them taking my passport off me. That episode taught me to tread softly with the Arabs: they are not a humorous race. I readily exchanged a reprimand on the whys and wherefores of letting myself into a country in return for my passport.

We still had to obtain Syrian visas: the officials by this time were not in any mood to rush around doing us any favours. An hour's wait and we were supplied with the necessary visas. Now we had to change our currency. "Sorry, the bank manager is away saying his prayers, come back in an hour," said the official. If I have to hang around this place much longer I am going to have to join him myself, I thought.

At long last, visas obtained, money exchanged and we were on our way through one of the world's 'hotbeds'. Barren desert terrain heralded our introduction to Syria.

Navigating was not made any easier by the fact that all the signposts were written in Arabic; luckily there are very few roads in Syria. More by luck than judgment we arrived at the ancient city of Aleppo. A modern, palm-lined dual carriageway welcomes you to the city, that being the sole evidence of the 1970s.

Aleppo dates back to at least the second millennium BC and is Syria's second city, being about the same size as Damascus. It is one

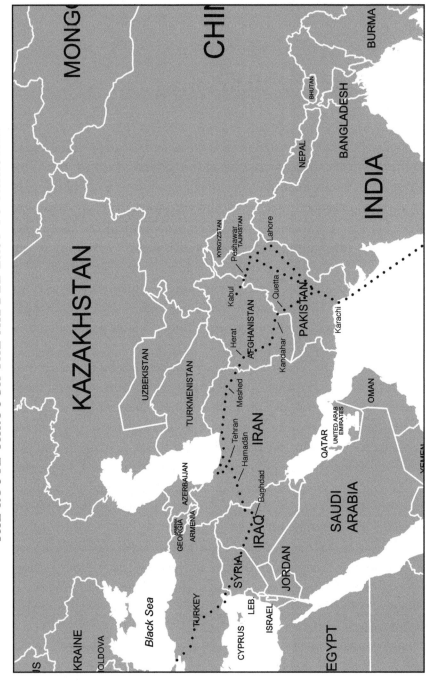

of the most ancient trading centres in the world. Through Aleppo
passed one of the great caravan routes of antiquity, being the shortest
avenue from the Mediterranean to Mesopotamia. Today the city is
Syria's chief industrial centre with food processing and cement plants,
textile and flour mills.

Dominating Aleppo is the imposing citadel, a 12th-century BC
castle constructed on a man-made hill encompassed by a deep moat.
It must have been an impregnable fortress in its day.

Approaching the castle, we were befriended by an Arab who insisted
we follow him to a small room, not much larger than a cupboard, at
the entrance to the citadel. Squeezing through the two-foot-square
opening, we joined two other Arabs squatting on their haunches.
We were soon sipping black tea whilst our 'credentials' were being
established. Evidently they were guides, no doubt hopefully awaiting
a customer since the end of the tourist season – that is if they have
such a season. Having been 'captured', we were compelled to follow
our guide on a conducted tour of the citadel.

I must be one of the world's worst sightseers, having distinct dislike
for guided tours, and preferring to discover local life sitting in cafés,
bars and tea houses conversing with newfound friends probably never
to be seen again. I had been to Athens three times before I got round
to actually visiting the Acropolis. To me, all the famous sights that
every good tourist must see are all rather a fraud: one sees them that
often on postcards, films etc., that by the time you actually visit them
you get the feeling that you have seen it all before. This was not the
case with this castle: it really was worth the guided tour.

Our guide knew every stone of the citadel, leaving none unturned
in his quest to educate four Englishmen. We followed him up and
down steps rubbed smooth by constant friction of shoes and bare soles.
Through long passageways, down to the cellars, dungeons, through
banqueting halls, crossing courtyards, look right, look left, look up,
look down, follow me, please keep together, so and so slept here,

etc. From what we could gather from our guide's pidgin English, the citadel housed a complete town within its walls, including a mosque, part of which was still standing. The view from the upper wall was quite amazing and gave one the impression of standing on the hub of a cartwheel from which the streets of Aleppo radiate.

Dusk was setting in as we left the citadel to set out in search of a campsite for the night. Allah must have favoured us that evening. Only a few miles outside the city we came across what looked like a camping ground at the rear of a shack that served as a café. A few enquiries and pleading looks and once again we were settled in an outhouse. What a pleasure to have a nice, dry stone floor to sleep on, plus the luxury of a roof over our heads.

During the evening we were invited by the owner to his home. Dick, Tim and I readily accepted: the experience was well worth it. His one-roomed home served as a café, bar and farmyard. Sparsely furnished, with a table, a few chairs and a bed in the corner, on which an ancient sheikh sat cross-legged engrossed in the Koran, looking rather like the local soothsayer.

Underneath the table an outsize turkey pecked away at our legs. Completing the motley crew were two sinister-looking Arabs and a German journalist driving on his way to Germany from Thailand. The solitary lighting from the dimly lit hurricane lamp, coupled with the glow from a roaring drip-fed heater, created a rather unreal atmosphere. A bottle of rakı went a long way in loosening tongues for what good it did, as we could not understand a word of Arabic.

Later on in the evening a huge bowlful of the local 'diet' was placed in front of us. A man was cooking pancake loaves (chapattis) over the heater: he must have made a pile well over 12" high and half a square yard in area. It was a case of literally all hands in. No knives or forks were used (fingers were invented before cutlery anyway). We were hesitant at first until hunger persuaded us to join in the melee. 'Chapattis' have a practical as well as a gastronomic use. Pieces ripped off to make a kind of lining for thumb and finger which would be used like a pair of tongs to pick up meat and vegetables etc., then the whole lot is unceremoniously shoved into the mouth. We soon got the hang of it!

The finale to the evening was a snuff-taking session, in which the Arabs were rather concerned because I would not sneeze. In the end, to prevent them shoving the whole tin down my nose, I faked a sneeze, which seemed to satisfy them. The following morning, tea was brought out to us by our 'hosts' to help us on our way.

Returning to Aleppo we visited the local representative of the engineering firm that Tim worked for in England. He was overjoyed to meet us, and after a long chat over numerous cups of black tea he insisted on showing us around the city.

Aleppo is a typical example of an Arab town, dirty streets, hawkers and beggars are aplenty. The flat-roofed buildings of yellow sandstone cluster together in protective huddles.

We found out with the loss of our mascot that it was unwise to leave the Land Rover unattended. No sooner would we stop than we would be surrounded by inquisitive onlookers fingering and pawing at the vehicle, giving one the feeling of a caged animal.

Before leaving Aleppo we had a look around the bazaar. A long, narrow, covered alleyway, literally seething with life, not an inch of ground could be seen for men, women and children elbowing their way about with jars and baskets on their heads filled with vegetables, skins, wools and dried roots. Occasionally a laden donkey with barely room to traverse through the alleyway would cause chaos as it nonchalantly went its way casting all before it in its efforts to evade its master's stick.

Hundreds of minute stalls, some little more than holes in the wall, spread either side of the alleyway crammed full with foodstuffs, spices, silks, leathers and skins. The fragrance of spices mingled with the smell of donkey dung, fish and body sweat. Babbling, screaming, muttering human voices crying their wares and haggling in excitable octaves. Tim, after much haggling at numerous stalls, managed to obtain, at a ridiculously low price, an excellent sheepskin waistcoat, which I half-expected to 'baa': it certainly smelled alive.

Rejoining Ron, who had been custodian of the Land Rover whilst we were at the bazaar, we made our departure from Aleppo. By the time we left Aleppo it was almost midday, giving little time to add many miles before dark.

Passing through arid desert wastes, the monotony was broken only by the occasional mud hut settlement. As we neared the River Euphrates the road degenerated into a boulder-strewn, rutted dust track. Evidence of a partially constructed bitumen road was visible nearby, though the rubble from this project only added to the hazards. Darkness came with the suddenness that befalls you in these latitudes as we approached Raqqa, a small town straddling the Euphrates.

The hopelessness of finding a campsite at Raqqa was soon evident, all our enquiries being met with blank stares. Tim thought he had seen a suitable site about ten miles back on the bank of the Euphrates. Having no better suggestions, we about-turned and retraced our tracks until we arrived at a little-used side track to our right. The track ran along the riverbank, being concealed from the main road by a huge mound.

"Ideal spot," said Tim. "A nice piece of flat ground just wide enough to pitch our tent and with the mound on one side concealing us, and the river on the other." I only hope the river does not rise too far, I thought. Unfortunately we were not sheltered from the high wind that was blowing across the river. As a precaution we gathered some of the numerous rocks that were handily piled in cairns close by, to batten down the tent. Imagine our surprise when we awoke in the morning to find the stones we had used to hold the tent down were in fact headstones to graves. We had pitched the tent in the middle of an Arab graveyard! Little wonder we were not disturbed during the night. I do not think I would have slept so well if I had known what I was lying over.

Beating a hasty retreat from our cemetery camping ground, we drove on, crossing the Euphrates by the road bridge, to Raqqa, a bustling, 'one-horse' Arab town, whose main street was a collection of shanty buildings. Most of the buildings were makeshift shops where a brisk trade in skins, pots and pans, dubious meats, fruit, vegetables and spices was taking place.

No sooner had we stopped than we were surrounded by inquisitive Syrians. I felt rather like the Pied Piper of Hamelin as I wandered through Raqqa's main street followed by a cortège of children, many tugging at our coats and hopefully thrusting out their hands. Ron, as generous as ever, usually obliged with a few coins. As for me, I do not like to encourage 'bad habits'. Even the dogs sensed that we were different as they yapped perilously close to our heels. Having purchased our daily bread, still hot from the clay ovens, we ran the gauntlet of staring eyes back to the Land Rover.

From Raqqa we carried on following the route of the vast, muddy Euphrates through the arid wastes of the Syrian Desert towards Deir ez-Zor.

Whilst stopping for a 'brew-up' on the riverbanks we were approached by a young student teacher who was elated at having the opportunity to practise his English. "Come over to my house," he said, pointing to a collection of mud hut dwellings about a hundred yards away.

Soon we were being introduced to his whole family, including his two wives and numerous offspring. Continuous cups of tea were brought out to us, it being seemingly impossible to empty a cup. No sooner would we take a sip when one of the children would be around refilling the cup. Crouching down in a circle in front of the huts, we proceeded to give our Syrian friend an instant English lesson, gathering a sizeable crowd of onlookers in the process. Turning down

Aleppo Citadel, Syria.   *Top of Citadel, Aleppo, Syria.*

Babylon, Hanging Gardens, Iraq.
The gentleman at top right was our minder.
(See Chapter 6)

an invitation to spend the night with the family, we bade our farewells amidst much handshaking and waving.

We were still following the course of the Euphrates, the green banks of which made a sharp contrast to the wide, rusty expanse of desert. Soon we were passing the cotton-manufacturing town of Deir ez-Zor with its line upon line of cloth hung out, giving the impression of a gigantic jamboree of tents. In January 2016 a massacre of the civilian population was reported to be perpetrated by ISIS. In September 2016 US planes struck targets at Deir ez-Zor.

Darkness was falling as we passed through the village of Qatat-es-Salihaya, so we decided to call it a day and look out for a place to camp. For lack of any decent sites, we pitched our tent by the side of the road, there being practically no traffic to bother us.

We were just settling down for the night, having pitched the tent, when Ron exclaimed, "There is something moving over there." Sure enough in the blackness of the desert night, broken only by the flickering of our hurricane lamp, we could see a ghostlike figure standing a few yards away. Slowly it moved closer, until before us stood the imposing figure of an Arab with his long, white, flowing garments, looking rather as if he had just stepped out from the pages of *The Arabian Nights*. He just stood there eyeing us up before nonchalantly strolling around the Land Rover, peering inside the tent and returning to us, vehemently spouting a load of Arabic. Rather at a loss as to what to do with our 'friend' we tried a fruitless attempt to converse with him. Then, as fast as he appeared, he disappeared only to return thirty minutes later with two more Arabs. Soon we were all sitting cross-legged in a circle around our lamp having a 'powwow', them gibbering away in Arabic and us in English. We did eventually manage to find out that the leading Arab's name was Josef and that he had six wives. He indicated that we could each have one if we followed him back to his village. Discretion being the better part of valour, we reluctantly refused his most generous offer.

Getting up, Josef moved over to the Land Rover and pointed to Tim's camera that was hanging up inside, then pointed to himself, indicating that he wanted his photo taken. To humour him, Tim agreed. The four Arabs (we had now been joined by yet another) spruced themselves up before standing rigidly to attention, waiting apprehensively as if half-expecting to be shot, rather like children awaiting their first school photograph. A quick flash and it was all over. They seemed very relieved that it did not even hurt.

We soon realised we had snapped ourselves a problem. Josef wanted the photograph right away. No matter how much we tried to explain to him that this was impossible, he remained adamant and was beginning to get quite upset. "It's got to be sent to London," said Tim. "You go London now, I wait here," replied Josef. Evidently he expected Tim to pop off to London, get the film developed, and return all in about an hour. Not satisfied, Josef went into consultation with his compatriots. A short burst of staccato Arabic and they swept off into the darkness.

Relieved to have been let off so lightly, we returned to the more domestic duties of cooking a meal. Our relief was short-lived. Returning was Josef and his three cronies. Back to the conference table, with Josef demanding his photograph and us trying to explain why he could not have it. Evidently Muslim Arabs believe that the camera is capturing their spirit as well as their image, and Josef did not relish us taking his away with us. It was beginning to get rather warm for us, especially when one of the Arabs produced a gun, taking great pains in showing us it was loaded. Two of Josef's friends were similarly armed, one with a knife, the other with a lethal-looking axe. My mind revolved like a one-armed bandit. Bristol man axed in Syrian Desert: I could see the headline blazoned across the front page of the local paper. Recognition at last. I only hope they find out how we went and do not just file us in the ignominy of the middle pages as 'person missing in Middle East'. Surprisingly Josef appeared to be calming down. Our efforts to get his mind off the camera by giving him an English lesson seemed to be paying dividends. By the end of the evening they all appeared to have forgotten about the camera. With much relief we watched them disappear into the night, but I could not help feeling that they might just return, possibly whilst we were sleeping.

It was a fatigue-induced sleep I had that night, with my hand resting on my knife.

Daylight arrived and we were relieved to find us all still in one piece. Crawling out of the tent we were greeted by a crowd of about twenty locals who had gathered round. The finale? No, they were only being inquisitive, no doubt surprised to find a strange 'tribe' appearing overnight in their territory. We dismantled the tent and made a hurried departure watched closely by our attentive audience.

An hour's drive brought us to the Syrian border town of Abu Kamal. Enquiries to the whereabouts of the border post led us to a few dead ends, but eventually we got onto the right track which took us to the border post. Out of Syria into Iraq.

CHAPTER 6

Into Iraq

A three-hour drive and still we had not sighted the Iraq border post. We began thinking that we had somehow bypassed it, there being no definite road to follow. Eventually we arrived at a small outpost standing like an oasis in an endless sea of sand. A group of military police came out to 'greet' us. On completion of a few questions and an inspection of our passports, they allowed us to move on.

That was easy, I thought, we were expecting a more thorough interrogation coming into a country like Iraq. Our relief was short-lived: two miles further on, a reception committee was waiting for us. Presumably the outpost was just an advance warning post, and we were only just arriving at the border post. We were rather apprehensive as to what sort of reception we would receive in Iraq (they only recently having broken off diplomatic relations with Britain).

Our fears were unfounded. We were taken into a small office where courteous but aimless officials entertained us with cups of tea whilst seemingly trying to decide what to do with us or why they wanted to interview us. One felt that this profusion of bureaucratic formality was a game, as none of these men seemed to comprehend the nature of his job clearly enough to take it seriously. Whilst conversing with the military we asked advice on the best route to Baghdad, to which they replied, "There are no roads, but as long as you keep to the left of the oil pipeline and do not cross the Euphrates before Fallujah you should end up in Baghdad." A great assurance.

Whilst at the border we had to obtain insurance cover which is compulsory in Iraq. Visas and passports returned and customs clearance given and we were once again on the road, though not literally. A few miles from the border post and any semblance of bitumen was purely coincidental. All we had to guide us was a few tyre marks in the sand and even those radiated in diverse directions so were not a lot of help. Luckily we had a very good car compass which proved invaluable in these conditions. Apart from the compass we found that telegraph wires were a helpful guide, going on the assumption that they must be heading for some sort of civilisation. If all that failed, we had a standby system. Our portable radio stood by as a prehistoric sat nav. If you tuned into Radio Baghdad, and when you got the best reception, you headed Sweaty Betty on that course. One could easily start heading in the wrong direction and there are over 1,500 miles of desert to the south. A sobering thought. On one of our stops Dick decided to explore a rocky hilly outpost, thinking he must be the first European to venture on it, only to find an old Coke bottle on it.

Regarding petrol, we had topped up at Abu Kamal and advocated that we would have sufficient to enable us to reach Haditha, pending no unforeseen mishaps. We were finding travelling really cheap in these parts. Petrol costing little more than 14p per gallon and vegetables and meats really cheap if purchased at the side stalls.

A 20-kilometre drive brought us to an oilfield guarded meticulously by the militia who stopped us for yet another inspection of passports. In the distance the oilfield looked like an oasis with its clusters of palm trees standing out like asterisks against the deep blue sky.

From the oilfield ran the pipeline which, although mostly underground, could be readily identified by the mounds of sand running parallel, and the inspection stations spaced at regular intervals.

Sand, sand and yet more sand, as far as the eye could see, nothing to break the monotony. At least we were saved the headache of searching for a campsite. As soon as it got dark we just pitched the tent where we were. Since leaving the Iraq border post that morning we had only encountered one other vehicle, so we should not have any worries about being disturbed.

Our next sign of habitation was the oil pipeline station of Haditha, a small collection of tumbledown dwellings close to the banks of the Euphrates. A short stop at this wild-looking Arab village gave us the chance to stock up with fresh vegetables and fruit. The dubious-looking fly-covered meats we gave a miss.

We were getting rather confused with the local currency. The Arab coins not only were written in Arabic, but also had Arab numerals, so extra care had to be taken when making any purchase. The Arabs were not slow in making a few cents for themselves at the expense of innocent tourists. So it was more a case of necessity than interest that we quickly learnt the Arabic numerals.

After satisfying the Land Rover's thirst for petrol we departed from Haditha. The going gradually went from bad to worse, conditions not being helped by a sandstorm that suddenly blew up. Sand was getting everywhere. The inside of the Land Rover was a fog of fine sand, necessitating us covering our mouths with handkerchiefs to prevent ourselves from choking.

The sandtrack we were following was quickly deteriorating, getting much bumpier, and worse still was that most of the previous tracks were being obliterated by the sandstorm. Luckily we did not have far to travel in these conditions as we were soon to join up with the main Damascus-Baghdad road. What a contrast, driving on the good bitumen road after the recent trek across the desert wastes. I could not help thinking just how much quicker and more comfortable it would have been if we had travelled down to Damascus from Aleppo and driven on the first-class road right through from Damascus to Baghdad.

We had just passed through the town of Ramadi, the first town of any size since we had arrived in Iraq, when we realised that once again we had allowed the darkness to overtake us, something we were endeavouring to avoid after our recent escapades. Our main objective now was to get away from the road, which, being the main road to

Baghdad, was comparatively busy. Once away from the built-up area of Ramadi we drove across the sand until we came to an ideal camping spot sheltered by large sand dunes. And so we nestled down for the night.

The following morning whilst brewing up a cup of tea, we were disturbed to hear strange rumblings, sounding close by. Climbing to the top of a nearby sand dune, we were shocked to see about a dozen tanks circling us, their turrets and gun muzzles probing menacingly. We rushed back to the tent and commenced packing, which, I believe, was in record time. All stops pulled out as we raced across the sand back towards the road, half-expecting to hear the whine of a shell following us. Just our luck: we had camped in the middle of a tank training area. I dread to imagine what would have happened if they held a live shoot during the night. Back on the road we passed, at regular intervals, large signs written in about six languages stating "Military Area – No Stopping" etc etc. It looks as if we had just spent the night in the lion's den. Once more we vowed to always find a camping 'patch' whilst still daylight.

The vast expanses of sand were now dwindling as we travelled through increasingly fertile and cultivated terrain. Our last sight of the River Euphrates was as we crossed the road bridge at Fallujah, leaving it to meander lethargically on its homeward stretch southwards to the Persian Gulf.

A considerable increase in the volume of traffic and industrial sites heralded the approaches to Baghdad. On the horizon we could see the tall minarets of the numerous mosques standing erect on the skyline.

First impressions of Baghdad are of an ancient city rapidly heading to the familiarity of a city of 'little boxes'. Tall, modern blocks tower over the numerous pockets of squalid shanty towns.

As we intended staying in Baghdad for a few days, our first objective was to visit the information bureau to arm ourselves with local maps and enquire about campsites. On recommendation we went to an excellent site just outside the city, close to the banks of the River Tigris. An ideal spot, a copse of palm trees sheltering numerous straw huts, one of which we commandeered. The site was practically deserted apart from a couple of Dormobiles, and by coincidence the Land Rover party on an identical trip to us whom we had previously met at the campsite in Istanbul. The party, Bo, Peggy, Mike and Tony, had travelled a different route from Istanbul, having journeyed via Damascus and arriving in Baghdad only an hour before us.

Apart from cleaning ourselves there was plenty of work to do on the Land Rover. The exhaust had taken quite a battering during the drive through the desert and was deteriorating rapidly. There was also plenty of cleaning to do, both inside and outside the vehicle. Sand had got everywhere. The engine was full of it, as were our cases and food boxes.

Once the chores had been completed we settled down to a couple of days sightseeing the city. Baghdad was not the city that I had imagined it to be. Where were the myriads of naked belly dancers? To me it was a disappointment, having become a very commercialised, bustling city. It seems to have lost whatever glamour it had in the days of the Arabian nights, though there are still some very good bazaars where craftsmen in their souks still pound their copper vessels out in flat sheets, and artisans still make shoes and other everyday items alongside gold- and silversmiths in their tiny shops.

Narrow alleyways jammed solid with bodies, veiled women, chanting men, yelling children, scarred faces, bright probing eyes, angry looks, and laughing glances. The sun blazed down on them all. A bargain hunter's paradise, a Baghdad bazaar has everything and anything, from a rusty, bent, second-hand nail to a Persian carpet or a dining room suite: it was all there. The open market was not so attractive, being one wide open space of filth, cows, goats and sheep mingling freely amongst the vegetables, fruit and spices.

Because of our concern over the increasingly explosive situation between India and Pakistan, we went to the Air India office in the hope of gleaning some information on the latest situation report. An extremely friendly Indian went out of his way to tell us all he knew, and to show all the Indian reports, all of which seemed predictably biased. Over cups of tea he assured us that by the time we reach that area, it would all be over, and India, of course, would have won. I am afraid we did not share his confidence.

By the time we had come out of the office it was dark, giving us the opportunity to see Baghdad by night. Most of the life was on the streets, there being very few bars or nightclubs. Sweetmeat stalls were everywhere, lit by glowing lanterns, temping selections of Turkish delights and succulent, coloured delicacies. We rounded off the evening with a visit to a nightclub on the banks of the Tigris, where we were entertained by a rather second-rate band and two 'go-go' dancers whose looks far surpassed their ability. With beer at 50p a bottle we made one bottle last all night, which brought disconcerting looks from the waiters.

I had always imagined Baghdad as being a very hot, fly-ridden city – a myth that was shattered the first night, which was bitterly cold, in fact so much so that our water canister had frozen, though it did get quite warm during the day once the sun came out.

A pleasant surprise was the friendliness of the Iraqis, especially the more educated ones, who all bade us well.

It appeared that our campsite doubled up as a public park: we were continually being visited by the locals, many of whom appeared extremely interested in our trip. The Friday, Iraq being a Muslim country, was a rest day, and the site was packed. Whether we had been advertised as a tourist attraction I do not know, but we certainly got attention. The following day we made an early start to go on the 160-mile round trip to see the Hanging Gardens of Babylon, taking the main road southwards out of Baghdad through Al Mahmudiya and on to Babylon. The two and a half-hour journey brought us to the imposing main gateway to the Hanging Gardens, a replica of the original and only a fraction of its size. After paying our admission fee we were allowed through the gates, whereupon we were presented with a military 'guide' who was to follow us, at a distance, until our exit.

Our initiation to the gardens was a small museum, with an excellent mock-up of the 'hanging gardens' in their prime. The gardens themselves are a bitter disappointment. As they were one of the seven wonders of the world, we had expected to see something spectacular. "Where are all the flowers?" asked Dick, "It's nothing but a load of old ruins." True, there was not anything that resembled a garden, and unless one is an archaeologist, historian or has a really vivid imagination, there is not really a lot to see, the only credit being prestige value in saying you have been there. Attempts are being made to restore some of the ruins to their former splendour, work on which was in progress. We spent a few hours leisurely strolling around the ruins with our faithful watchdog of a guide never far behind us, no matter how much we tried to elude him. Perhaps he was afraid we might procure some ancient relic. The fabled Lion of Babylon stood forlorn in its near-headless state, looking every day of its age. From the high point of the 'gardens' we had a commanding view of the surrounding countryside. The meandering Euphrates in the distance, in the foreground the small town of Hilla completely encompassed by palm trees. Futile attempts were made to try and piece together the ancient city. We could make out the main cobbled thoroughfare of Nebuchadnezzar's procession street, and the partly restored main assembly throne room hall, which dominates the whole scene; also an assortment of buildings still sunk below ground level, which we presumed were the local red-light area. There is a fine collection of stereotyped figures moulded out on the stone walls, mostly depicting ancient Mesopotamian warriors. Having seen all there was to see, we returned to the main gates feeling rather conned.

Just outside the gates there was plenty of activity in the way of further excavations of recent discoveries, though we were not allowed to inspect these. On the road back to Baghdad we passed the other Land Rover crew (Bo, Penny, Mike and Tony) who were on their way to see the sights of Ur and Basra. Before returning to our campsite we visited the Baghdad Museum, which was well worth the effort. A whole kaleidoscope of Mesopotamian history with the many interesting finds from Babylon and the Tombs of Ur.

Back at the campsite we prepared for our departure from Baghdad. With our food supplies diminishing we were able to obtain much-needed breathing space in the Land Rover. Prior to our departure, Ron caused a stir at the campsite by complaining about the state of the wash houses. Such a rumpus was caused between the management and the cleaners that they overlooked to charge us for the night's camping.

It was pouring with rain as we left Baghdad, passing through flat, sandy countryside with sparse vegetation. Through the townships of Baqubah and Sharaban (Miqdadiyah) and through rich oilfield country to Khanaqin. Evidence of the approach to the border could be seen in the increase of military presence. Between Khanaqin and the Iraq border post we were stopped three times by the Army.

The border post was a hive of activity. The large reception hall was full of Arabs, tribesmen and Iranians, babbling away in little groups, making a colourful scene in their diverse costumes. Many, no doubt accustomed to the long delays at the border posts, had squatted down drinking tea out of their small glass containers or had lain out on their instant beds. Custom officials were methodically going through the travellers' piles of skins, silks, leathers and carpets, no doubt all heading for the Baghdad bazaars. Outside, officials were swarming like ants over an ancient bus whose roof rack was piled high with merchandise, chickens and hobbled sheep.

Luckily, after a short wait we were apprehended by an Army officer who directed us through various offices, and with preferential treatment soon had our passports cleared and we were once more heading on our way eastward across the short 'no man's land' to the Iranian border post, having just clocked up our 5,000th mile since leaving England.

CHAPTER 7

Into Iran

Dusk was approaching as we arrived at the barrier to the Iranian border post. As we already had our visa for Iran we were hoping for a quick clearance, but no: "Please fill in these forms. May I have your passports and Carnet?" said the desk-bound official. After an hour's wait we were allowed to proceed, though not before customs had searched through the Land Rover. Whilst at the border we took the opportunity to cash some traveller's cheques.

As you start to travel in these parts of the world you discover that crossing borders can often be a tedious and time-consuming business to which you soon become accustomed.

At long last we were on our way again. The two miles between the Iraq and Iran borders had taken up three hours of our time. It was dark, cold, wet and windy as we left the Iran border. I think we were all feeling rather disgruntled at this point. In pouring rain we drove on to the border town of Qasr-e Shirin.

Whilst stopping at a garage for petrol, Dick got into conversation with an affluent-looking gentleman who claimed he knew of an excellent cheap hotel where we could spend the night. Tim, as usual, was rather reluctant, preferring to camp, regardless of weather. A big decision! Up to now we had relied on our tent for accommodation. A show of hands. Even though I was always on the side of the cheapest way out and having got quite 'hardened' to the gypsy life, I had to admit that camping in these conditions, heavy rain and below-freezing temperatures was inviting trouble. Ron, as usual, was always on the side of comfort. And so the decision was made, we would be lax for one night. Tim was quick to add, "Let's not make a habit of this."

Once we had made up our minds, the person with whom Dick had been chatting jumped into the Land Rover and guided us to a run-down-looking hotel. No doubt our 'guide' had connections with the hotel manager and conveniently posted himself at the garage in the hope of directing wayfarers – the likes of us – to the hotel. We were taken to a room, which was just enough space to cram in four beds and a washbasin which, after all, was all we needed. The price of such luxury was 70 rials (35p) each. Against regulations we managed to smuggle our Primus stove into the room to enable us to cook a meal.

Seeing as we had paid for a night's luxury we lost no time in getting between the sheets. What a fantastic feeling, our first bed for six weeks. I never realised just how much I had missed it. I tried to stay awake to revel in the comfort, but it was too comfortable: soon I was fast asleep. Happiness is in the shape of a Persian blanket! It took great willpower to drag myself out of my bed in the morning after such a perfect sleep. The memory of that bed still lingers on, even though it was only a metal frame with a horsehair mattress.

Reluctantly we left our hotel. Before moving on, we had a stroll around Qasr-e Shirin. A scruffy-looking border town seething with beggars with their hands out, hopefully for their 'baksheesh'. Small shops full of Persian carpets, blankets and silks gave it the appearance of a trading post, which to all intents and purposes it was, being the nearest Iranian town to the Baghdad markets.

From Qasr-e Shirin we headed through the province of Kermanshah towards to the Zagros Mountains, home of the nomadic Karuk, Bakhtiari and Qashqai tribes. An hour's drive and we were once again up amongst the mountains and the snow. Driving was hazardous, the roads having been turned into a veritable skating rink. The snow thickened as we gained altitude, ascending towards the Gaduk Pass. The beautiful scenery more than compensated for the arduous going. Lush green plains nestled between peaks of snow-white mountains, resembling very much Switzerland minus trees. Many of the Zagros Mountain peaks attain a height of nearly 12,000 feet.

Even though the sun was shining in a cloudless sky, the temperature was dropping considerably. Ice was giving way to hard, packed snow well over a foot deep. Despite the intense cold the view from the top of the mountains made it all well worthwhile.

After passing through the small mountain village of Kirind we descended to Kermanshah, capital of the province. From Kermanshah to Hamadān we noticed numerous piles of snow-covered turnips by the roadside, presumably waiting to be 'picked up'. Such an opportunity to live off the land we could not pass. Discreetly parking the Land Rover between two piles of turnips, we commenced filling every available container. A couple of meals of turnips, okay, but two weeks of eating turnips is just a bit too much.

Our harvesting completed, we continued on our way through the mountainous countryside passing the villages of Bisotun, Kangavan and Asadabad, eventually arriving at dusk at Hamadān, which was certainly living up to its reputation as one of the coldest towns in Iran. That assumption is not surprising considering that it's over 7,000 feet above sea level.

The adverse weather had already made up our minds to again settle for a night in a cheap hotel. The ground was so frozen I do not think we could have hammered in a tent peg anyway. The whole area was one solid pack of frozen snow: sounding like a multitude of people eating potato crisps simultaneously, we crunched our way into Hamadān. Stopping alongside a policeman we enquired where we could obtain a cheap hotel for the night. Without further ado the policeman got into the Land Rover and directed us to a small hotel in the centre of the town.

With the willing help of the hotel staff we unpacked the Land Rover and settled into our room, which at 70 rials (35p) we certainly could not complain about. The water container, which was stowed on the front of the Land Rover, had frozen into one complete block of ice – not surprising considering the hotel manager had informed us that the temperature outside was 28 degrees Fahrenheit, below freezing. He advised us to park the Land Rover in the yard opposite the hotel, where there was at least some shelter.

No sooner had we settled in our room when we were brought in cups of tea and informed that a meal was ready downstairs. We were served with an excellent dish of kebabs and rice with a bowl of yoghurt, which appears to be the local staple diet. Also dining in the small hotel restaurant was our friendly policeman: perhaps he, too, had shares in the business.

During the evening Tim and I took a walk in the crisp night air. Hamadān, we found, was a pleasant change from the customary unkempt Middle East towns. Whether the ice and snow were hiding the dirt, it certainly gave the impression of a very clean and well-planned town. All the streets radiated from a central roundabout which was brilliantly decorated with a colourful display of lights. A very interesting conversation was had between Tim and me and a policeman who was on sentry duty outside the police station. Although his knowledge of English was limited he proved to be a very amusing character, intimating to us how much he loathed standing around the streets in such dastardly weather. He thought us mad to be out walking the streets by choice. It seemed that all Iranian policemen look-alike, very stereotyped, carbon copies of each other, giving the impression that they are mass produced, all being turned out with 'Viva Zapata' moustaches.

Before departing from Hamadān we spent a couple of hours admiring the frozen wastes by daylight, confirming the previous night's opinion of Hamadān as a clean, well-designed town, with a very good, bustling bazaar. 'Our' policeman was there to wave us goodbye as we left Hamadān and rejoined the main road which was one solid sheet of ice.

We 'waltzed' our way for a few miles before deciding to stop in a lay-by for a 'brew-up' in the hope that, meanwhile, the sun would rise enough to break the ice. A humorous hour was spent watching the antics of passing vehicles. A police patrol car driver's confidence was shattered as he sped past us, only to do a 180-degree coup de grâce, finding himself heading from whence he came. Deciding to once more try our luck on the 'rink', we 'tiptoed' our way cautiously onwards, doing our best to keep our nose heading in the right direction and avoiding contact with other vehicles. Thick snow, glistening from the brilliant sunshine, gave a fairy tale atmosphere amongst the towering mountain peaks which spread out either side of us like decorated icing on a birthday cake, the dominating peak being the Alvand to our right, which rises majestically to a height of 11,000 feet.

Occasional interludes from the mountainous 'helter-skelter' were provided by long stretches of flat plateaux, which joined the mountain ranges with the similarity of barbells.

Road conditions were gradually improving: as the sun shone, temperatures rose, clearing much of the ice. In fact it was quite pleasant driving, provided we kept our circulation moving. Unfortunately the vehicle was far from draught-proof, canvas not being the best insulation from the elements, and there not being any heater fitted. We were constantly changing drivers: after only a short spell at the wheel our hands and feet would become numb. The area we were now passing through was the scene of a major earthquake in 1962 in which some 6,000 people perished. Many of the villages have been restored with the help of American aid.

The villages of Rajan and Aveh passed, we were soon approaching our target for the day, Qazvin. As in common with most Iranian towns, Qazvin had a very imposing entrance, an archway of coloured lights, crowned with a laminated coronet.

Again we found ourselves in a cheap hotel, right in the main street, with a handy backyard to park the Land Rover. No sooner had we settled in our room than we were visited by a student who gave us the 'rundown' on where to go and what to do in Tehran.

All the small Iranian towns appear to have been built from the same blueprint, consisting of a main street leading on to a large, central roundabout from which radiate numerous side streets. Coloured lights in abundance, giving the impression of a promenade of an English seaside resort. I was surprised to find just how Westernised Iran has become and how forward in comparison to its Arab neighbours.

From Qazvin we joined the main road to Tehran which took us through flat, prosperous-looking countryside. Evidence of the proximity of Tehran could be seen by the increasing number of industrial projects. We were now travelling parallel to the Elburz mountains which run the length of the Southern Caspian Sea coastline. A wide dual carriageway and an imposing modern structure of concrete enormity crowned a large roundabout which heralds the entrance to Tehran, Iran's capital city.

Tehran, a charming city, a city of contrasts, where the ancient and modern go hand in hand. Tall, modern office blocks, wide, tree-lined boulevards, parks and supermarkets mingle with bustling bazaars and mosques. Factories with their mass-produced products rub shoulders with the ancient crafts still being plied. Set in beautiful surroundings, with the snow-covered Elburz mountains supplying the backcloth. Much of the city is built on the slopes of these mountains. I got the impression that the higher up the slopes, the more affluent the houses. Rather as if the rich were trying to creep away from their poorer counterparts, who lived in the lower half of the city.

Although it was only two days away from Christmas, there was little evidence of the festive season, apart from an abundance of Christmas trees on sale outside the British Embassy and a few shops selling Christmas cards.

A visit to the British Embassy to collect any mail was met with an indifferent reception from the staff who informed us that our mail had been returned to the Tehran Post Office. The British Embassy is a bastion of colonial England dropped right in the heart of Tehran, surrounded by a high brick wall enclosing a church, houses of the Embassy staff, a modern Embassy building, plus lawns and gardens. Guarding the entrance to the Embassy are lion and unicorn statues either side of large, heraldic wrought-iron gates, a spoonful of England in the heart of Iran.

A cheap hotel in a back alley near the centre of the city was to be our abode for the Christmas period. Dick was in his element, the hotel being situated next to a yoghurt shop. The hotel certainly would not warrant an AA rating. Our room consisted of just the bare essentials, four beds and a washbasin, which left little room to stand up in. The toilets at the end of the passageway were the typical 'stand-up' type. The comfort of a 'sit-down' loo was left behind as far back as Greece. Still, at 60 rials (30p) a night we did not expect The Dorchester. From the window of our room we could look down on our Land Rover which was taking up most of the space in the busy alleyway. Even though it attracted much attention, and there being no way of locking the vehicle, there was no attempt at souvenir hunting, which was a pleasant surprise considering we were in the poorer part of the city.

On the recommendation of an English-speaking student who had befriended us, we patronised a very good cheap restaurant close to our hotel. For 35 rials (17p) we were able to obtain excellent meals, mostly consisting of rice and kebabs. There was no menu and the waiter spoke no English. But that did not matter as we were allowed to go into the kitchen and make our selection from the meats and vegetables in the cooking pots on the charcoal stove.

I was impressed by the friendliness of the Iranians, most of whom went out of their way to assist us. The majority of people we conversed with preferred to be known as Persian as opposed to an Iranian; this also applied on a national basis, preferring Persia to Iran. I suspect this goes back to the deep-rooted pride in the bygone greatness of the ancient Persian Empire.

As darkness descends, the city turns into a blaze of neon lights advertising cinemas and clubs, though by 10 pm most of the entertainment seemed to finish. The lights went out and the streets became deserted. We visited a cinema where we saw a Greek film with Persian subtitles. What did surprise us was the total absence of females in the cinema.

On Christmas Eve we treated ourselves to an evening out at a club. Unfortunately if we wanted a drink we were to have a meal, which we did not want. No amount of arguing with the waiter and manager would make them change their minds. Eventually we settled on a compromise of a bowl of fruit. On completion of the floor show, which was a mixture of second-rate singers, gymnasts and comedians, we once more crossed swords with the management, this time regarding the bill: they were trying to charge us for four bowls of fruit instead of one. Heated exchanges between us and the increasing number of staff who gathered, neither side being able to understand each other. It was beginning to get ridiculous, though to an outsider it must have looked quite humorous. We ended the bout by putting what we thought was a reasonable sum of money on the table, and walking out, leaving them to sort it out amongst themselves.

Christmas Day 1971, coffee in bed by courtesy of Ron. In the morning Ron and I walked to the north of the city to attend a carol service at the Anglican church. As it happened, we turned up at the wrong church. Fortunately, an English couple in the same predicament gave us a lift to the right church, where we joined ambassadors, embassy staff and other dignitaries in a short bout of carol-singing. Tea and biscuits afterwards, though the hoped-for invite to a Christmas dinner with some rich white was not forthcoming.

Our midday Christmas meal consisted of a small Christmas pudding divided between the four of us and a small bottle of whisky, both religiously saved for the occasion. With all the shops and offices open and being a normal working day, it was a job to get into the Christmas spirit. A visit to an excellent German restaurant, seasonally decorated, in the evening for a slap-up Christmas dinner of turkey, red cabbage, Russian eggs and caviar went some way to rectify this.

During our stay in Tehran we visited various airline offices and travel agencies in an endeavour to obtain information on the latest situation of the Indo/Pakistan crisis. Our efforts were met with conflicting reports, which did not help in clarifying our position. By now we were too committed to turn back, so we had to press on, in the hope that by the time we reached Pakistan the conflict would be over. Though it was a black cloud on the horizon and a constant source of concern.

We departed from Tehran on Boxing Day, leaving by the same road from whence we arrived, heading back towards Qazvin, our intentions being to cross the Elburz mountains to get to the Caspian Sea coast. We had already been informed that the easterly route across the mountains was impossible due to snow.

About ten miles west of Tehran we took a minor road heading north up into the mountains. A continual series of hairpins as we ascended the mountain trail soon brought us to the snow line which rapidly deepened as we ascended. Conditions deteriorated, with hard-packed snow making hazardous driving. Halfway up the mountain we were stopped by the police, who informed us that they had strict instructions to refuse passage to any vehicle without snow chains, a commodity which we had neglected. Even Tim's insistence that we had an "instant tyre chain" in the form of an aerosol can, and the fact that we had four-wheel drive, would not make them relax their strict instructions. After an hour's arguing we finally succumbed, realising that they were remaining adamant in their decision. So there we were, the easterly route across the mountains blocked by snow and now the westerly route impassable. We had little option but to about-turn and backtrack our way down the mountain. The only alternative left open to us was a 250-mile detour via Qazvin which would take us around the Elburz mountains to the Caspian Sea. At least there was some consolation from our wasted morning's effort: beautiful scenery, huge mountain gorges and deep river valleys.

Back on the main road we drove west towards Qazvin, a town where we were four days previously. I felt as if we were heading further away from our objective, rather than nearing it. It was a dejected crew who drove through the flat countryside towards Qazvin.

As if we had not had enough disappointments for the day, we ran out of fuel about seven miles from Qazvin. Having no spare fuel, we emptied our gallon can of paraffin into the tank. Surprisingly enough, after a lot of coughing and spluttering and the inevitable pinking, we managed to get to a garage in Qazvin.

From Qazvin we journeyed through rice-growing land, crossing the River Sefīd-Rūd close to the vast dam project which irrigates the paddy fields. Turning north, we crossed the dry, rocky, volcanic surface of the westerly fringe of the Elburz mountains.

After passing through the small town of Rasht the scenery changes dramatically from the charcoal volcanic surface to lush-green, English-looking countryside. The temperature had also risen considerably. We were now at long last on the Caspian Sea side of the Elburz mountains, an area known as the province of Mazandaran.

It was dark by the time we had reached the Caspian Sea. Our initial sight of the sea was the flickering of the moonlight dancing on its surface away to our left. To break the monotony of the long day's drive, we stopped for a drink at a small tea house at Lahijan. I think we were all too tired to take much notice of the disconcerting stares from the local inhabitants.

Prior to the small town of Rudsar, Dick noticed a small plot of vacant land, just off the road and adjacent to the Caspian Sea. A lucky break – an ideal spot for the night, sheltered from the road by tall trees and only a few yards from the shore.

By now we were ready to call it a day, having driven 350 miles and with nothing to eat all day. At least we had achieved our objective in reaching the Caspian Sea and had made up much of our lost time.

By the light of the moon we erected the tent and Dick soon had the two Primuses going flat out to provide a meal. With our bodies refuelled we lost no time in crawling into our sleeping bags, to be lulled to sleep by the soothing lapping of the waters of the Caspian Sea.

All too soon dawn was upon us. Crawling out of the tent we were greeted by the bleating of a herd of sheep, inquisitively invading our privacy. Shooing away the interlopers we went down to the shores of the Caspian Sea for our first look in daylight. It seemed incredible to think that opposite shores were over 700 miles away in the depths of Russia. It is the largest inland body of water in the world, and the home of the world's best caviar.

Taking advantage of the fresh, clear and practically salt-free water, Tim drove the Land Rover over the pebbled beach and reversed into the sea where it was given a well-needed wash. I was tempted to go for a swim, but settled for a stripped wash. There is nothing like a midwinter swill in the Caspian Sea to freshen you up!

We were well rewarded for our long detour to get to the sea. Not only was there a marked rise in temperature, but also a very pleasant change in the countryside, which was not unlike England, now 6,000 miles behind us. A sea of undulating grasslands, green and cultivated. This time to our right, our friend the Elburz mountains majestically stretched a parallel course to us. To our left we got intermittent peeps at the Caspian Sea. Nestling between the mountains and the sea are the coastal resorts of Rudsar, Chalus, Amol and Babol, all fairly prosperous and well kept. No doubt gaining much income from rice, sugar cane, oranges, tobacco and tea which abound in this area, reflecting the warm and moist climate.

Poets speak of this area as "enjoying perpetual spring". Many of the larger houses in these towns are artistically decorated with colourful drawings, similar to those seen in Austria and Switzerland.

The Caspian borderland includes, in part, a humid lowland below sea level, in part glacier-clad peaks which rise to heights of nearly 6,000 feet.

To our right we could see the stark, volcanic peak of Mount Damāvand, Iran's highest peak and Asia's highest volcano, some 19,000 feet high standing proudly above lesser peaks of the Elburz range. A flawless, snow-capped cone against a backcloth of orange cloud. The Elburz mountains, 500 miles long, form a major climate boundary, wet on the northerly slopes and dry on the southerly. There are three main ranges, cut by deep gorges and susceptible to severe earthquakes. The few transverse highways reach elevations of almost 9,000 feet. Vegetation matches altitude and exposure.

Although we were now driving in near perfect conditions, we were not allowed to relax our concentration. Apart from the suicidal driving of the Iranians we were continually having to be on the alert for horses, sheep, cattle and geese, who wandered nonchalantly into the road. Much of the local mode of transport appeared to be the horse, and we passed many bare-back riders.

Our concern over the state of one of our rear tyres finally came to a head with a bang. We had just got our first blow out, which was not entirely unexpected, we had been recently reflating it with increasing regularity. All the tyres had taken a pounding and were beginning to show distinct signs of wear. A swift roadside wheel change and we were once again on our way.

Darkness was approaching as we reached the eastern extremities of the Caspian Sea near Bandar Shah, a mere twenty miles from the Russian border. Top priority was a campsite for the night. In pouring rain we explored every side turning in our quest for a suitable site to pitch our tent, all to no avail. As a last resort we enquired at a roadside police traffic checkpoint. "You are more than welcome to pitch your tent alongside the police buildings," said the officer in charge. "There are also toilets and washing facilities if you need them." And so we made camp for the night under the protective wing of the police.

Any hope of settling down for an early night's sleep was shattered by the insistence of the police that we join them in their office for the evening. Tea, cake and oranges were served up during a very entertaining evening with the friendly Iranian police. In fact they were a bit too friendly: they would not let us go. They retained our interest with 'hot' magazines and books, and a rundown of various 'tricks of the trade'. The police post was a checking-in point for all vehicles. Transport lorries are weighed and their speeds checked off the vehicle's speed disc which is compulsory on all lorries in Iran. During our stay in the office we saw many drivers pay out instant fines. One driver was paying his third fine within three checkpoints for having an invalid driving licence. He came into the room with his money ready to pay the impending fine before even showing his driving licence. It was well after 1 am before we managed to get away from our evening on duty.

The following morning, after a rather damp night's sleep (it rained all night), we took advantage of the rare facilities to have a good clean-up and to restore the Land Rover which was now lighter by one tyre, having rid ourselves of our blowout.

On completion of weighing the Land Rover on the police weighbridge, we bade our farewells to the friendly bunch of cops who all came out for a round of handshaking.

Farewells over, we continued the short distance to the nearby town of Gorgan, where we stopped to purchase an inner tube to replace the one ruined the previous day. From Gorgan we drove within a few miles of the Russian border through attractive urban countryside.

The friendly waves we received from the local populace were a far cry from the warnings of stone-throwing from the children in these parts, which we had received prior to our departure. I think the answer was in having someone on hand to do duty as a waver, rather like royalty in a state procession. Failure to return a greeting would probably be answered with a hail of stones.

The further east we travelled, the poorer the people became. Gone were the smart stone houses of the Caspian Sea coastal towns: in their place were mud hut villages. To our right the Elburz mountains still dominated the scenery. The vast plain along which we were travelling seemed endless. Apart from a few small farming communities, there was very little sign of habitation. The only village of any note was Shah Pasand, where we stopped to barter for provisions at the local market.

Our session of easy driving was all too soon over as we started to climb for our final battle with the Elburz mountains. On unsealed roads through thickly forested terrain, we commenced our laborious ascent of the eastern fringes of the mountains.

Not wishing to find ourselves having to camp above the snow line, we decided to make an early camp. We found a very good site just off the road adjacent to a fast-flowing mountain river.

Shortly after pitching the tent, we were visited by a game warden who informed us that we should not be camping here, it being a government game reserve. Our plea of ignorance paid off: reluctantly he allowed us to stay, though not before pointing to our bamboo fishing rod and shaking his head. Being a game reserve, poaching was not allowed. Confirmation of this we saw in the numerous signs to that effect in the area. Exactly what sort of game inhabited these areas we did not know. "Maybe wolves," said Ron. It certainly had the right setting for such imagination.

Undeterred, we made ourselves at home in our forest patch. Before long we had a roaring fire going, providing not only warmth, but also the means to cook the evening meal.

Dick went poaching for fish by moonlight in the nearby river. He managed to catch three, which by the time they had been cooked on a spit over the fire had frizzled down to a bare mouthful. At least we got the taste.

Efforts to screen ourselves from the road by suspending blankets from the branches of trees were only partially successful. The reflection from the fire must have stood out like a sore thumb for miles. Luckily there was very little traffic on the road, perhaps at the most one vehicle an hour, so we were left virtually undisturbed.

Ideal weather and a near-perfect site prompted us to stay a further day, enabling us to catch up on many of the outstanding chores.

Tim spent a busy day changing two tyres and once more having another go at bodging up the Land Rover's disintegrating exhaust. Even though we were within walking distance of the snow line, the weather was pleasantly warm, the temperature probably being in the tropical 40 degrees Fahrenheit.

Dick had a further attempt at catching our supper, his day's efforts being rewarded with two small fish.

With the cool, clear waters of a mountain river on our doorstep, I could not resist the temptation of a stripped wash. There is nothing like it to wax a waning spirit!

As we dismantled the tent the following morning, little did we realise that we had just spent our final night under canvas.

Leaving our game reserve, we proceeded eastwards towards Meshed. It was not long before we were up amongst the mountains again, along with deteriorating weather and of course the snow. Once at the top of the range we were confronted by vast expanses of rolling, arid plains. Very little vegetation grows at these heights, giving a rather desolate scene, not enhanced by the miserable weather we were experiencing: cold, windswept and snowing.

We made a somewhat costly error whilst stopping for a brew-up at the side of the road. Underneath, the snow was soft, oozy mud. All too late we realised, as Sweaty Betty sank up to the axles. Not even four-wheel drive could free us; we were only sinking deeper. Luckily, a lorry driver pulled up, seeing our predicament. Gleefully rubbing his hands, he watched us struggle. When Tim asked him if he would pull us out, he intimated that he would for a fee of 100 rials (50p). This transaction we refused. He obviously was not the Samaritan type and could only see the $ signs.

Returning to Sweaty Betty, we made further futile attempts at moving it. It was to no avail: even with Ron's weight behind, it refused to budge. Having no option, we returned to the lorry driver who had been eyeing the situation from his lorry with a grin akin to a new moon. No amount of persuasion would lower his price, he knew he was on to a winner, there being very little other traffic on the road. Reluctantly we agreed to pay the 100 rials. With very little effort he towed us back onto the road. The easiest 100 rials he had made for a long while. Apart from a change in colour, Sweaty Betty was none the worse for her mudbath.

Not wishing for a repeat performance, I kept well into the centre of the road (the edges were undetectable, being covered in snow). This strategy nearly proved fatal. A bus, being driven at its limits, charged down the road towards us. "Move over!" yelled Tim. Too late, away went our offside wing mirror. Another coat of paint would have probably had us all pushing up daisies. With no insurance and knowing the biased legal battles and delays we could involve ourselves in, we made 'post-haste', not waiting to retrieve our wing mirror which we left for the bus driver who had by now stopped.

After a short stop at Bojnord we proceeded through mountainous countryside where the road degenerated into little more than a cart track – quagmire-ish, potholed and literally strewn with rocks and boulders. The remnants of the Kopet mountains stretched down from Russia to fade out near Meshed.

Having passed through Quchan, the going improved, the terrain having flattened itself out and the roads once again being bitumenised.

It was getting dark as we neared Meshed. Not only did we have the snow to contend with, but the incessant flashing of the Iranian drivers whose headlight-dipping was more often than not full beam plus any extras they found to throw in.

A blaze of illuminations greeted us as we entered the Shia Shrine city of Meshed. Coloured lights were strung gaily across and along the streets, giving a carnival atmosphere.

Whilst slowly driving through the streets looking for somewhere to spend the night, a man drew alongside us and offered to take us to a cheap hotel. As it was by now getting late and snowing heavily, we agreed to follow him. A short drive brought us outside a dingy-looking hotel just off the main street. At 25p a night we agreed to stay and were taken to a small upstairs room which led out onto a verandah. With windows all round it looked like a conservatory and with no curtains, privacy was non-existent. Still, four beds were all we needed and that was all we got. The toilets at the end of the corridor were, even by Arab standards, pretty poor. A ceramic hole in the floor, the roofing having fallen in, which to some extent was a godsend as it let some of the smell out, though at the same time it let the snow in. From the customary crouching position one could look down through the missing floorboards into the kitchen below.

Promising to return tomorrow to show us around Meshed and his turquoise factory, our guide departed.

From the window of our 'glasshouse' we could see the floodlit silhouette of the imposing mosque, from which we could hear the chanting, or rather, wailing calling the 'flock' to prayer.

We awoke the following morning to find Meshed covered by a thick blanket of snow.

True to his promise, our guide arrived to take us on our tour. His tour consisted of taking us straight to his turquoise factory which was in a narrow alleyway off the main street. The factory was a small room about ten feet square fitted with a desk, a few chairs, an archaic wooden stone polisher, and a small grinding machine. His staff consisted of a wizened old man who silently went about his work of sorting and polishing the turquoise stones, and a small boy whose duties appeared to be those of messenger, factory minder and tea boy. Obviously, our guide's intention was to arouse our interest into buying some of his stones, and his offer to show us around Meshed was just a cover to get us to come into his shop.

We sat for over two hours drinking continuous glasses of black tea whilst he showed us his stock of turquoise amateurishly set out on cheap cards. Great lengths were taken to show us his references from satisfied customers – many, he stated, were from his contacts in England who were making massive profits reselling his stones. We were not impressed, the letters looked as if written by an illiterate; maybe he had written them himself. Seeing our interest waning, our guide excused himself, saying that he had to go to meet a friend and would be back in a few minutes. Having no intention of making a purchase, we took our cue and left.

The remainder of the day was spent looking around the city. Meshed is the fourth largest city in Iran and the main religious centre, being the Mecca for many Muslim pilgrims. It was founded around the tomb of two Mohammedan princes. The centrepiece of the city is the enormous mosque, home of the Shia Shrine. Surrounded by beautifully designed, turquoise mosaic walls and an impressive arched gateway. Inside the walls is a large courtyard fronting the huge dome and surrounding minarets. Being Friday (the Muslim Holy Day) we were not allowed inside the building, though we did get an excellent insight from the main entrance gates. Apart from the main entrance, many cloistered bazaar alleyways, alive with people, shops and stalls lead up to the mosque's courtyard.

Snow had been falling all day, but now Meshed was under a thick, white carpet, giving the city an unreal fairyland atmosphere with a grey sky backcloth to the domes and minarets.

The Caspian Sea, Iran.
Tim washing Sweaty Betty,
Dick overseeing.

Meshed, Iran,
New Year's Day.

Village at sunset between
Meshed and the Afghan
border.

Camel train on the road
between Meshed and
Afghanistan.

The population of Meshed is swelled at religious festive times by the influx of the thousands of pilgrims. Luckily we were there during the off season, so were able to see the sights at our leisure, though the inclement weather did not encourage much sightseeing. Apart from being a religious centre, Meshed is the main trading outlet to Afghanistan and the East.

Back in our room we took the opportunity to catch up with the much-neglected washing, drying the garments over the large, drip-fed oil stove which served as the room's heater. Our room seemed to be an open house: people were constantly walking in and sitting on our beds, no doubt to observe the strange ways of the English intruders.

Our conversations usually revolved around our trip and intentions and were accurately portrayed by our spread of maps. This usually satisfied their curiosity, though some were more interested in our gear, much of which seemed strange to them. We had to keep a wary eye open for souvenir hunters.

It was New Year's Eve. For two hours we paced the streets of Meshed in search of somewhere to celebrate. All enquiries were met with a shake of the head. Alcohol of any shape or form just could not be found. Meshed was certainly living up to its religious identity. Resigned to a dry New Year's Eve, we gloomily trudged our way through the snowbound streets back to our hotel. Not even waiting to see the New Year in we dejectedly went off to sleep on our flea-ridden straw mattresses.

The following morning whilst Tim and Ron were getting provisions at the bazaar prior to our departure from Meshed, Dick and I were approached by a man who insisted on showing us his carpet factory. "We are just about to leave," I excused. "It will take about five minutes, it's only around the corner," he replied. Curiosity getting the better of us, off Dick and I went.

Down the street we hurried, through narrow alleyways full of cross-legged craftsmen, carpenters, blacksmiths and artisans, making shoes and other everyday items in their little shops. Through courtyards we sped, sending chickens scattering in our wake. "It's just around the next corner" was the reply to our protests. At last up a flight of steps and we were in a small room. "My factory," our friend triumphantly announced. Glasses of tea were thrust in our hands as he started to unfurl carpet after carpet in front of us, explaining how good his carpets were and what a good price he could arrange for us. "I could even send the carpets home for you," he said, indicating to a pile of ready parcelled carpets in the corner. No doubt he was genuine and sincere in his intentions, but buying Persian carpets was not exactly what we had come all this way for. Explaining that our friends were waiting for us, we made a hurried exit and endeavoured to retrace our steps through the maze of alleyways back to the Land Rover where Tim and Ron were impatiently waiting for us.

Through thick snow, treacherous icy conditions and sub-zero temperatures we left Meshed. Confronting us was an endless frozen waste, with any scenery that would have been seen camouflaged by a thick layer of snow. A vast, forsaken wilderness broken only by occasional wretched mud hut villages. Little clusters of 'beehive' houses snuggled behind the protective perimeter of a high mud wall.

A hair-raising few seconds were experienced when the ice decided to take over control of the vehicle. With Dick wrestling at the wheel, we did a 100-yard tango, 50 yards on two wheels (off and nearside alternatively), another 100 yards crab-fashion, before finally coming to rest in a pile of snow. Prayers over, we stepped a little shaken out of the Land Rover only to be greeted by a burst of laughter and a familiar voice shouting, "Bloody hell, not you lot again!" There behind us were Bo, Peggy, Mike and Tony, the other Land Rover crew on a similar venture to us, whom we had last seen at the campsite at Baghdad. "We were just laying bets on whether you were going to roll the vehicle," said Bo.

They, too, had spent New Year's Eve in Meshed and had managed to unearth what must have been the only beer supply in the city, which was little consolation to us. A cup of tea and a reminisce and we were on our way after our unscheduled stop.

We agreed to go in convoy with the other crew: not only would it give us a change of personality to converse with (by now we were all getting a bit edgy with each other, understandably so after close contact for such a length of time), it would also be an added safety precaution for the more primitive lands ahead, where banditry is still a viable proposition.

Together we proceeded towards the Iranian exit. The only sign of activity on the road was heavily laden camel trains lurching awkwardly through the snow. The soft thudding of their pads and the moans of the baby camels swam into sound focus above the waspish drone of our Land Rover and the hiss of the icy wind on the screen. Occasionally the low oasis of a village could be seen. A small cluster of dome-roofed mud hut dwellings, completely enclosed by mud walls. From the distance, they looked like a decoration on a gigantic birthday cake with a liberal helping of icing supplied by the surrounding snow.

The sun like a ripening orange slid down behind the snow-clad desert as we approached the Iranian border town of Torbat-e-Hayderieh, still some twenty miles from the actual border. This is where the controls start. Our passports were checked before we were allowed to go on. These controls were (I think) customs, yet no one as much as glanced at our luggage.

After Tim's recent successful attempt at bogging us in the mud, he produced an encore within a few yards of the Iranian border. Fortunately, the other Land Rover crew were able to tow us out.

The Iranian border post consisted of a small mud building marooned in the middle of nowhere. A couple of offices harboured a handful of bored-looking officials. This was passport control which entailed filling out a sort of visitors' book with our personal data, and eventually receiving the inevitable stamp cancelling our visas. After doing so they nonchalantly informed us that the Afghan border was closed for the night.

Destined to spend the night stuck between two countries, unable to get into Afghanistan and unable to return to Iran, having just been 'stamped' out of the country which now made our visa invalid. None of us were enthusiastic about pitching the tent in the adverse conditions, so we ventured a few miles through 'no man's land' towards the Afghan border.

We had not gone far when a figure ran out in front of us frantically waving his arms. Stopping, we were confronted by a young, sinewy-looking person, with a grin like a watermelon segment. "You want room for the night? I have cheap hotel, good food, very cheap, for you a special price" (we had heard that one before). "All borders closed until the morning," he unnecessarily informed us in a high-pitched, boyish voice. "It's either that or the tents," said Tim, so we all agreed to give it a try.

The hotel was a ramshackle, flat-roofed building looking rather like a faded carpet. A passageway led to the main room which was devoid of any furniture apart from a few low tables and a wood-burning stove supplying the heating. A few bedrooms led off from the passageway which also housed the kitchen.

An amusing hour was spent haggling with our 'captor'. In the end, with the added bargaining power of the other Land Rover crew, and the threat of leaving and pitching our tents, we managed to get him to accept our price of ten rials (5p) each for the use of the main room. Even that price was probably twice as much as a local would pay. Being the only building between the borders, he had the monopoly. I should imagine there is a lucrative business going on between the hotel owner and the border guards who conveniently let you into 'no man's land' before informing you that you cannot get out until the morning, rather like a lobster trapped in a pot.

Barely had we settled down in the room when we were joined by six others, four Americans and two Canadians; the former we had met previously in our hotel in Tehran. One of the more pleasant aspects on the 'hippie' trail to Afghanistan is the continual meeting-up of old acquaintances.

The evening passed pleasantly enough, playing cards and exchanging experiences and intentions. A meal of rice and chunks of camel meat was dished up to us all for which we paid the exorbitant price of fifteen rials (7p). The owner was certainly cashing in on the day's catch.

As all power was shut off at 10 pm we were forced to have an early night, though not before being joined by two others, an elderly Afghan who coughed and wheezed all night, and the owner who informed us he was Nepalese and tried to convince us that he could speak six different languages, his favourite words being "f... off", which he used to gay abandon, and was usually the answer to any question put to him. Long after the lights were out he continued to chatter, mostly about his female conquests. He finally quietened after threats of us all heaving him out of the door. So there we all were, in the middle of nowhere, a cosmopolitan mixture of four Americans, two Canadians, eight English, one Afghan and a Nepalese sleeping like sardines on the floor. I slept in the windowsill, there being little room left on the floor. Murmuring voices lost themselves in the darkness, seemingly unrelated to individuals, moods, emotions and thoughts.

A rude awakening to the morning by the shouting of the manager who revelled in his self-appointed role of 'sergeant major'.

Outside the weather had taken a turn for the worse. By Bo's thermometer the temperature had dropped to 20 degrees Fahrenheit, below freezing point, a barren, inhospitable waste of snow and ice.

Near the 'hotel' an ancient bus, The Afghan Post, was refusing all attempts by the crew to start. Obviously it had frozen solid. The crew, rather unwisely, had started a roaring wood fire underneath the engine in an effort to defreeze it. Our offer of a tow was readily accepted. "We should charge them, they would us," said Dick.

Feeling charitable, we gave them a free tow. Three attempts and two broken ropes, and the bus burst into life and was on its way. We also tow-started a car that was similarly frozen. To date we had had no trouble through the adverse weather with our Land Rover, which had behaved perfectly and always started at first kick.

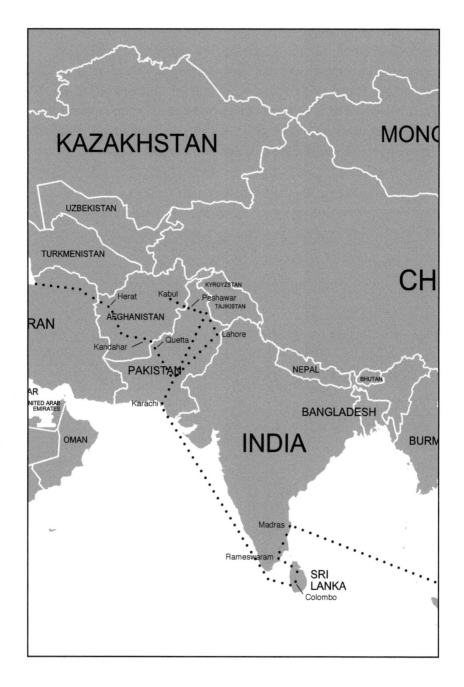

CHAPTER 8

Into Afghanistan

We were advised, prior to arriving at an Afghan border post, to check the vehicle to ensure there are no signs of sheep's blood on the vehicle as there is a common practice of throwing sheep's blood at vehicles and being accused of knocking down someone, therefore requiring to pay cash in compensation at the border before being allowed to continue your journey. Together with the other crew we drove the short distance to a cluster of buildings that represent the Afghan border town of Islām Qala. In bitterly cold weather we were kept waiting for over two hours whilst petty officials passed us from one office to another. Forms to be filled in, medical cards checked, Carnets to be cleared and passports stamped. All around us were sombre-looking Afghans and Iranians jabbering away, squatting in little groups, as though they were waiting for the world to pass them by.

At long last the necessary forms were completed, our passports stamped and we were ready to move on. Before leaving we managed to get our currency changed at the hands of the many black marketeers, each trying to outbid the other in an effort to obtain our custom. It was quite an art playing one against the other to obtain the services of the highest bidder. We were warned by a policeman not to change money except through a bank – rules and regulations, he stressed, then promptly offered to change it himself at the current black market rate.

Being short of fuel, we attempted to obtain some petrol at the border. The only source available appeared to be an antique pump where a lethargic Afghan pumped away as we watched the dial move round to show ten gallons. Turning on our ignition, we found that our gauge still showed just under quarter full. The pumps were empty and only air had been pumped into our tank. A profitable business if you can get away with it. Our initiation in the shrewdness of the Afghans. Leaving the protesting Afghan to yell abuse, we departed from the border followed closely by Bo, Peggy, Mike and Tony in their Land Rover. At least we had the sobering thought that we would have someone on hand if we did run out of petrol, one of the many advantages of having such company. Useful in case of a breakdown and also as added bargaining power when bartering for a room at a hotel (one could usually get a cheaper price with a party of eight as opposed to four) and also the added security and companionship.

Bo's Land Rover was better equipped than ours, being a hard top, long wheelbase, fitted out with a refrigerator (an unnecessary luxury in the present climate) and a gas cooker, and the added attraction in having Peggy in our midst, a welcome change from the all-male company.

The 75-mile journey to Herat took us through flat, bare and inhospitable, snowbound desert, though the snow decreased as we neared Herat. Very little traffic was encountered, though we did pass numerous herds of camels, shattering my childhood visions linking camels to sweltering deserts. It seemed strange to see them roaming wild through snow and ice.

Not unexpectedly, we eventually ran out of petrol, though luckily only a hundred yards from a petrol station. Having quenched the vehicle's thirst we drove the short distance into Herat, where 200,000 acres of cultivation stand out as a green island in a lifeless sea. Situated on the River Hari in the flat, low-lying area at the base of the Paropamisus range of mountains. Encompassing the town is the old city wall with its many ruined towers. The one main street is unsealed with the earth trodden down to a hardcore by the countless hooves of camels, donkeys and humans, and in later years by the intrusion of motor vehicles, the majority of which would have graced any vintage motor museum. Most of the town buildings were of mud structure, those in the process of being constructed held up by rickety bamboo scaffolding. I got the impression of Herat as a town that has been put in the deep-freeze for the past few hundred years and has suddenly been dropped into the melee of modern life, slowly and reluctantly catching up with its Western counterparts, though still 200 years behind.

We had little trouble in finding a room to stay. At the nominal price of 80 afs (40p) for the eight of us, we obtained two small rooms in the backyard of a hotel on the main street. Except for a small, wood-burning heater, they were completely bare and windowless, but at least they had a roof, which was the main thing. Our group was no exception for the hotel which was full of penniless European hippies and fellow-travellers, and obviously catered for the likes of us. A chance at last to catch up with the news, though news in these parts is mostly of travel and exchange of experiences. There was much talk of sickness, people with dysentery, hepatitis and other such travellers' diseases. In fact our hotel resembled a hospital ward, so much talk of bowels.

A stroll through Herat is a stroll through time. Horse and carts, donkeys and camels are the main mode of transport. Horse-drawn carriages decorated gaily with tassels and polished brasswork, and jingling bells jog noisily through the streets. Dingy shops abound with bric-a-brac, ancient guns, antiques and leather goods. Almost anything can be bought, sold or exchanged. We sold our wrecked used tyres to the local cobbler to be turned into shoe soles. Bartering is expected and a cunning art: even without bartering, everything is so ridiculously cheap. Tim exchanged his worn-out boots for a pair of robust Pakistan Army boots. Dick exchanged his hat for a leather money pouch, and I exchanged my hat for a leather waistcoat. No doubt one could exchange an unwanted mother-in-law for a pair of leather trousers. Evidence of previous European travellers could be seen in the shops by the way of discarded Western clothes: everything appeared second-hand.

Main street, Herat, Afghanistan.   *Main street, Herat, Afghanistan.*

At a checkpoint between Herat and Kandahar,
Afghanistan. Tim getting friendly with the official.

Herat reminds one of a theatrical changing room, people walking in wearing Western-style clothes and emerging in way-out leathers, knee-length boots, sheepskin waistcoats and long, gaily embroidered Afghan coats. Dick just about kitted himself completely in leather, the only missing items being leather underpants and socks.

Poverty was everywhere: the town abounds with beggars, many of whom walk around with a permanent hand out crying for their baksheesh. Wizened, walnut-faced knife-grinders relentlessly hawk the streets with their ancient treadle machines. Females in their burkhas, a garment concealing head, face and body, leaving only two eye slits, glide along dreamily with their ghostly egg faces. A sharp contrast to the many Western hippies dressed in their acquired gear.

Herat, hippies and hash go hand in hand: 'pot' is smoked openly and is obtainable as easily as a packet of cigarettes, and a lot cheaper, too. The sweet smell of hash and opium is everywhere.

The evening was spent playing cards in the hotel dining room, mostly by candlelight as the power is turned off at 10 pm. Not that that affected our room which was devoid of any lighting at all. A hearty meal of rice, camel, spinach and swede at the hotel for about 7p gave me the thought that with £50 in my pocket I could spend a year here without doing a day's work. Fortunately, it was only a thought: no doubt the novelty would soon wear off.

It was foggy as we drove away from the hotel, maybe that could be our excuse for spending an hour driving around in ever-decreasing circles. Realising where we would end up if we continued in this way, we asked a policeman (like all good travellers do) the way out of Herat. The policeman, who might just as well have been a farmhand, directing horses, goats and camels from a traffic pedestal, pointed us in the general direction.

A short tour through the bustling backstreets of closely packed mud hut suburbs brought us onto the sealed main road out of town. An avenue of trees heralded our exit from Herat with cultivated fields either side. Like an opening curtain to a concert, the fog lifted, presenting the desert stretching itself in the sun before us, like some satisfied giantess.

In pleasant, warm sunshine we travelled along the excellent Russian-built road. The building of the 700 miles of roadway between Herat and Kabul was shared by Russia and America. Plaques on the roadside indicated over whose money you are driving.

Thankfully we had by now left the snow behind us, apart from a few isolated patches on the higher lands. Our short 'honeymoon' with flat terrain was soon over as we started to ascend over one of the extending ribs of the Hindu Kush, that vast, barbaric range that straddles Afghanistan rather like the roof of a house. The interior of the country is a land of barren mountains with irrigated valley bottoms fed from distant snow peaks. A hive of tribesmen and ancient cults, where tribal law is still the rule.

We heard many stories of travellers being waylaid by bandits coming down from the mountains, robbing, raping and even murdering. It was some comfort to have the other Land Rover crew accompanying us.

Some spectacular scenery could be seen, rugged and stark, barren and inhospitable, but at the same time ruggedly attractive. At 6,000 feet we went through a mountain pass before starting the descent to the small town of Shindand. Once out of the mountains we took the opportunity, whilst having a brew-up, to dry out our tents in the warm sun, our first real chance to do so.

The scenery changed dramatically. We looked out over the arid land, a land that, from its colours, might have been burnt, tawny, ochre, or perhaps it was warm brown? Beyond, the wonderfully pure and luminous sky rested upon the motionless waves of mountains. Ahead and to our right stretched the Khash Desert with only a few bulges to temper the flatness. Small clusters of sheep and goats grazed on apparently nothing. Camels were plentiful, inhabitants few, apart from isolated mud hut settlements and the odd black umbrella of a nomadic encampment where tribesmen squatted down in huddles, as though they had settled down for a slightly longer stay than usual. The few villages were of the domed roof, mud hut type, small-roomed houses clustered cosily together. From their isolation I should think each settlement was practically self-sufficient with its own artisans, carpenters and blacksmiths to furnish the needed tools, and probably a store to supply the few material wants.

Very little traffic was on the road; occasionally a gaily decorated lorry would pass us, more often than not overloaded mostly with wools and skins. Quite often above the load of goods was a human cargo piled up until they made a seething unstable pyramid topped with wisps of cloth blowing to and fro in the wind. The bodywork of these lorries was gaily decorated with multicoloured inscriptions and artistically painted floral wreaths and medallions containing tiny landscape scenes.

Whilst dreamily driving along in the warm afternoon sun we suddenly realised that the other Land Rover was no longer with us. Turning around, we sped back to find them a couple of miles behind us having experienced a blowout. Bo and Mike were busily changing a front wheel.

With the other Land Rover back in circulation we proceeded through the desert, our only witness being camels and the occasional eagle. At regular intervals (too regular) we had to stop at toll gates where, for your fee, you are given a ticket which you have to hand in at the next gate, and so on. Not satisfied with having the road built for them, they also want payment for its use! Oh well, that's Afghanistan.

Dusk was approaching as we arrived at the small village of Delārām, where, according to our guidebook, we would be able to acquire a room for the night. Unfortunately the only hotel was full up, having just accommodated a busload of travellers. Whilst debating our next move we watched with fascination while the recent arrivals from the bus, silhouetted against the flaming sunset, prostrated themselves to the sinking sun in their ritual praises of Allah.

We had hoped to have found accommodation before dark, not wishing to pitch our tents in these inhospitable parts. We all agreed to carry on to the next village of any size, which would be Girishk, some 70 miles away. As we had not eaten all day we decided to try and obtain a meal whilst we were at Delārām.

Amongst the small collection of mud-walled dwellings that comprised the village was a hut, outside of which stood a dilapidated sign proclaiming that it was indeed a restaurant. Dubious-looking or not, a combination of curiosity, rumbling stomachs and persuasive Afghans who were crowding round us, decided for us.

Ducking under the low doorway (yes, even I had to!), we entered the restaurant, the likes of which were never entered in the tourist brochures. An earth floor, with the occasional straw mat, not a scrap of furniture apart from two wood-burning stoves. Three rooms, each about eight feet square, joined into one, separated only by a partial mud partition. The only lighting was from a few hurricane lamps suspended from the ceiling. Around the rooms squatting or sitting cross-legged were a motley array of Afghans. A cruel sea of unsmiling, mocking mouths, weather-beaten, wrinkled faces stared persistently at me, barefooted, turbaned and wearing their loose-fitting pyjama costumes. Always on the point of spitting somewhere, anywhere, with enormous skill and self-satisfaction, leaving their red or green betel trademarks. The odours of charcoal, animals and hide mingled with those of unkempt cotton clothes and the human bodies they covered. Room was made for us to sit down on the floor. A plate of rice, some chunks of dubious-looking meat and spinach, all of which we devoured ravenously with our fingers. I think by now our constitution had hardened to so many changes of diets and dubious local foods that we were able to eat practically anything and suffer no ill effects. Washed down with some green tea, boiled in a tottering samovar, the meal at least bridged that gap.

Leaving the 'restaurant' we rejoined the road and headed in darkness towards the town of Girishk, where we hoped to be able to obtain accommodation for the night.

The 70-mile journey took us along the edge of the Khash Desert, with the dim outline on the horizon of the Hazarajat mountains to our left. "There are the lights of Girishk," said Dick, pointing to a bright yellow glow on the horizon. Our suspicions were confirmed when the lights of Girishk were in fact the before glow of the most brilliant moon I have ever seen. As it crept out from behind the mountains, the brilliant orange ball gave an unnatural aura to the landscape. Shortly before 10 pm we arrived at Girishk, a tumbledown shanty town straddling the Helmand River.

After an unsuccessful attempt to obtain a room at a hotel by the river we slowly drove down the main street, which was in darkness, the only light coming from the occasional lantern in a window. Squatting in a doorway was a small group of people who, on our enquiring as to where we could obtain a room for the night, put themselves at our disposal to direct us to a hotel with one of the strangest characters I have ever come across. Barefooted and clad in only a loincloth, looking like a combination of a product of Frankenstein and a starving Yul Brynner. Beckoning us to follow him, he limped, leaped and sprinted, spotlighted in front of the Land Rover, a macabre edition of the Pied Piper.

Stopping outside a brick-cum-mud dwelling displaying a hotel sign, he intimated that this was where we could obtain a room for the night. Before we had a chance to thank him, he disappeared into the blackness of the night.

A reception committee was waiting for us: news travels fast in these parts. A bunch of foreigners in such an outpost as this is indeed news.

A burly Afghan, who appeared to be the boss, confronted us. "Have you a room for the night?" we asked. He indicated for us to follow him. The sight that beset us as we filed into the hotel was as if we had stepped back into a bygone era. Inside the front door, a steaming cauldron was gurgling away alongside an ancient 'chai' boiler. A man was kneading dough in the process of making chapattis – this, then, presumably was the kitchen. We followed the leader through a maze of honeycombed passages, passing through a gauntlet of recumbent Afghans bedded down for the night. Some were just squatting, chatting, playing cards or drinking their 'chai', whilst others, their recumbent figures stretched out on mats, looked as if they had passed out until further notice. Though with the sudden invasion by eight foreigners they awoke to fix their bleary eyes at the intrusion to their slumbers. Along the passageway hung cages of quail birds who squawked incessantly, as if protesting at our arrival. Chickens roamed freely, their smell mixing with the aroma of unwashed bodies, spices and human waste.

We were directed to a small room, about three yards square and barely six foot in height. Windowless and void of any fittings, the entrance being by a small four-foot door. A concrete floor and mud walls. The hotel's only toilets were about 100 yards down the road in a backyard which appeared to be the local bus depot and lorry park. In the corner of the yard was a floodlit open toilet with no privacy or sanitation whatsoever. The overpowering stench and risky route march through dark alleyways certainly limited our visits.

I have dossed down in many low dives, but this place just about beat the bunch. The customary argument of prices pursued: we eventually settled for 50 afs (25p) for the eight of us. Each trip to the vehicles to unload baggage was an ordeal in itself, as we had to pass through the gauntlet of staring, inhospitable faces, weather-beaten, wrinkled and mocking, looking like shelves of papier mâché busts.

We were reluctant to leave the Land Rovers in the darkness of the street, easy prey for anyone out for a quick profit. Luckily Bo's vehicle was lockable, which enabled us to transfer all our loose gear into the other Land Rover where at least it should be comparatively safe. With the vehicles secured as well as possible, we returned to our 'cave' to settle down for the night, though that was easier said than done. The curiosity of three small boys who loitered in our doorway, eyeing our every movement, saw to that. No amount of abuse would rid us of them: they must have thought we were being friendly, as they revelled in their given names of 'F… Off', 'B… Off' and 'P… Off', which we had kindly given them.

When our sleeping bags were laid out there was literally no room to walk without stepping on someone. A very restless sleep followed, interrupted by the incessant squawking of the birds, plus the heavy snoring, coughing and spitting of the locals. The claustrophobic atmosphere and the nauseating stench contributed to a somewhat uncomfortable night. As dawn approached the screeching of the birds reached a crescendo, dispelling any hope of any more sleep. Not that any of us were sorry to get up, we were practically suffocating by now; anyway, it would give us the opportunity of an early start. The only casualties of the night were Peggy and Bo who were attacked by fleas.

We crept past the gauntlet of recumbent figures who lay as if dead, probably trying to get through much of the day by refraining, as far as humanely possible, from showing any life whatsoever. The fresh air and sunlight hit us, a refreshing blow as we stepped out into the street, but the sight that greeted us was not one we relished. We could not see the vehicles for bodies. It looked as if the whole village had come out to stare at these two strange vehicles that had invaded their village under cover of darkness. Pushing aside a gangway, we hurriedly threw our gear into the Land Rover, watched closely by our attentive audience of barefooted, ragged-looking children, and equally ragged adults, staring, pointing, laughing and jabbering away incessantly. "Let's get the hell out of here," said Tim. "We can sort the gear out later." Followed by a cavalcade of running children and yapping dogs, we drove off, making a quick tour of the village before heading for the open road.

Girishk, a poverty-stricken village: filth and refuse lay in heaps, stench from open sewers and decomposing matter. Buildings were either mud dwellings or makeshift shanty town huts thrown together from bits of old wood and corrugated iron. Shops or stalls were assembled from flattened-out biscuit tins, kerosene cans and tea chests. A mosque dominated the village supplying their religious needs.

A short distance from Girishk we pulled up at a lay-by alongside the Helmand River, where in comparative seclusion, apart from a few interruptions from a goatherd and his flock, we managed to restow the vehicles after our recent emergency exit. Whilst having a brew-up we were joined by a GB-plated Dormobile whose husband-and-wife crew were on a reciprocal trip to us, having come from Australia and returning to England. They were able to give us many useful hints on what to expect on the long road ahead.

Following Bo's Land Rover, we proceeded in brilliant sunshine through flat desert scrubland toward Kandahar. There being very little to break the monotonous terrain apart from the low oasis of the mud hut villages of Khugiana and Sinjiri and the frequent camel. The rare dose of sunshine was really a luxury, a pleasure we had become accustomed to being without.

Greenery and an escalation of cultivation announced the approaches of Kandahar, Afghanistan's second city and the principal entrepôt for trade with Pakistan.

Being only midday, we had plenty of time to search for a decent 'pad'. After two or three attempts at hotels in which either the price was not right or they would not accommodate all eight of us, we found a hotel which, by our by now low standards, was luxurious. Although the price of about 15p each per day was way above our normal price, it was well worth the extravagance.

A fairly large room, with four beds (leaving only four of us to sleep on the floor) and a wood-burning stove in the centre of the room. A small restaurant was available in the hotel and, the height of luxury, a European loo, and – this is just too much – soft, pink toilet paper (which was soon exchanged for one of our rather coarser rolls). "Hey, there is nowhere to put your feet," said Mike. We had to excuse him: it had been such a long time since we had used a toilet with a seat. The hotel even had a bath, that is if one was energetic enough to stoke up the boilers first.

Barely had we time to settle into our room when the manager brought in a hubble pipe. A ceramic pot about two feet high with a slender neck which housed a small bowl, and extending from the base of the neck was a long tube with a mouthpiece. "For you, my friends, I have the best hash in Kandahar," he said whilst grating a toffee bar-looking block into the bowl. We watched as he lit the shredded pieces. A bluish haze of hash smoke rose from the bowl, causing a distinctive sweet smell to waft around the room. A smell that we were soon to become all too familiar with.

Whilst eating our daily bowl of rice in the restaurant that evening, we met some of the other inmates of the hotel. Mostly Europeans and members of that ever-increasing army of dropouts of the new generation, who see countries the likes of Afghanistan, through the haze of blue smoke, as the key to eternal enjoyment and freedom. A gaunt, pale-faced Scotsman, powdering his hash in the palm of his hand and mixing it with tobacco from his cigarette, re-rolled it and continued to puff away as if playing a mouth organ. He informed us that his brother had recently been taken to hospital in Kabul suffering from dysentery and hepatitis, a result of "this key to eternal enjoyment". Others excused themselves by saying smoking hash is the only way to make the local food taste good.

Discussions that evening resulted in the decision to rid ourselves of the two Land Rovers, a decision brought about by our increasing concern over the India/Pakistan crisis which had resulted in the closure of the border into India. With no indication as to when the borders could be reopened, our only alternative was by air, other than retracing our steps to Iran and chance a boat from one of the Persian Gulf ports, a costly and unpredictable business. Consideration also had to be given to the fact that entry of the Land Rover into Afghanistan had been recorded in Tim's passport, which meant that the vehicle would have to be taken out of the country or else be burdened with a considerable import duty fee. In places like Afghanistan there must be ways and means, we consoled ourselves, but first of all we would have to find a buyer.

Whilst Tim, Dick and I had little to lose, having paid only £160 between us for the vehicle, we were rather pessimistic about Bo's chances, having paid over £1600 for their vehicle, including the small fridge. Who in Afghanistan is going to have that sort of money in a land of poverty and penniless hippies? As the saying goes, "where there is muck there is money", and there is certainly plenty of muck around Kandahar.

The following day we had our first real look at Kandahar and to solicit for prospective buyers. Notices were placed at various hotels and feelers extended in the more affluent quarters of the city. It was now a case of waiting for the result of our day's labour. Dick and I found an interested buyer at the local airline office who promised to come around to our hotel the following day to discuss terms.

Kandahar certainly lives up to its reputation as 'The Fly Capital', filthy but fascinating. As with Herat, the main mode of transport is horses pulling gaily decorated carts, and camels whose dung constitutes a substitute for tarmac. The occasional pre-war truck and an array of vintage buses, decorated with motifs and bursting at the seams with people, their cotton robes fluttering like pennants from the open windows and doors. As a European, both the buses and the passengers were an extraordinary sight, but if you happen to be an inhabitant of these parts such a sight is perfectly normal. Apart from a few almost westernised houses on the outskirts of the city, most of the buildings look as if they were dropped from a passing aircraft, left where they fell, then covered with a layer of mud. Kandahar is a maze of narrow, winding lanes and blind alleys, stalls, shops and mud dwellings; and everywhere the sun flickered through the straw mats and foliage set up to shade the alleys. The main thoroughfares and side alleys were an entangled, milling swarm of men and beasts.

The hurly-burly of the market, where the aromatic odour of spices, rotting fruits and vegetables mixes with the stench of open sewers, excreta and decomposing matter, plus the ever-prevailing sweet smell of hashish smoke. Black pyramids of dates change colour at the flick of a feather duster by the squatting hawker, as the flies shoot off to mass together for their next attack. Bisected camels hang obscenely by hooks outside the meat stalls, a haven for flies. At food stalls the weights used were an assortment of washers, cog wheels, petrol caps and other such ironmongery.

I would now well believe the many stories we had heard that no one escapes Afghanistan without having a dose of gastric troubles, hygiene and sanitation being virtually non-existent. Much of the tinned foodstuffs displayed in the stalls and shops was of pre-war vintage. The streets abound with beggars and stone-throwing children, Europeans being the obvious target.

The lackadaisical attitude of the country was brought to light on our visit to the city's main post office, to purchase some stamps: "Sorry, no stamps today, all gone, maybe some tomorrow?" we were informed, as if it were a regular occurrence.

Our first good meal for some time was had at one of the larger restaurants, though having just come from the market I seemed to have lost my hunger. The cashiers at the restaurant were two anaemic-looking English girls, both broke and trying to earn enough money to get themselves out of the country.

Back at our hotel we were given some promising news. The hotel manager informed us that his brother was interested in our Land Rover. "Tonight he will come to see you," he said. Sure enough, that night we were introduced to Aziz; whether he was the manager's brother or not, I do not know, but as we were soon to find out almost everybody we were introduced to was Aziz's brother, so I had my doubts.

Aziz, a friendly character, as crooked as they come: short, thin and home to a permanent grin, sparkling eyes and humour to match. Said to have travelled to Europe on illicit trading and had been imprisoned. His ambition was to go to England, find an English girl and marry. "Afghan girls no good, I should know, I have one for every day of the week," he chuckled. He could speak fluent English, always wore Western-style clothes and was never without his English-looking raincoat. Occupation – shop owner and hashish farmer, being the owner of a large hashish farm in a village near Kandahar. "I grow the plants for medicinal purposes only," he said with a wry smile, "I send opium to hospitals in Iran." A cover for his conscience, I mused.

During our conversation in our hotel room Aziz certainly showed his keenness in purchasing the Land Rover. "I will give you $400 cash," he said, fondling a large bundle of notes. "No deal," we replied, nothing under $500. "Too much," said Aziz. "My last price $400 plus four females, and a promise to return tomorrow to renegotiate."

With the prospect of a sale we now had the problem of ridding ourselves of our excess gear. And so we set about the task of sorting out our gear, keeping only the essential items of clothing and personal gear. Knowing that what we kept we would have to carry on our backs in our rucksack for the remainder of the journey to Australia made us quite generous in our discarding. "Why not try and sell the gear?" suggested Dick, and we all readily agreed.

The backyard of the hotel seemed an ideal site. And so, in brilliant sunshine we set up our own bazaar. Pots, pans, cutlery, Primus stoves, heater, blankets, shirts, trousers, jackets, coats, vehicle spares, even our tent, everything and anything, leaving ourselves with just a skeleton wardrobe. Bo and his crew understandably were a little more cautious, having had no offers yet for the purchase of their Land Rover. They were hoping for about $2,000 for their vehicle and obviously not expecting to find a buyer as quickly as us. Nevertheless, they, too, had a good clear-out.

We still had some tinned food left, which we pooled with Bo's reserves. After sharing out some of the tinned eats as individual emergency rations we mixed together the remainder for one final slap-up hash. Any food that did not go in the hash was put in the bazaar.

News travels fast: no sooner had Ron and Dick gone round to the main hotels to advertise our sale when crowds began to congregate. Soon we were doing a brisk trade, Europeans and Afghans alike were pouring in, trying on the clothes and fingering through the goods. Some items just disappeared, others were sold in bulk, lots at ridiculously low prices. Gradually our pile of goods diminished, leaving only a few of the larger items, such as heaters and tents. Dick made one of the best bargains by selling his airbed which was riddled with punctures. "I only hope he does not try and inflate it before we leave," said Dick.

Eventually the tent was sold and Aziz came along and bought our heater. Bo even managed to sell the recently blown-out tyre at a cobbler's shop, to be used in soling shoes. It appeared that half the population of Kandahar were wearing some item or other of our clothing.

All morning Aziz had been jealously guarding 'his' Land Rover, even though both sides were sticking to their prices. We even went as far as obtaining a bogus buyer from another hotel in the hope that Aziz would raise his offer. Aziz was not impressed: as far as he was concerned the Land Rover was already his.

During his demonstration ride he told us all the alterations he intended doing to the vehicle. He persisted in calling it 'his' Land Rover and we had to constantly remind him that it was not yet his until he met our terms, a reply that was always met with a hearty laugh.

As with most dealings in Afghanistan, it takes time, nothing is rushed. A day of bargaining, a night to think it over, more bartering, and so it goes on, a game of cat and mouse.

Aziz even suggested that we all spend a few days with him on his hash farm to come to some arrangement. "Plenty hash and women," he tempted. We declined his generous offer, being keen to settle as soon as possible and be off on our way again.

Eventually we decided to accept Aziz's latest offer of $420, approximately what we paid for the vehicle, it being unlikely that we would receive a better offer. "What do you want to be paid in?" asked Aziz, "Dollars, pounds, marks or kilos?" the latter referring to blocks of hash. We decided on dollars and Afghanis.

During the afternoon Tim and I went round to Aziz's shop to finalise the deal and collect the cash. Outside the small Afghan gift shop, Aziz proudly showed off to his friends his latest acquisition, rather like a child receiving his first train set.

Plans were made as to how we were to get the Land Rover entry cleared from Tim's passport and the Carnet, both necessary if we wanted to clear the country without paying the high import duty on the vehicle. To do this we would have to take the vehicle out of the country and cleared at the customs post. Though once through the Afghan border post, we would not be able to proceed through to the next country, Pakistan, without having the vehicle recorded once again on our passport and Carnet, in which case we would not have gained anything and Aziz still would not have his Land Rover.

He was as keen as we were to evade the duty, as it would probably double the cost of the vehicle, plus the rigmarole that would have to be gone through, a process in Afghanistan that could take weeks.

Eventually, a plan suggested by Aziz, with a few amendments from our side, was agreed upon. Tim and I would pick up Aziz from his shop early the following morning, proceed to the Afghan border post, having discreetly dropped Aziz off just prior to the post. Then, having gone through the formalities of clearing our passports and Carnet, we would drive on through into no man's land between Afghanistan and Pakistan and pick up Aziz, who in the meantime had bypassed the border post and placed himself somewhere along the two-mile stretch between the two countries. Tim and myself would then hand over Sweaty Betty to Aziz and make our way on foot into Pakistan. "How will you get the vehicle back across the border without being recognised as the vehicle that had just passed through with two Englishmen?" we asked Aziz. A vehicle like that, painted bright blue with GB number plates did, after all, stand out like a sore thumb. Not only that, but by now the exhaust had just about disintegrated and the vehicle sounded like a Centurion tank, so you could hardly creep up without being heard. Aziz scoffed at our concern. "It is easy," he said. "I drive out into the desert and cross the border where no one will see me, I know the country well. Anyway, these officials can always be bribed." To us it did not sound too foolproof, but once we had relieved ourselves of the Land Rover, that was Aziz's concern and he was confident.

From the Pakistan border Tim and I intended to travel by local transport through Pakistan to the north of the country and back into Afghanistan via the Khyber Pass, meeting the rest of the gang in Kabul.

By now, Bo had resigned himself to not selling his Land Rover in Kandahar and was placing his hopes on the greener pastures of Kabul. Ron and Dick would join Bo's crew for the journey north to Kabul.

The evening was spent sorting ourselves out in preparation for an early exodus the following day. Tim and I packed just the bare essentials for our journey, a sleeping bag, toilet gear and a few tins of emergency rations. Bo would take the remainder of our gear up to Kabul.

With the prospect of an early start in the morning, we all bedded down fairly early, although it was some time before I finally dozed off. I could not help musing over the recent change of plans and the impending journey. I think I was somewhat exhilarated at the thought of doing some border smuggling, a far cry from the daily monotony of my old 9-5 job.

Morning was all too soon upon us: the sun was peeping over the distant hills as we make our final preparations for our departures. Throwing our two small bags in the back of the Land Rover, Tim and I embarked for our final drive in Sweaty Betty. We bade our farewells to Ron, Dick, Bo, Peggy, Mike and Tony, who would be driving up to Kabul later on in the morning. "See you in about six days' time in Kabul!" we shouted optimistically. "I will send out a search party if you do not arrive in seven days," joked Bo.

Aziz was waiting for us as we arrived at his shop. With him was an Arab who, Aziz informed us, was his aide and would be his driver on the journey back to Kandahar.

Barely had we travelled any distance when Aziz told us to pull in at a side street. "The roof rack has to come off," he said. "Why?" we queried. "Too recognisable. Anyway, it will make us go faster," he replied amidst a burst of laughter. Ah well, it's his Land Rover now so we did not pursue the matter. Aziz disposed of the roof rack in a nearby workshop. "Okay, let's go," he said. "We are running short of fuel," said Tim, who was driving. "We have enough to get us to the border" – which was about 60 miles away – "but not enough to get you back to Kandahar." "Okay, let's fill her up, then," replied Aziz. We drew up at the first filling station and topped the tank up. Tim and I turned to Aziz with our hands out for cash to pay for the fuel. "It's your vehicle now, Aziz, so how about paying for the fuel?" "Oh no, I take over at the border, you pay," he protested. "We already had enough fuel to get us to the border, so what we have just put in is for your use," replied Tim. Aziz submitted with a futile "I am a poor man, you strike a hard bargain." He pulled out a wad of notes and paid the attendant.

At last we pulled away from the sprawling mud huts of Kandahar and out through the sand-choked Registan Desert, a desert of sandy wastes, completely desolate in places, with a thin and scattered vegetation of stunted, thorny scrub.

As we pulled up at a toll gate, a few words from Aziz to the official and we were allowed through free. Aziz turned to us with a broad grin. "Here in Afghanistan everything is free, if you have money: I bribed him."

The road was practically deserted and we made good progress along the straight desert road with only a few bulges from the remnants of the Hada mountains to temper the flatness. Apart from the small settlement of Hal Karez, we passed little sign of habitation before the border.

"I often hunt in these parts," said Aziz. "Next time you come to Kandahar you must stay with me on my hash farm, we could go hunting in the Land Rover." We thanked him, but doubted if we would ever be seeing Kandahar again.

Squatting in the rear of the Land Rover was Aziz's aide, a silent passenger, his muteness only broken by a few utterances of Arabic.

Prior to reaching the border post we stopped to let Aziz and his partner out, leaving them to make their own way around the rear of the building to their hideout in no man's land. Meanwhile, Tim and I proceeded to the customs post.

Inside the dilapidated building, we were confronted by a shabby bunch of officials. They must have smelled a rat: they seemed more officious than we had become accustomed to with the Afghans. "Your passports have not been stamped, you must go to the police post further down the road." We walked the hundred yards to the police post only to be told: "Your vehicle has not been cleared from your passport by the customs, this must be done before we can stamp your passports." Back we trudged to the customs building.

The irate customs officer, his efficiency being questioned, began a verbal barrage with his assistants whilst we looked on as our passports were passed from hand to hand. Presumably the senior official looked up at Tim. "This your passport?" "Yes," said Tim. "You have a radio stamped as being brought into the country, where is it?" The radio had been transferred to Bo's Land Rover; we had overlooked the fact that it had been recorded on entry into Afghanistan. Fortunately, Tim's excuse that it had been stolen was accepted. "Let me have a look at the vehicle," he said as he pushed past us and went to the Land Rover. He made a thorough search, inside, outside and underneath. It must have looked highly suspicious, two men journeying from England to Australia and carrying only an overnight bag, apart from which the vehicle was completely empty. "Where is all your baggage?" he asked. "We like travelling light," I replied. Seemingly satisfied, they cleared the Carnet, deleted the entry in Tim's passport and allowed us to proceed to the next obstacle, the border police.

Shortly before reaching the police checkpoint our curiosity was aroused by a large gathering of men on the roadside. We were about to witness the local sport of dog fighting. Another form of the ancient sports of cockfights, camel fighting and bear-baiting.

Three dogs, one a bitch, participated. The scent of the bitch was rubbed onto the two contestants, both held firmly by their owners. The two dogs were then teased, provoked into a height of hatred for each other. Once they were worked up to a sufficiently ferocious state they were released, to go tearing into each other, locked in mortal combat. For a few minutes they were merged as one, rolling over and over in a cloud of dust, sending the existing spectators scattering. Money was changing hands as bets were cast for the winner. We did not see the eventual outcome as we still had an appointment with Aziz to keep and having yet to survive the border police check.

Confronting the long line of turbaned police officials sitting behind a desk gave one the impression of being interviewed for a job. "Where have you come from, where are you going …?" questioned the senior official as he flicked through the pages of our passports. Rather reluctantly, it seemed, he put the magic stamp to our passport. Much relieved, we returned to the Land Rover and drove through the barrier.

About half a mile down the road, stepping out from behind a tree, was Aziz and his aide. To save ourselves a two-mile walk we drove to within sight of the Pakistan border post before handing over the vehicle to Aziz.

A quick farewell and they were off. I stood watching as Sweaty Betty disappeared over the desolate wastes towards Afghanistan, its exhaust pipe literally dragging in the dust. I could not help but wonder as to what future lay ahead for the 21-year-old vehicle. To be resurrected from the obscurity of a Somerset pig farm to a 7,000-mile, trouble-free journey across Europe and half of Asia, only to end its career on an Afghan hashish farm. Goodbye, Sweaty Betty, you served us well, even though you did not live up to your adopted name.

CHAPTER 9

Into Pakistan

Now we really were on our own, but perhaps we could console ourselves that the budget traveller on foot has a better chance of meeting the local character than has his car-bound counterpart – little consolation as we picked up our bags and started to walk, in the midday sun, the final half-mile towards the Pakistan border.

There was little activity at the few scattered buildings that indicated the border into Pakistan. A few military personnel idly resting on their rifles, ragged-looking children on dilapidated bicycles, and a sprinkling of old men bent under the weight of heavy baggage.

"So you want to enter Pakistan," said the solitary police inspector as he unlocked his office door, ushering Tim and me inside. "Where do you intend going? Where from? What for?" questions and yet more questions. "Fill in these forms. Do not forget there is a war on. I will stamp your passport to allow you to travel to Rawalpindi and Lahore."

"There is a minibus waiting outside that will take you as far as Quetta, about 70 miles away."

Formalities over, we were directed to the waiting minibus. "You going to Quetta?" we asked. "Yes, yes, all the time I go to Quetta, get in, I go in a minute," replied the driver. "We have no rupees, only Afghan money," said Tim. "That is alright, I shall show you where you can change your money."

Picking up two other passengers, we were soon on our way. This is going too smoothly, I thought. A short drive brought us to the border town of Chaman. "We stop here for a while, this is where you can change your money," said the driver. "I will take you to the

best money changer who will give you good price for your Afghanis."
We followed him down a side street where a collection of money
changers squatted or sat cross-legged behind piles of banknotes of
various currencies. "This is your man," said the driver pointing to a
turbaned Sikh. He was right: it was in fact the best offer we received
whilst in Pakistan.

Our money changed, we returned to the bus, expecting to be
off any minute, but no, it was over an hour before the driver drove
off, and then it was only for a slow tour of the village soliciting for
customers in a rather novel way. A small boy attached himself to the
rear bumper, shrieking at the top of his voice in a quick-fire verbal
barrage of incoherent advertising. Having picked up a few passengers,
we returned to the original starting point. At least we had a chance of
seeing Chaman. Children in discoloured rags of cotton peeped through
dusty and lice-ridden hair. Goats, hens, mangy dogs and children
scattered before heavily laden bullock carts. Shops made of mud, stone
or the sides of rusty kerosene cans and tea chests. Shirts and blouses
were being made in the street on archaic sewing machines. Stalls of
rice, spices in earthenware jars, betel, sweets and sticky sweetmeats
which became the resting place for thousands of flies.

After a further 'promotional' tour of the town the driver assured us
that we were about to leave.

Our relief was short-lived. Instead of heading for Quetta, we were
returning towards the border. After two and a half hours in the bus we
were back where we started from. A further wait at the border before
we once again moved off towards Chaman. Back at Chaman we had
another couple of 'publicity' tours before finally moving off in the
right direction towards Quetta.

With Chaman behind us we headed across flat, arid desert land
towards the rambling Toba Kakar range of mountains which stretched
before us like a giant barrier. Leaving the flatness of the desert we

started the steep, twisty ascent towards the Khojak Pass. From our dizzy height we could look down on a vast golden sea of desert which glistened in the afternoon sun.

The tough going soon began to take its toll of the bus. It had to be constantly stopped to cool down, as it was overheating. To make matters worse it had to be push-started, which required the help of volunteers from the passengers.

After much coughing and spluttering the bus finally made it to the Khojak Pass and could now look forward to the somewhat easier descent. Though even that had its hazards. As we careered down the mountain at breakneck speed, we were periodically encountering opposing vehicles, often on blind corners and hairpins. Gaily painted overloaded vintage buses and lorries crept upwards in clouds of exhaust smoke.

For most of the journey our fellow passengers sat in silence. A cosmopolitan bunch: a couple of Afghans, a Sikh, the remainder being Pakistanis.

Having negotiated the mountain barrier, we resumed along the flat, desolate lowland countryside. Occasionally we would stop at some isolated settlement to embark or disembark a passenger.

Most of the people in these areas are of the nomadic type, rearing goats, sheep, camels, cattle and a few horses. They practise transhumance, moving up into the mountains in the summer and returning to the plateau and valleys in the winter. The winter is spent in village settlements, mud huts thatched with palm leaves or tamarisk. In the summer they live in goat-hair tents or rudimentary shelters made from branches.

We were still experiencing overheating and had numerous unscheduled stops. The final indignation came when the vehicle refused to start. We all got out and pushed: it must have been nearly a mile. We were all pretty well exhausted. The driver flagged down a passing bus to recruit some help, but the few volunteers soon gave up after an unsuccessful 100-yard dash. It was all very frustrating: it was now getting dark and we were getting nowhere, and still about twenty miles from Quetta.

"Maybe we have run out of petrol," suggested the driver. Sure enough, his unmechanical mind was correct: the tank was dry. Miles from the nearest habitation, by now dark and in a rather hostile country. Fortunately a lorry stopped and we were able to dispatch a small boy to go to the nearest petrol station, which was about five miles away, to obtain a can of petrol.

After an hour's wait the boy returned with a gallon of petrol, which we were assured was sufficient to get us to Quetta.

At long last we were once again on our way. By now there were only five passengers left and I think we were all feeling a bit restless.

The lights of Quetta shone ahead, and I breathed a sigh of relief. It had taken eight hours to cover the 70-mile journey. Quetta, the centre of Balochistan and the old British military and administration centre. Destroyed by earthquake in 1935 and now rebuilt as a commercial centre for woollen textiles.

In a muddy backstreet the driver stopped, informing us that this was as far as he went. Begrudgingly we paid him the fare, asking him where we could obtain a room for the night. "Follow me, I shall show you, it is where I stay." We did not like the look of 'his' place so we headed for the centre of the town to see what that had to offer.

Even though it was only about 9 pm the town appeared practically deserted. We managed to find a seedy hotel off the main street. A small, dingy room with a couple of wooden spring beds, and dirty mattresses and blankets. We were given a bucket of coal to feed the metal can that served as the heater.

Not having eaten for over 24 hours, we were feeling rather peckish, so we went out in search of food. A short walk from the hotel brought us to a respectable-looking restaurant practically devoid of customers and with an abundance of disinterested waiters. An ample portion of chicken curry soon accounted for our hunger pangs.

Replenished, we set off in search of the station to check on the train times for tomorrow's departure. A passing three-wheeled minicab was hailed and we climbed into the miniature 'gogo-mobile', joining a third passenger. The driver sped recklessly, reminiscent of a Japanese suicide pilot, though a maze of back alleys with their dilapidated lamplight, shanty stalls blaring out exotic Eastern music.

During the journey we got into conversation with our fellow passenger, who unfortunately for us was very anti-British. According to him, the British had committed just about every atrocity possible during their occupation of Pakistan, and was the cause of the present strife with India. Our protesting arguments fell on deaf ears, and it was some relief when our irate driver reached his destination, leaving a gobble of spit in our direction. We were later to find that this attitude towards the British is not uncommon in Pakistan.

At the station we found that our train left at 0730. "You will have to get here early," said a station official. "Many soldiers on that train."

Even though we left our hotel at 0600, we caught a minicab, arriving at the station at about 0630: the platforms were already crowded and long queues were forming at the ticket kiosks. 90% of the intending passengers were Army personnel complete with armoury and stores. Dressed in various outfits, some with boots, some with sandals, some in bare feet, some lay prostrate on the platform, whilst others squatted or lounged around in babbling groups. An undisciplined slipshod rabble. 'Tepees' of guns and boxes of ammunition lay unattended in piles on the platform.

We joined the rear of one of the queues which gradually became more disorganised as people ignorantly shoved, jostled and fought to get a ticket. It was an hour before we reached the kiosk, only to be informed that we were in the wrong queue. We rushed to another kiosk and managed to obtain third-class tickets just as the train was starting to move. Grabbing our bags, we ran to the moving train and managed to barge our way into one of the carriages.

Not a vacant space could be found: every wooden seat was occupied, and the passageways were full to bursting point with smelly, unkempt bodies. It was an understatement when Tim said, "I think we were economising a bit too much by getting a third-class ticket." The prospect of standing in a crushed corridor for thirteen hours prompted us to seek greener pastures of the second-class compartment. Fortunately, although still crowded, we managed to squeeze in on a hard and dusty second-class seat. We just had to hope that a ticket inspector would not turn up.

The initial part of the journey was very slow and tedious as we crawled up the barren, stark and lifeless mountains towards the Bolān Pass. Speed did increase slightly once we had accomplished the Bolān and Harnai Passes and began the gradual descent to the lower plains towards Sibi.

Very few inhabitants abound in these parts of Pakistan, being the abode of the nomadic rather than the settled farmer. A few isolated mud huts, the occasional camel and oxen broke the monotony of the vast expanses of arid desert in which any vegetation has to struggle to survive, though in the monsoon season the dry riverbeds become raging torrents.

Our travelling companions in our compartment were an inhospitable lot whose sole source of pleasure seemed to be staring at Tim and me. Even our retaliating stares failed to have any effect, a motive which we gave up, leaving them to their ignorance and us with the consolation that at least we had provided them with some entertainment during the journey. Some squatted on the seats rather than sat, giving the impression of a monkey on a barrel organ. Most wore the traditional dhoti – a large cotton sheet wrapped round the waist and drawn between the legs, rather like an outsize nappy. They would constantly chew on betel nut, spitting out huge blobs of red with much skill and satisfaction. The betel nut chewers looked as if their gums were continually bleeding. Many smoked 'bidis' – minute, cheap, cigar-tasting cigarettes.

The train slowly jerked its way through monotonous desert land, stopping with frustrating regularity at every village and township.

Perhaps the journey could have been enjoyed if the environment could have been improved, but travelling on hard seats in a hot, overcrowded train such as this is not the ideal way to enjoy the passing countryside.

For lunch we finished off the remnants of our canned supply we had brought from the UK. "I hope we do not offend any Muslim," I said as I opened a tin of pork luncheon meat in front of the staring eyes of our fellow passengers.

From Sibi we continued through desert waste to Jacobabad, which is at the tail of the Sulaiman range of mountains. By now the terrain had become more fertile, with an increase of habitation. What farming we saw was very rudimentary, ploughs pulled by oxen are simple, iron-tipped sticks which appear to stir but not turn the soil. Crops are reaped with a sickle, threshed by the feet of horses or cattle and winnowed in the wind.

Dusk was approaching as we neared Shikarpur. Shortly after Sukkur we were rumbling over the bridge which crossed the River Indus, on its way southwards to the Indian Ocean, having survived a 600-mile journey from the Himalayas.

Barely had we crossed the Indus when we were entering the railway terminus of Rohri, which is where we thankfully had to change trains for our journey northwards.

It was 9 pm: we had a two-hour wait on the crowded platform before catching the train to Lahore. We took advantage of our long wait to get ourselves a rather dubious curried meal at the station restaurant.

There was a stampede as the already overcrowded train pulled in at the station. Every seat was occupied, the corridors bulging, and even the luggage racks were occupied. It looked very much as if we were about to spend a very uncomfortable night. We pushed our way towards the teeming mass of bodies making our way towards the first-class compartment, where we found a vacant piece of ground space in the corridor. Staking out our claim, we settled down on the floor to prepare ourselves for the coming ordeal. Fortunately we were at the end of the corridor so we were not disturbed by the passing passengers. To make sure, we locked the two outer doors.

We were joined by two young students who settled down beside us. They were keen to hear of our travels and were envious of our experiences. Such travelling appeared to be out of reach of the average Pakistani. The students endeavoured to teach us a few words of Urdu, though I am afraid we made poor pupils.

We awoke in the morning, after an intermittent sleep, to find ourselves covered with sand, the result of having passed through the extremities of the Thar Desert during the night.

As we shook the sand from ourselves the train was just pulling away from Bahawalpur, a town whose main claim to fame was that it was the capital of the former princely state of the same name.

The countryside had changed considerably overnight. Being in the plains of the Indus, the terrain had become very fertile and a rich farming area. Palms, sugar cane and orange groves in abundance, all very subtropical-looking.

During the morning we passed through Multon, a market centre for textiles, notably cotton, silks and carpets.

Many small villages snuggle against the railway. The early morning sun breaks up the deep shadow of houses and mud huts, which are plastered with dung fuel cakes (which we nicknamed 'dung patties'). Slapped on the walls to dry, still bearing the imprint of the fingers of the women who squat down turning the cakes from one hand to the other before slapping them on the walls. Where cakes have dried and fallen, there are round stains on the walls.

The poverty of the people and the mud and straw houses reflect the marginal livelihood of this overcrowded country. Industrialisation increased as we neared the educational city and ex-capital of the old Sikh empire, Lahore. The large, imperial-looking station building of Lahore marked the end of another stage of our journey back to Afghanistan.

With a 16-hour wait before the midnight train to Peshawar, we had ample time to explore Lahore. Straddling the River Ravi, the old walled city has become a centre for Muslim learning, textiles, engineering and food processing. The oldest part of the city is at least 1,000 years old and is surrounded by a 15-foot-high wall. The main business areas of Lahore are relatively modern and clean, though hiding behind this façade are the dirty backstreets.

Much evidence of the present hostilities with India could be seen. Most of the main buildings were camouflaged with mud and had their windows taped and were heavily sandbagged. Trenches had been dug at vantage points and in the parks and wastelands. Road signs had been blacked out or daubed with mud.

After the customary haggling, Tim and I hired a tonga, a small, gaily painted gig drawn by muscular little horses, to take us to the fort, which is one of the few tourist musts of Lahore. Built in yellow sandstone, its main minareted building and walled 'arms' cuddle an impressive courtyard of lawns and gardens. Closing the far end of the courtyard is a beautiful mosque. Inside the spacious, barely furnished mosque (the only extravagance being a thick, wall-to-wall carpet) little groups squatted down comfortably, chatting to each other as though they were in a bar. Others were standing or even asleep, just as if it were the local club rather than a church.

The war seemed far away as we laid out in a nearby park watching a cricket match in the warm afternoon sun.

Lahore, Pakistan.
The author having a break.

Khyber Pass.

Typical street in Karachi.

Beach near Karachi.
Dick (head in sand), trying to
save on suntan lotion.

Like most Eastern peoples, the Pakistanis are very curious about any foreigner's way of life, and their respect for privacy is nil. Tim and I were getting agitated by the incessant staring we received: we only had to pause for a few seconds before we would be surrounded by staring faces. I think we would have received less attention if we had just landed in the centre of a Martian city. The braver ones would attempt to open a conversation, which usually consisted of ascertaining our origin followed by a query as to our views of the war. I had no views, though the more I travelled through Pakistan, the greater the feeling that I was on the wrong side of the fence.

As dusk approached we slowly made our way back, via the backstreets, towards the vicinity of the station.

In the evening the dim and teeming life of the bazaars erupts. The din reaches a crescendo with the clamorous crowds and the hoarse cries of the stallkeepers coupled with the exotic sound of Eastern music blaring from invisible speakers. The aromatic odour of spices, the tasty smell of roasting meat and the smell of fruits and other sweetmeats mix with the stench of drains and excrement, dominated by the reek of oiled butter and curry spices. Pyramids of swelling cucumbers, strange, phallic-shaped fruits and baskets of curries, beanlike vegetables and nuts spread out on portable market stalls, illuminated by kerosene lamps which from a distance look like the march of a column of glow-worms. A dancing bear, towed by its ancient owner by a piece of cord, pranced across our path, though reluctant to do any special performance for our benefit.

Leaving the humdrum of the bazaar we returned to the station, intent on arriving early enough to obtain a seat for the 18-hour train journey to Peshawar. After much shoving and bustling we managed to win for ourselves a seat. Hard though it may have been, it was a seat, which was an achievement in itself.

Once again it appeared we had caught the slow, stopping train, giving cause to a rather intermittent sleep as we were constantly being woken up by the cries of the vendors as we pulled into the stations. Being European we were obvious targets for their promotions; the same applied to the constant stream of beggars who paid us much attention. I think they all have the impression that Europeans wear gold underpants. If only they knew: we were probably as broke as they were. Well, perhaps not quite, but we were slowly heading that way and we had a lot further than them to go.

During the night we had passed the industrial outskirts of Lahore heading northwards through Gujranwala and Gujarat. Through flat, uninteresting countryside we meandered passing the occasional poverty-stricken shanty village, where ragged, pathetic-looking villagers went about their daily chores in derelict carts pulled by oxen. Sari-draped women squatted beside muddy pools pounding their washing on stone slabs or methodically slapping dung patties for their day's fuel, whilst near-naked children watched wide-eyed as the train trundled past. Few patches of greenery stood out like grass stains on a rusty dress.

At Jhelum, close to the Kashmir border, we crossed the River Jhelum on its southerly journey to swell the River Indus. A lengthy stop at Rawalpindi, whose duties as capital city have been taken over by the nearby new city of Islamabad, enabled us to stretch our legs on the crowded platform.

Nearing Peshawar the terrain took on a more mountainous and fertile character. On the horizon we could see the city, a skyline of cupolas and minarets. It was late afternoon when we arrived at Peshawar, an old British garrison town. A city that commands the old caravan trade route between the Indus Plain and into Afghanistan via the Khyber Pass.

Stepping from the station we were immediately accosted by a regiment of tonga drivers. It took thirty minutes of hard bargaining before arriving at a realistic price to transport us to a cheap hotel: a clause in the arrangement was "no like hotel – no pay".

The hotel we were taken to was near the centre of the city, and up to our usual dubious standard, though the price of six rupees (24p) for the two of us was rather exorbitant. Still, as it was getting late and having spent the previous two nights travelling, we were pretty well dead beat and only too pleased to have a stinking, bug-infested mattress to sleep on. By now we were both beginning to 'hum' profusely. The hotel's solitary handbasin of cold, muddy water went little way to alleviate the problem. At least we could console ourselves that our odour appeared to keep the bugs at bay.

Unfortunately, our room was adjacent to the toilet. The thin partition had little effect on muffling the continuous grunts, groans, coughing and spitting, and the smells of the hotel patrons going about their 'business'.

Top priority whilst in Peshawar was to locate the Afghan Embassy to obtain visas to enable us to return to that country. After a couple of hours of fruitless searching, we eventually found the Embassy. Situated in a pleasant district of Peshawar, an area of tree-lined streets and colonial-style houses, though many in a state of neglect. Close by was the rambling Army barracks, remnants of the bygone British presence – a sharp contrast to the squalor of the remainder of the city.

Whilst at the Embassy we met Dave, another Englishman, who had unsuccessfully attempted to cross the border into India and was now returning to Kabul. Having completed the necessary forms and with a few hours' delay before being able to collect our visas, we took the opportunity to see the sights of Peshawar.

The main street teems with life, and the noise of the chanting of the mosques mixes with the yelling of the street vendors, hawkers, moaning of the beggars and screaming urchins – a cacophony of sound. It appeared that every other shop was either a dentist's or a chemist's, most of which had prominently displayed advertisements for the cure of piles.

Filth is everywhere, narrow alley betwixt congested shacks, poverty and misery. Alleys strewn with animal dung, accumulations of rubbish and open sewers. Slimy gutters issue from kitchens, forming greenish puddles. Animals wander with protruding ribs and backbones; emaciated, mangy dogs fossick through piles of rubbish.

Nowhere have I seen so much deformity: surely it cannot be accidental? And it must stem from the sadistic practice of deforming at birth to rear a beggar for much-needed cash for the family coffers. The pathetic sight of limbless beggars dragging themselves through the streets on their stumps, yet still able to raise a macabre smile. No one excused, all ages, from minute children to the aged, thrusting out their hands or tin mugs, pitifully bleating for baksheesh. Even women holding a bundle of rags in which dead-looking babies lay huddled, would plead for our monetary sympathy.

A labyrinth of narrow backstreets heralded the fascinating bazaar, peopled with characters in 'Arabian Nights' costumes. Gaudy jewellery, beaten silver and gold, coffee pots, jars, tankards, copper dishes and cauldrons, lengths of cotton printed in gaily coloured patterns, plus the usual pyramids of foodstuffs, fruits, vegetables, curries, spices, cereals and pus-coloured, fatty, sticky substances. Sickly-looking coloured sweetmeats lay with a thick coating of flies. The streets were daubed with the scarlet stain of the betel nut, the result of the incessant spitting from the betel chewers.

Fortunately the weather was pleasant; the stench from the open sewers and inadequate sanitation must also be asphyxiating in the summer heat. Ancient Bedford buses rattled along in opposition to the jingling of the numerous tongas. Having collected our visas, we bought tickets for our departure the following morning on the daily bus to Kabul. Our newfound companion, Dave, informed us that he was residing in a hotel at half the cost of ours (three rupees), resulting in Tim and myself having a quick change of hotels for our final night in Peshawar.

All day I had been suffering from an unpleasant bout of food poisoning. A not entirely unexpected condition, having been promised it ever since our arrival in Afghanistan. I had been extremely fortunate to escape such discomfort up until now. Coupled with diarrhoea, made even worse by the fact of having virtually nowhere to go. The toilets at the hotel could only make one feel worse. Just a plank with a hole, no flushing or drainage system, excreta piling up, waiting for the daily shovel to take it away. I was still groggy the following morning and was not relishing the 7-hour journey on the bus to Kabul, though it was a better alternative to staying in Peshawar.

A tonga took us from the hotel to the bus depot for our 9 am departure. The customary argument with the tonga driver over the fare persuaded the driver to succumb to our threat to take what we offered or nothing at all.

A strange sight greeted our arrival at the bus depot – a line of about ten men, presumably convicts, joined together by lengths of chain, rather like the paper doll cut-outs we made as kids. They greeted us with ironic waves and cheers.

Our bus, though not quite as ancient as the majority in these parts, was nevertheless not quite what one would wish to travel in for seven hours. The bus was practically empty as we departed from Peshawar. Leaving the built-up area of the city, we headed through the fertile valley where the Kabul River is joined by the Swat.

Wheat, maize, sugar cane, cotton and tobacco are grown in this area, mainly by irrigation. At the small village of Jamrud we stopped to pick up a few more passengers before proceeding through the barren, inhospitable hills of the frontier. These hills house the Afridi, Orakzai and Waziris tribes who collectively belong to the larger group known as the Pathans, renowned for their toughness and bellicose characters. These tribes are herders of sheep and goats, and cultivate plots. In the past they were not averse to doing a little raiding and plundering. Their warlike nature resulted in military garrison towns such as Peshawar.

Prior to reaching these hills we were stopped at a roadblock at Landi Kotal, where large signs warned us that we were about to enter a tribal area (meaning under local administration). For the privilege of entering this domain we all had to forfeit one rupee before being able to proceed.

The terrain became more rugged as we ascended towards the western gateway to Afghanistan, the Khyber Pass – famous not only for its grandeur, but also for the battles fought in these inhospitable mountains, memories of which are still preserved in the participating regiments' crests hewn out of the rocks. An impressive array of forts stand like sentinels against the rugged backcloth.

CHAPTER 10

Back into Afghanistan

The bus rattled its way along the hairpinned road, taking us through the mountains which towered either side of us. Having successfully accomplished the Khyber Pass we made the gradual descent to the Pakistan border town of Torkham. There was a short stop at the border post whilst our credentials were given the once-over and the bus searched.

As we were leaving the customs post, half a dozen men boarded the bus and proceeded to conduct a verbal barrage with the driver and his mate. Although not being able to comprehend, we gathered that they wanted to be smuggled into Afghanistan. No sooner had we passed the Afghan checkpoint than the 'invaders' alighted, but not before being seen by a handful of locals who gestured wildly at the driver who in turn appeased the mob by throwing a handful of coins out of the window.

Proceeding through mountainous countryside we were entertained by beautiful views of fertile river valleys. We were now running parallel with the Kabul River which escorted us for much of the journey to Jalalabad, a resort for the richer merchants of Kabul. A short break at Jalalabad enabled us to obtain a chapatti and a bowl of yoghurt at one of the many chai- khanas.

From Jalalabad, we continued to follow the River Kabul through fertile plains before commencing the assault on the final barrier of mountains before Kabul. This range being one of the extending ribs of the Hindu Kush, that large expanse of inhospitable mountains whose name derives from Hindus Killer, from the Indian slaves killed whilst crossing the range in severe cold. We passed through the amazing Kabul Gorge where the road lies in a deep cutting with the Kabul River rushing alongside. It winds through a series of tunnels and curves to drop more than 3,000 feet. At times we were engulfed by sheer walls of rock with only a thin strip of blue sky way overhead.

This final range even surpassed the Khyber in grandeur, crowned by the magnificent Tangi-Garu Gorge. An area of vast gorges intermingled with fertile valleys and the occasional dam to remind one of the 20th century.

With a rather unexpected abruptness we arrived at the outskirts of Afghanistan's capital, Kabul. The outskirts of the city are relatively modern with the Army barracks and tall concrete office blocks, but the closer we came to the centre, the older the buildings became, rather like a casual journey in a time machine.

Luck was with us as we were proceeding through the city, Tim noticed Bo's Land Rover parked outside the Khyber restaurant, which would give us a good lead to the whereabouts of the rest of the gang. Alighting from the bus at the beautiful central mosque, we walked the short distance back to where Tim had seen Bo's Land Rover parked. There it was, parked outside the Khyber restaurant; attached to the windscreen, in anticipation of our return, was a note informing us that they were staying at the Abaseen Hotel.

Being unfamiliar with our surroundings, we took the uncharacteristic step and hired a taxi to take us to the hotel. We should have known better: the taxi took us on a three-mile tour of the city before alighting us at the hotel which, we discovered, was only a hundred yards from where we had hailed the taxi – the driver's excuse being that, unknown to him, the hotel had recently changed its name. It was useless to protest: we put it down to experience.

A long flight of stairs leading from a back alley brought us to the manager's office. Informing him that we were looking for six Englishmen who had booked into his hotel, he replied, "Ah yes, you must be the other two they were expecting: follow me." Another two flights of stairs brought us to a verandah-style corridor. "You will find them in the end room."

It was good to see the gang again: even though it was only six days since we parted in Kandahar, we had much to talk about. The gang had had an uneventful journey up to Kabul; since their arrival they had not been idle, and already they were working on prospective buyers for the Land Rover.

Agreement was reached with the manager, for Tim and myself to take up residence in the room along with the other six. A fairly large room (by our, by now, low standards) with four beds and an ancient heater providing the only furniture, leaving just enough room for four sleeping bags on the floor. Where else could you find such luxury for about 7p each per night? With the prospect of an indefinite stay in Kabul or at least until Bo had unburdened himself of the Land Rover and the Indo/Pakistani border situation eased, it was essential to find as comfortable and as cheap a 'pad' as possible.

Even a shower was provided, though operating times were rather limited, depending on the bacha boy's generosity in supplying logs to light the boiler for heating the water. The fringe benefits did not cease there: the hotel was equipped with European-type loos – yes, actual sit-down loos. Though the rarity of such modern commodities was just too much for some of the patrons (or staff), as we often found footmarks on the seat accompanied by the resultant 'missed aims' (old habits die hard). Below our room was the hotel restaurant, a very pleasant dive, with low lights and Western-style music, and offering a panoramic view of the city. For about 12p one could obtain a reasonable three-course meal, though there was very little selection and after a few days of camel or goat meat, spinach and potato, it did become rather monotonous. The restaurant was also a meeting place for many European hippies and overlanders; we had many a reunion with travellers whom we had met previously on the 'milk run' to Afghanistan.

Tim and I were only too pleased to have an early night's kip after our somewhat fatiguing six-day jaunt through Pakistan. Bo awoke the following morning feeling, and looking, pretty ghastly, and raised no objection to our suggestion of fetching a doctor. Whilst Peggy and Dick went to organise a doctor I accompanied Mike and Tony on a visit to a prospective buyer of their Land Rover.

Already three days of hard bargaining had been pursued: this was just another round on the way to the final. The customer was a prosperous tobacco dealer whose office consisted of a three-yard-square 'box' alongside the smelly Kabul River. Inside the office were stacked thousands of cartons of cigarettes, leaving barely enough room for us all to squat down. Glasses of tea and sweetmeats were brought in by the bacha boy before commencement of talks with the turbaned buyer and the middleman who had brought the two parties together. Agreement had previously been reached on a price of $1,600, but there were still differences to be ironed out: one was the commission the middleman wanted for his part in the deal. After nearly three hours of haggling it appeared that the deal had almost been finalised apart from a few minor details like currency exchange rates and the import duty which Bo would have to settle, being the registered owner of the vehicle. Monetary bargaining is par for the course in Afghanistan: it appears that when rumours that a large deal is about to be brokered, as with Bo's Land Rover, it rocks the Afghan currency market.

Back at the hotel we found that a doctor had visited Bo and diagnosed a fever, confining him to bed with numerous bottles of lotions and pills which he guaranteed would cure him within 48 hours. Surprisingly enough, it did. In return for his services, the doctor asked Bo to write him a letter of reference, stating what a fine doctor he was.

The weather, although considerably colder than it had been in Peshawar, was quite bearable. The colder temperature was not unexpected: after all, Kabul is almost 6,000 feet above sea level. The mountain slopes of the Hindu Kush ran almost literally to the backyards of the hotel. From our window we could see the timber shanty shacks which congest the sides of the mountains, each shack appearing to be perched on top of the other, looking rather like steps up the mountainside. These dilapidated, weather-beaten slums house the majority of Kabul's 300,000 population. One resident of one of the nearer shacks had us puzzled. All day he would stand on his roof waving what appeared to be a giant-sized butterfly net. It took many days before we realised he was guiding his pigeons home.

Each day one of us would do the three-mile mail run up to the British Embassy – an imposing, white neo-Georgian building surrounded by well-kept lawns and gardens, on the outskirts of the city. Unfortunately, mail deliveries in Afghanistan are rather erratic: there always seems to be an element of maybe/maybe not about their postal system. A visit to Kabul Post Office would certainly confirm this. Afghans have absolutely no concept of queueing: one is immediately caught up in a loose scrummage of tattered bodies, each with an arm thrust out to the clerk in whose face envelopes, money and forms are waved vigorously while requirements are yelled as though, by the rules, the loudest yell must win. The clerks seemed to avoid Europeans as if they know that 'here comes a problem'. The cost of sending a letter to the UK varied from day to day; determining the airmail fee for such an outlandish place as England resulted in a series of weighing and reweighing on ancient scales of doubtful accuracy. Even though we would watch the stamp stuck on and franked, we always had the feeling that there is only a 50/50 chance of the letter ever reaching its destination.

Kabul, the metropolis of Afghanistan, even though the capital city, gave one the impression of a small market town. Many of its population live in the myriads of small mud hut dwellings which balance on the sides of the mountains that surround much of Kabul. For a capital city the traffic is light, mostly vintage: American cars of dubious roadworthiness and the occasional Bedford bus with its customary farmyard assortment on its roof, and of course the camel and donkey trains which come in to trade in the city.

Kabul is the Mecca for hippies who thread their way through Europe in the hope of finding their utopia through the haze of hash smoke. A pilgrimage of many nationalities. In following the trail as we did, you meet people from Britain, Europe, Australia, America and Canada. For many it's a journey of degradation, hardship and suffering disease, hunger and indignities. Many practically starve themselves. Even though we lived on the borderline we were never on the point of starving (Ron saw to that!). I suppose this kind of life is in keeping with the hippie philosophy of sharing and living in a spirit of peace and love, the true dropout philosophy which is all too prevalent in Kabul where they are not only tolerated, but also catered for. Hotels supplying cheap food and accommodation have mushroomed.

Hashish is readily obtainable in all shapes and forms, from hash cookies to hash candy. In fact the small blocks of hash seem to have more buying and selling power than the local currency.

In Chicken Street, numerous shops supply good leather and skin products at ridiculously low prices. Here can be bought the chapan, a handsome, colourful longcoat which has become the uniform of the overlander. Colourful, embroidered leather waistcoats, tailor-made leather trousers and knee-high boots can all be bartered or bought for a fraction of the cost in the world's boutique fashion centres. As its name implies, Chicken Street is a poultry paradise (providing you are not one of the species). Stacks of caged chickens await their inevitable fate. More fortunate ones mix with grubby ducks and geese and congenitally mangy dogs, rumbling around together in filth-blocked gutters filled with a greenish, glutinous liquid. Narrow, muddy, dirty streets are frequented by Europeans, many of whom have reached their lowest ebb and are reduced to begging, to obtain 'afs' for some 'bread'.

As in common with the rest of Afghanistan, sanitation and hygiene in Kabul are minimal. Apart from in the hotels, toilets are practically non-existent. Any stretch of wasteland serves as a public convenience. It is not uncommon to see a person stop and squat in any convenient spot and answer the call of nature, his 'dhoti' conveniently covering any source of embarrassment as if designed for this purpose. One particular area close to our hotel was a favourite 'release' centre which we always made sure to give a wide berth: the stench was overpowering from the piles of human faeces.

The Kabul River runs through the city, furnished from the snows of the Hindu Kush, meandering its way through stinking, garbage-strewn banks. Kabul is rich in colourful and well-stocked bazaars, where animal skins, lapis lazuli (a semi-precious stone) jewellery, silverwork and local exotic clothing can be bought cheaply if one is willing to spend a few hours bargaining – which is expected and enjoyed.

To vary our diet from the monotony of the ditto meals of our own hotel we would occasionally experiment in other establishments, though wherever we went the choice was very limited. One experiment that backfired was a meal in the German restaurant, on the recommendation of the British Embassy, where we certainly overstepped the mark in monetary extravagance. A Dutch sandwich (the cheapest item on the menu) costing us 60 afs (30p), three times our normal daily food allowance. At the opposite end of the scale was Siggis, a hole in the wall-type restaurant-cum-lodging house, inside of which small, hushed groups of dropouts and hippies (or travellers, as they prefer to be called) sat cross-legged or lounged on the floor, in a completely naked room, picking with their fingers at bowls of rice and meats, with the sweet smell of hash overpowering the smell of cooking.

To eliminate any threat of boredom, Dick found a novel way to amuse himself. At a nearby pond he would feed hash cookies to the fish and watch as they went round in ever-decreasing circles before finally giving up the fight and passing out. This confused the hotel manager, as the pond supplied the water for the hotel and he relied on the fish being active to let him know the water wasn't contaminated.

Intriguing are the multitude of kites which assemble over Kabul, rather like miniature colourful barrage balloons. Invisible strings follow the swooping protagonists, whose owners are never seen, as if the kite is equipped with an alert, built-in brain.

On our second day in Kabul snow began to fall: as it happens, this appears to be a very satisfactory arrangement as it lessens the stench of excrement and rotting garbage that accumulate in the streets.

Since arriving in Kabul most of our time had been spent in acquainting ourselves with the city and reassessing our position, much of which depends on the Indo-Pak situation and pending the sale of Bo's Land Rover.

Our names were placed on a waiting list for a flight to Delhi with Ariana Airlines. Although all flights into India had been suspended, we were informed by the airline that they were expecting to be granted permission to fly limited flights to Delhi very shortly. Frequent visits to the airline office only served to add fuel to our frustrations: we were constantly fed contradicting information. First we were on a waiting list, next there was no such list, then there was a list but our names were not on it. Yes, there is a flight, come back tomorrow, we did, only to find the office closed for the day. I got the impression that if we ever did manage to get on one of their flights it would have been a case of 'Hands up those who want to go to Delhi, and now those who want to go to Baghdad': the majority show of hands wins.

Our urge to move on escalated with a sudden turn of events. Ron, returning from one of his daily walkabouts, informed us that he had met our old friend Aziz who had just flown up to Kabul from Kandahar. He was waiting to see us in the hotel restaurant.

Aziz greeted us with a loud chuckle: "Hello, my friends, good to see you." We did not quite share his enthusiasm at the unexpected meeting: we smelled trouble. "What brings you to these parts?" I asked. "I am here on business," replied Aziz.

Giving in to interrogation, Aziz confirmed our apprehension: he was in trouble concerning the Land Rover. Evidently, he had been caught bringing the vehicle back into Afghanistan; he had Sweaty Betty impounded and himself put in jail, charged with illegally bringing a vehicle into the country, evading import duty and stealing the Land Rover (he had no legal document to say that he was the rightful owner). As if that was not enough, they also had him on the possible murder charge, being suspected of killing Tim and me and stealing our vehicle. He was now out on bail (or bribe) to try and prove his innocence on the murder and stealing charges.

Knowing our intentions, Aziz had come straight to Kabul in the hope of persuading Tim (the official owner of the vehicle) to accompany him back to Kandahar to prove he was still alive and that the Land Rover had been sold to Aziz. We were baited with offers to stay as guests at Aziz's hash farm. As much as we would have liked to have helped, the risk of getting involved was too great. On the other hand, there was a chance that Aziz would pull a few strings and try and stop us leaving the country. If the implications of the latest developments were not so serious, it would have been quite a comedy. Tim wrote out a receipt saying he had received the said sum from Aziz for the Land Rover and also handed over all relevant documents appertaining to the vehicle. This temporarily appeased Aziz, who left the hotel promising to return the following morning, having reported to the Kabul custom authority.

Meanwhile, Bo, Peggy, Mike and Tony had been busy in further transactions concerning their Land Rover. The price had been agreed upon; all that was left to do was the legal transfer of ownership and the customs. The latter task being hastened by a monetary bribe to the customs official to push the necessary documents through, a task which normally takes many days. All part of the lackadaisical business atmosphere of Afghanistan.

Even the banks run short of cash or are unconversant in the latest currency exchange rates, giving rise to a flourishing black market where a far better rate of exchange could be obtained – though in Bo's case, where a transaction of over $1600 was being activated, the price of the pound mysteriously rose. Obviously prior warning of an impending 'big deal' had reached the ears of the black market. Nevertheless, Bo completed the deal which was a great relief to us all, leaving us free to proceed on our journey as soon as the opportunity to get into India arose.

Concern over the latest developments with our Land Rover led Tim and me to seek advice from the British Embassy. As much as the Vice-Consul sympathised with our predicament, there was not anything he could do, apart from offering his advice, as legally we were in the wrong. Tim was advised to go with Aziz to the customs authority in an attempt to clear everything up whilst we were still in Kabul. We were advised against returning to Kandahar where they would more than likely intern us for aiding and abetting the evasion of import duty. It appeared there was a different set of rules in Kandahar than in Kabul, the country still very much affected by tribal differences. Many tales were heard of overlanders interned for trivial offences only to be released after being milked dry of their monetary resources.

Tim and Aziz went to the customs office but were told to report to the public prosecutor the following day.

Aziz's constant fingering of his worry beads and his unusually sad expression portrayed his genuine concern over the whole business.

Meanwhile, Ron had contracted a severe bout of 'Afghan gut-rot' which put him out of circulation for a few days. This was a condition that we all appeared to have suffered in some way or other; in fact, we all seemed to be suffering from a permanent sore throat, a condition that could hardly be unexpected considering the state of hygiene and food and the conditions we were living in.

Whilst Tim and Aziz went to the public prosecutor, Dick and I visited the Indian Embassy in an endeavour to glean some information on the latest border situation. The news was not good, there being no indication as to when the Pak/Indo border would reopen.

Feeling rather dejected and not relishing a lengthy stay in Kabul, we decided to try the Pakistan Airlines office to see if they had any suggestions. "Yes, we are still operating, though not into India. Why not try our scheduled flight from Karachi to Colombo? Then you can make your own way from Ceylon to India by boat," said the airline official. "How many of you are there?" he queried. To our reply of eight he informed us that if we could find two more passengers he would allow us 10% discount on the £60 fare.

The idea certainly met with Dick's and my approval: at least it would offer us an escape route and enable us to proceed with our travels. Elated, we returned to our hotel to ignite the gang with our enthusiasm. They did not need any persuasion, they were as keen as Dick and me. Our spirits were somewhat dampened by the return of Tim from his visit with Aziz to the public prosecutor: Tim's passport had been taken off him and handed to Aziz on the assurance that Aziz would return to Kandahar with Tim.

This was the last straw, a blow below the belt which put us in an awkward position. We could not very well leave Kabul and leave Tim to an unknown fate in Kandahar. On the other hand, Aziz had been forced to give an assurance to return to Kandahar with Tim: failure to do so would no doubt have dire results between him and the police. Roguish as he was, we had become very attached to the friendly cheerfulness of Aziz, and the last thing we would wish was for him to sink deeper into trouble, even though he had brought it on himself by his own carelessness. Nevertheless, our loyalties lay with Tim; we would have to get the passport off Aziz and get Tim out of the country.

Retrieving Tim's passport was easier than anticipated. On the pretence that the British Embassy wanted to see the passport, Tim managed to persuade Aziz to hand the passport back.

Plans were made for Tim, accompanied by Dick, to leave Kabul the following day on the early morning bus to Peshawar, whilst the rest of us would follow a few days later, during which time we would do our best to forestall Aziz and finalise the arrangements for our flight from Karachi.

We had little trouble in finding two more travelling companions to make up a party of ten for the flight: two Danes, Bow and his attractive girlfriend Dorte who were on their way to India.

Firm bookings were made with the airline office. As we had had to change our pound traveller's cheques into dollars for the fare, a visit to the black market necessitated, two hours of hard bargaining with the unscrupulous black marketeers.

Situated near the banks of the Kabul River, the monetary black market was an organised grotto of cupboard-sized shops sited in a small square. Much expertise and patience were required to play one shop off against the other to obtain the best deal. Mike and I would start at one end whilst Bo and Tony the other, until we arrived at the highest bidder for our traveller's cheques. Not only is this an enjoyable game, but also profitable, as a much better rate can be obtained than from a bank. It is said that in countries like Afghanistan, with an unstable currency, traveller's cheques are never cashed, but are passed from hand to hand as legal tender.

Clutching our newly acquired dollars we returned to the airline office where we were presented with our tickets for the flight to Ceylon leaving Karachi in a week's time. Overjoyed at having made a scoop booking of ten seats, the manager invited us to tea at his house in the evening.

Back in the hotel we were confronted by Aziz with the sad expression of a Boxer dog. "Where is Tim?" he asked. We had been prepared for this question. "He has gone up to Kunduz to see the Buzkashi [a national hair-raising game where horsemen fight for the carcass of a calf or goat]," we lied unconvincingly. "When will he be back?" replied Aziz. "We are not sure, probably tomorrow, he just left a note in the room saying he had got a lift up to Kunduz and would see us later." We were not very convincing, but as long as we could stonewall Aziz until 1300 by which time Tim would be safely out of Afghanistan and his last chance to prevent Tim leaving the country would have gone.

It was an embarrassing and nail-biting situation; none of us enjoyed being deceitful to Aziz, but it was for our own good. A phone call to the border police could make it rather uncomfortable for us. Even once Tim was safely across the border, no mention could be made of our intending departure, as there was every chance that Aziz, once cornered, would try and prevent us from leaving the country.

Aziz phoned the British Consul, endeavouring to confirm Tim's story that the Embassy required his passport. Luckily the Consul would not entertain Aziz's questions. Once midday was past we could relax a little: at least we were almost certain that Tim and Dick would by now be in Pakistan.

Most of the afternoon was spent bartering or selling off more of our excess gear and trying to evade Aziz, but he watched our every movement. Positioning himself strategically near the door of the restaurant, he would watch our comings and goings as we came up or down the stairs leading from our room.

An awkward moment arose when a Pakistan Airlines minibus drew up at the hotel to collect us to attend the tea party with the airline manager. We could see Aziz staring wide-eyed out of the restaurant window as we piled into the bus. Surely his suspicions must by now be confirmed.

We were taken to a large, fashionable house on the outskirts of Kabul where we were welcomed by the manager, his wife and various other airline dignitaries. Drinks were served whilst we chatted amiably with our hosts before being led into an adjoining room where a fantastic spread of food was laid out before us.

The extravagance of such luxurious sweetmeats was elaborated by our long abstinence from such luxuries, having become accustomed to a plate of rice and meat per day. Whilst taking full advantage of this gastronomic orgy, photographs were taken of "this happy bunch of travellers sensibly travelling by PIA and being feted by the airline". Obviously good publicity.

Feeling better for our rare feed, we were driven back to reality as we were taken through the snow-covered streets back to our hotel, where we were informed by the manager that Aziz had only just left, having made numerous phone calls.

We tried as inconspicuously as possible to prepare ourselves for an early exodus the following morning. Hotel bills were paid and a feeble attempt was made at laying a false scent by telling the manager that we intended going up to Kunduz to join Tim and Dick and would probably be returning in a few days. At least if Aziz enquired as to our whereabouts, there was a chance that he would believe the story, thus delaying any action to prevent us leaving the country, by which time we should be safely in Pakistan.

Dawn was breaking as we crept out of the hotel, fully laden with rucksacks and sleeping bags. It was a bitterly cold morning, a thick carpet of snow spread out over Kabul, and it was still snowing as we trudged the mile-long route through deserted streets of tumbledown dwellings to the bus departure point. Although there was a nearer pick-up point, it was situated close to the hotel Aziz was staying at, and we did not want the risk of him seeing us. We knew of his habit of rising at dawn to pay his respects to Allah.

Already a small collection of passengers had gathered to await the arrival of the bus which turned up at 0630. A short delay whilst the classic Asian array of luggage was loaded on to the roof. Bedrolls, tin trunks, wooden boxes, cardboard cartons unceremoniously roped together, canvas satchels, cloth bags, biscuit tins plus bundles tied up with filthy rags.

At about 0700 the bus moved off, winding its way through Kabul until we were at long last on the road to Pakistan. In Arctic conditions the bus rattled its way through scenic mountains and passes arriving about midday at the border post and our final barrier, the police and customs checkpoint. The bus conductor collected our passports and took them into the police office where, without further ado, they were stamped and handed back to us.

Our final obstacle was the customs post, about 100 yards further on. On arrival, a stern-faced official boarded the bus, affording cursory glances through all foreigners' passports. Glancing through Mike's passport, he noticed that a tape recorder had been entered as having been brought into the country.

"Show me your tape recorder," he asked sourly. Mike had completely forgotten about the tape recorder's entry in his passport (which was the same problem Tim had had with his radio on our recent exit from Afghanistan when smuggling the Land Rover out of the country). It had in fact been sold at one of our grand sales. "I have mislaid it," replied Mike, looking for some compassion on the official's face. "If you have not got it with you then you must pay duty," was the unfriendly reply. "How much duty?" asked Mike. "I do not know, for that you must return to Kabul." Our faces dropped: here we were a few yards from the border and now the distinct possibility of having Mike sent back to Kabul.

Such a move would create serious problems for us. We would be reluctant to let Mike return on his own to Kabul, where he would be at the mercy of the customs and no doubt Aziz's fury on hearing of our escape. Apart from that, Tim and Dick were waiting for us in Peshawar, and with our seats booked on a flight from Karachi in four days, we could hardly afford any delay.

Our protests to the official that Mike had to catch a plane landed on deaf ears. He was adamant: Mike was going back to Kabul.

"Get his luggage off the roof," he told the conductor. This was done whilst the official escorted Mike to his office. Fifteen minutes later, Mike returned; we were optimistic on seeing a hint of a smile on his face.

"It's all okay," said Mike. "I slipped him £10 which changed his whole attitude: in fact he almost apologised for the inconvenience."

That is just about a synopsis of the Afghans, I mused. We all breathed a sigh of relief as, with Mike's bags back on-board, the bus trundled across the border and into Pakistan.

A short delay prevailed at the Pakistan border post of Torkham in Khyber Province whilst the customary entry formalities were completed.

Alongside the customs shed a derelict array of abandoned vehicles, many sporting GB number plates, lay huddled forlornly together. Abandoned by whom? I do not know: maybe their owners could not afford the import duty and had abandoned the cars betwixt the Afghan and Pakistan border posts, a common sight at many international boundaries, or maybe they had just broken down, or outlived their usefulness, especially as road and rail transportation in these Eastern countries is so cheap.

Having run the gauntlet of money changers, beggars and vendors, we returned to the bus to continue on our way through the ramshackle border town before ascending the familiar hairpin road towards the Khyber Pass.

An uneventful journey pursued as we survived the Khyber Pass and descended through the tribal areas of Landi Kotal and Jamrud, following the fertile valley of the Kabul River to Peshawar.

CHAPTER 11

Back into Pakistan

Heavy rain greeted our arrival at Peshawar which only helped to make the town look even more uninviting and dirtier as mud and mire splattered through the street, though this was somewhat compensated for by the higher temperature, a pleasant change from the below-freezing temperature of Kabul.

From a traveller's point of view, January appears to be a good time for travelling through Pakistan and India, though having recently suffered our fair share of inclement weather we were very easily satisfied.

We were relieved to see Dick and Tim waiting for us as the bus pulled into the bus depot, a feeling akin to the relief at being able to stretch ourselves after eight hours of discomfort cooped up on the bus. Willing hands swarmed over the bus to unload our baggage, though it would be more accurate to say they were released from the roof. No doubt they were hoping that their small service would reap a rupee or two. Understandably they looked upset when we shook their outstretched hands! We were soon surrounded by crowds offering to change money at intolerable rates. Feeling like hardened travellers, we resolutely refused, used by now, to the ingenuity of such people when it comes to conning tourists.

"We haven't much time to lose, the train leaves early this evening," said Tim. A couple of tongas were hailed, we all piled in for the short journey in the horse carts to Peshawar station.

Apart from Dick and Tim, none of us had eaten all day and were feeling ravenous. Fortunately Tim had foreseen this and had forewarned the friendly railway restaurateur to prepare a meal in anticipation of the arrival of eight starving Europeans. Shortly after, we were sitting down tucking into a bowl of curry and rice.

Providing one is a curry fan, eating in Pakistan or India will be no problem. Not only is it the breakfast and dinner of the inhabitants (that is, those that can afford two meals), but more importantly it is cheap. One can manage on a few pence a day, though the monotony of such a diet would tend to limit one's eating enough to survive.

Our appetites sated, we made our way through the rambling colonial-style station to the booking office to purchase our tickets for the 1,000-mile journey to Karachi. With such a long train journey before us, we all agreed to up our status and travel second-class. To offset this extravagance we made a claim for a student discount.

"Where are your student cards?" asked the railway clerk. Between us we could only produce two student cards, belonging to Bow and Dorte, the two Danes. These cards, together with a collection of international driving permits, and anything else that came to hand that looked official, these were thrust before the by now confused clerk, succeeding in obtaining us a 20% reduction on our train fare. Armed with our tickets we proceeded through the barrier to the crowded platform to board the waiting train.

Luck was with us: even though by Western standards the train was already crowded, we managed to monopolise a small bunked compartment. With nearly two days on the train before us, it looked as if we were going to have a mammoth task to keep the compartment to ourselves, which even with just our party of ten seemed crowded, though to a Pakistani it would appear practically empty.

Dusk was falling as the train slowly slipped out of Peshawar to the sound of the wailing of the city's mosques, sounding as if they resented our departure.

So far we had managed to repel all attempts at an invasion of our compartment, though it was getting increasingly difficult. Even having locked the doors, the incessant banging on the other side would eventually activate one of us into opening the door, in which case a verbal barrage of dissent would usually discourage the offender, unless of course it was the ticket collector. Eventually even he would wait until the train arrived at a station, and go out onto the platform, bypassing our compartment. The worst problems arose when arriving at a large station, when hordes of people would pour onto the train. We were fortunate in having recruited the services of an excellent ally in the form of one of the train's butlers. Apart from supplying our gastronomic needs he would at every station position himself at the doorway of our compartment informing would-be intruders that it was a reserved compartment. This arrangement suited his purpose equally well, as he was an avid hashish smoker: the seclusion of our compartment enabled him to enjoy a smoke without fear of informers. We named him 'Butler No. 1', which seemed to please him, no doubt glad of the verbal promotion.

Once the train had left Rawalpindi we settled for the night. With only eight bunks between the ten of us, Ron and Dick opted to sleep on the floor.

The hard bunk and the shaking of the train, coupled with the shouts of vendors, beggars and passengers as we arrived at stations, guaranteed a sleepless night. Butler No. 1 ensured that we would not oversleep, as if that was at all possible in these conditions. "Who wants breakfast?" he cried. We settled for a cup of tea, preferring to sustain ourselves from the cheaper titbits from the station vendors.

The cheapness of these snacks hardly compensated for the dubious quality and lack of hygiene. Consolation could be taken for the apparent acceptance by our stomachs of even the most foul-tasting foodstuffs, whether it be evil-looking gobbets of mutton, camel or what-have-you being sold by some emaciated, betel-spitting old crone.

Each station suppled its own collection of beggars, each with their own party piece, some blind, some limbless, starving and diseased, many malformed. One could not help but take a more lenient view of our affluent society. People all around us seemed inwardly dead, mere mechanically moving puppets, their expressions dulled by permanent suffering. At the stations, beggars would crowd the train in an effort to make as much as possible in the short time allotted. Being Europeans, we were obvious targets, though their pleading looks fell on stony ground except with Ron, who could not refuse a beggar's plea. Perhaps our indifference seems a trifle callous, but when you are beseeched by hordes, how can you single out one to receive your favours?

Hard to get accustomed to was the incessant staring we received. Every station produced its collection of spectators who would press their faces against the windows in an ignorant gesture of inquisitiveness. Peggy and Dorte, with their blonde hair and blue eyes, seemed to them something rare and strange, which indeed they were, being so solitary creatures, a far cry from their own dark, sari-draped women who move mystically and noiselessly along in gold-sandalled feet, their heads poised and erect as though beneath the weight of an invisible water jug.

Amusing was the nonsensical roll of the head of the Pakistani men, as if the head was pivoted on a well-oiled ball bearing: this was usually the reply to any question they failed to understand, though many seemed to perform subconsciously.

The train lethargically rolled its way southwards through interesting terrain of sugar plantations and paddy fields where men stooped ankle-deep in water in the beds of rice seedlings, pulling fistfuls of plants, twisting the stalks to bind the bundles before parting with them to a child who passed them on to a woman standing knee-deep in the water in another allotment to replant the seedlings in erratic rows.

Bullocks toiled sluggishly in the fields or else were detailed off to pull dilapidated wooden carts complete with large, solid, wooden wheels, whereas their counterparts, the cows, appeared to be let off scot-free, being allowed to roam around of their own accord.

At Multon, police boarded the train: on entering our compartment they must have scented the sweet hash smell still lingering from a recent visit from our friendly Butler No. 1, as they searched and sniffed through our rucksacks and bedrolls. Finding nothing, they left, leaving the train to continue its way southwards to Bahawalpur.

From Bahawalpur the countryside became less fertile and more desert which resulted in a covering of sand dust in our compartment. The weather became noticeably warmer as we journeyed through the extremities of the Thar Desert, passing the townships of Khanpur, Rahim Yar Khan and Sukkar, after which the countryside took on a rather boring attitude, alternating between sandy wastes, cotton fields and date palms, with the occasional scruffy village to stir our interest.

Darkness put an end to the 'show'. With little else to captivate the audience, we settled down for the expected restless night.

Dawn was breaking as we approached Hyderabad. The red and ochre coloured horizon which merged with the blood orange sunrise indicated heat and dust, the latter confirmed by the fact that practically all of us awoke with sore throats, the result of breathing in the dusty sand that crept through every available opening, like a thick, yellow fog. By this time the heat and the train were making us resemble a group of half-consumed lollipops which had rolled around a cinema floor.

Hyderabad, a large city just north of the apex of the Indus Delta, an old caravan centre. As with most large cities at least a 30-minute stop could be expected, an ideal opportunity to stretch our legs, which were, by now, beginning to show signs of stiffness after nearly two days of inactivity apart from the odd stretch or two on a station platform.

The River Indus was crossed between Hyderabad and Katri, taking us on to the last leg of the journey to Karachi.

Everything seems the same tawny, reddish brown, occasionally shading into grey. Green is an exception rather than the rule, and unfortunately seldom to be found. One would search unsuccessfully for its cool relief which would be a comforting oasis in that barren, dusty wilderness.

The desert merges with Karachi's outskirts like a dusty tide having ebbed, leaving sandy puddles in the streets and wretched, shrivelled gardens. Approaches to Karachi are plagued with poverty. Contrasting with makeshift shanty town huts made from bits of old wood and corrugated iron, can be seen signs of improvement in the tall blocks of flats, which ironically alternate abruptly with marble palaces and splendid mosques.

It was mid-afternoon when the train finally pulled into the bustling Karachi station. Our introduction to Pakistan's leading port, as we struggled with our heavy rucksacks against the surging masses, was a legless beggar, whose sole contribution to life seemed to be his macabre smile, wheeling himself along on a miniature trolley, his tin mug thrust up at us.

People everywhere, many were soldiers. Sari-draped women, their ears ringed and noses pierced, sporting a coloured dot on their forehead. Yelling children, crying babies being unashamedly suckled. Men wearing the loose-fitting dhotis stood amongst piles of large cloth bags; many looked lost, confused or abandoned, and most looked poor. Uniformed turbaned porters darted about between people's legs on a variety of errands, vanishing and popping up again ready to do any meagre service.

We appeared to be the odd ones out, an impression substantiated by the stares and odd looks we received. Not just casual stares, but persistent glares, as if they could not believe what they saw. Efforts to outstare the offenders met with little success: either our time or our patience ran out first.

The chaotic kaleidoscopic hurly-burly of Karachi took us rather by surprise: having geared ourselves down to the leisurely pace of recent Arab countries, we were unaccustomed to such momentum.

With three days to go prior to our flight on January 29th, our initial objective was to find a cheap hotel. This problem was alleviated by the arrival of two horse and cart taxis (tongas) whose drivers claimed they knew of a very good, cheap hotel. From past experiences that could have meant anything from a mud hut to a shanty house, or even a brothel.

With no better suggestion, we soon had the overladen horses jogging us through the backstreets of Karachi. A twenty-minute journey brought us to a scruffy-looking building. "Here is your hotel, it is very good, eh?" said the driver. I could not share his enthusiasm, but we had landed at a lot worse. After a short inspection and the customary price haggle, we had a roof for the night. Three small 'cells' between the ten of us – rather extravagant, I thought. I am sure one would suffice, but there you are, as the manager said: "We have our standards to keep, we cannot have overcrowding." Coming from a Pakistani it sounded a wry comment; perhaps he has never been to Bradford. "Please pay in advance," said the manager. Obviously we were not the first Europeans to use his hotel. When only paying two rupees per night you must not expect the standards of, say, the Hilton. Looking out from an iron-barred window we had an excellent view of a rubbish-strewn backyard and a shelled-out building. One bed between four of us, though as most Pakistanis carry their own bedroll, this could be expected. Our door opened out to the hotel toilets, which were the typical hole in the floor-type (God help the ground-floor tenants); air conditioning was supplied by nature, there being no roof, which at least minimised the smell. All in all a hotel up to our usual standards.

Having sorted ourselves out we made off in search of the PIA office to confirm our flight. This done, we enjoyed the nostalgic luxury of a plate of fish and chips. With very little sleep the past two days, we were in no mood to spend the evening walking the streets, preferring to have an early night and leaving the sightseeing to the following two days.

Karachi, a stadium of chaotic streams of traffic, bicycles, three-wheeled scooter taxis, tongas, three- and four-wheeled delivery vans, lorries, overcrowded buses and huge drays drawn by camels who plodded in their slow, loose-jointed 'could not care less' gait, chewing away and peering at the world from a great height out of their small, bleary eyes. People of influence, wearing dark glasses, glide along in large American cars, impatiently hooting, adding to the nightmarish orchestra. Conducting this Oriental musical was a poor, disregarded traffic policemen, his legs and arms waving forlornly. In his mouth he had a whistle which he blew shrilly each time someone ignored his instructions, which seemed incessantly.

Soldiers walking hand in hand were a common sight. Beggars were everywhere, starved, malformed and pathetic. Children danced around us with outstretched hands, persistently tugging at our clothing. On the pavements barbers squatted in front of their customers, cutting hair and shaving men with huge, cut-throat razors, some were even cutting corns. Learned men would employ themselves as professional letter-writers, sitting cross-legged, their typewriters before them, drafting letters for the illiterate.

One marvels at the Eastern peoples' ability to crouch down, seemingly for hours, chatting, arguing or just whiling away the time, rather as if they were equipped with rubber haunches.

Dick and I spent much of the first day touring the shipping agencies in an effort to obtain information on boats leaving India for Malaya. There was very little to offer: either they were reluctant at any dealings concerning India, or else they just did not know of anything. Eventually we did discover that there was a boat which sailed monthly from Madras to Penang, though the agent was unable to accept any bookings owing to the present strife with India. At least it gave us some hope.

Much of Karachi's industrial and financial offices are housed in tall, modern buildings, many of which have been abused by the betel chewers. It's nothing to see a man spit and leave a huge blob of red on a new wall or floor. There was little sign of "the devastation by Indian planes"; what we did see was mainly in the dock areas, petrol storage tanks and a few collapsed buildings, though it was difficult to say whether the latter were through bombing, age or lack of maintenance.

Nightlife in Karachi is in the streets, which are full of people, colour and movement. The light dazzles, and neon signs and stalls lit by hurricane lamps provide an array of mystical foods, fruits and coloured alcoholic drinks, carrot juices and sugar cane squashes. The carrots and sugar cane are squeezed through ancient mangle-type presses.

An entertaining evening was spent in the cinema watching the 'blood and thunder' of *The Mercenaries*.

Taking advantage of the fine weather, we booked a minibus from the tourist office to transport us to Paradise Bay on our final day in Karachi. Sandwiches and fruit were packed and water bottles filled. Shortly after dawn the minibus arrived to take us the twenty-mile journey along the desert coast track, which brought us to the beautiful sandy cove of Paradise Bay.

A spotlessly clean and deserted beach. Presumably 80 degrees Fahrenheit is considered too cold for the locals to go swimming. To us it was perfect, well worth the effort in getting up early. A day spent sunbathing, swimming, crab hunting and searching for turtles.

Dorte, true to the sexual freedom of the Scandinavians, reverted to nature in an effort to get an all-over suntan. The remainder of us were not so keen, preferring not to expose our more sensitive parts to the viciousness of the sun. Dick went to the other extreme, though not entirely voluntarily: a hole was dug in which we placed him, leaving only his head exposed. Dorte, tantalisingly leaning over him, in no way helped relieve his discomfort!

A pleasant distraction during the afternoon was the arrival of a camel, whose owner could not resist the opportunity to earn a rupee or two. "You want ride on my camel?" he asked. "You can pay me what you wish." He obviously was banking on a more affluent crowd than us. Apart from the ungainly alighting and arising of the beast, it was an exhilarating experience charging up and down the beach, much better than the tame donkey rides of our childhood days. After returning the camel to its owner, we proceeded to the minibus for the journey back to Karachi, a little sunburnt but nevertheless feeling refreshed after a relaxing day.

Back at the hotel we packed our rucksacks in preparation for our late evening departure for the airport. Much of our winter clothing was given to the hotel manager, assuming that the likelihood of us experiencing cold weather before reaching Australia was slim. Arrangements were made for two taxis to pick us up later in the evening to take us to the airport to await the 0500 departure of our flight to Ceylon. This not only would eliminate the pain of having to get up early, but also saved us a night's hotel bill.

Our final evening in Karachi was spent strolling through the bustling markets and indulging in a sugar cane squash before returning to our hotel to pick up our gear and await the taxis.

We arrived at the airport shortly before 2300, giving us six hours to wait before our departure. Little time was lost in rushing us through the immigration control, but there we came to a grinding halt, being told that we would have to wait until 0400 before being cleared by customs and thus allowed into the comfort of the departure lounge. In the meantime, we would have to wait in the bare, chairless entrance hall, not the most comfortable place to while away a night.

As is common with most people, airports hold a great attraction for me. Different nationalities, creeds and colours, comings and goings, farewells and greetings, an atmosphere of apprehension and excitement. Virgin travellers looking rather pale whilst their more experienced counterparts go through the formalities with a superior arrogance.

Karachi's airport is not busy compared with London's Heathrow, but its steady influx of colourful travellers ensured us of an interesting night. Dick decided that this was an ideal time to try his hand at busking. With him on his banjo, Bo on his mouth organ and the rest of us on our vocals, we soon attracted a crowd of onlookers. Dorte, seizing the opportunity, went round with a hat. Surprisingly enough, she did receive quite a handful of coins of various denominations. It must have been Dorte's feminine charm – it certainly could not have been our talent.

Whether because of the noise we were making, I do not know, but the customs official decided to get us out of the way early. "Do you have any hashish?" asked the official. "Oh yes, our bags are full of it," we replied jokingly. "I do not mind you having a little as long as it's not too much," he said as he chalk-marked our bags and passed us on to the airline section where our tickets were checked, and bags weighed and taken from us. "Please wait in the departure lounge until your flight is announced," said the receptionist.

Shortly before 0500 our flight was announced. "Passengers for flight PK750 to Colombo, Canton and Shanghai, please proceed to the departure gate." Picking up our duty-free cigarettes and spirits, we followed the attractive, sari-clad hostess across the tarmac to the waiting Boeing 707C. The plane was practically empty. Apart from our group of ten there was only a handful of other passengers, mostly Chinese on their way to Canton or Shanghai.

"Would you like a boiled sweet, sir? Please fasten your safety belt and extinguish your cigarette." Slowly the aircraft taxied past the airport buildings until, gradually gaining momentum, it thundered down the runway and was soon up, up and away, leaving the 'Milky Way' lights of Karachi twinkling far below us. With so few passengers aboard we were able to spread out in comparative comfort.

CHAPTER 12

Into Ceylon

Dawn arrived with an unusual swiftness. The cloud cover looked like an Arctic ice field through which the occasional break would provide us with a glimpse of the Indian coastline. Above, the sky was a deep dark blue, harbouring a beautiful sunrise reserved for us privileged few above the clouds. The clouds cleared as we neared Ceylon, giving us a spectacular bird's-eye view of its coastline.

Beautiful lagoons, polka-dotted with 'Dinky Toy' catamarans peacefully fishing in the placid deep blue waters. Palm trees abounded, a luscious green, rimmed with inviting stretches of yellow, sandy beaches. Occasionally a mud or straw hut village would break the green monopoly. Little wonder Marco Polo described Ceylon as "the best island of its size in the world – the jewel of the East".

Gradually we lost height and were soon skimming over the tops of palm trees as we approached Katunayake Airport. The tarmac rushed up to greet us and with a barely perceivable bump we were brought back to earth. Stepping off the plane, the heat hit us like the blast from a furnace causing us to screw our eyes up against the assault of the sun. The air was stiff with heat.

We were unprepared for the reception we received: a full brass band fighting to make themselves heard above the roar of the Boeing's engines wanting to believe that this was especially for us, but I gather that this is a regular performance for visitors arriving at this delightful tropical island.

Our hostess escorted us to the ultramodern airport reception building, handing us over to the waiting officials. Formalities were brief and with the minimum of fuss.

THE ROUTE FROM CEYLON TO BALI

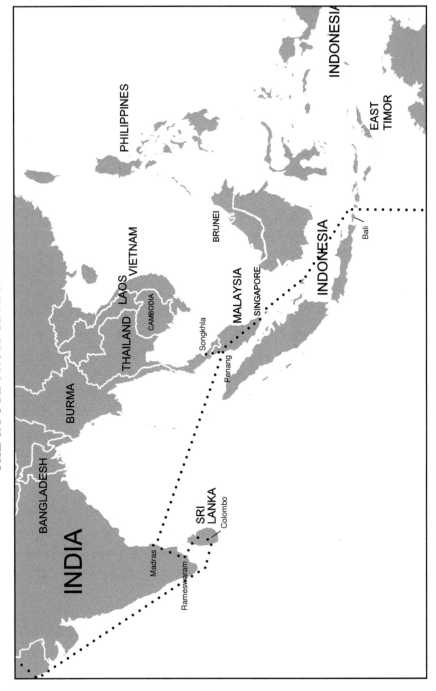

Whilst waiting for our rucksacks to appear on the conveyor belt we were approached by a gentleman offering to arrange accommodation for us in Colombo. With practically no sleep during the night we were not relishing the thought of traipsing through Colombo looking for cheap accommodation, and after all he seemed decent enough, so we took the easy way out and accepted his offer.

Our baggage had arrived and we had had a chance to change our money at the airport bank. Two cars were waiting for us outside. Had our friend been expecting us?

The twenty-mile journey to the island capital, Colombo, took us through many mud and straw hut villages snuggled amongst dense tropical foliage. Occasionally an ox and cart might hinder our progress, but nobody cared. What is time in such beautiful surroundings? A group of pretty girls alongside a stream busily beating their linen against a rock.

With very little warning we found ourselves at the outskirts of Colombo. Our apprehensions as to where we were about to be taken would soon be sated, though our friendly chit-chat with our adversary offered little hint as to our fate.

Our friend guided his ancient Morris car down a narrow lane into what appeared to be a very affluent area. Typically English, almost nostalgic, was the hoarding proclaiming we had just passed the "Redhill Convent School for Girls", a grey Victorian building. The end of the lane led onto a small sports field where boys were enthusiastically kicking a football around, their school satchels substituting for goalposts. The far side of the sports field bordered onto a large lake which glistened in the brilliant midday sun. Little, palm-covered islands dotted the lake whilst small, canoe-like boats ploughed peacefully to and fro.

Stopping the car, our "friend" informed us we had reached our destination. We were outside a pleasant, flat-roofed, two-storey, whitewashed building. A sign told us that this was 'Lake Lodge'.

"Here you are my friends, you like?" It did indeed look very attractive but surely way above our budget. Two smartly dressed Ceylonese came out to greet us. "Welcome, welcome," one said, obviously pleased with the prospect of a good catch.

Inside the small reception lounge we were given cups of tea whilst the usual round of talks and bargaining went on. A satisfactory monetary arrangement was reached: above our normal accommodation allotment, but seemed good value. A few days of real comfort would make a pleasant break. Ron had already decided that he was staying as he reclined in an armchair surveying the luxurious surroundings.

Having decided to stay, we unloaded our gear from the two cars and bade farewell to our 'agent'. Four rooms were allocated to us, each complete with showers, WC and comfortable beds.

This is the life, I thought, as I lazed in a deckchair, supping a beer on the rooftop patio which looked out onto the sports fields and the lake beyond. Beyond the lake, hiding behind the feather duster heads of tall palms, was the hubbub of the city, which seemed so far away from this peaceful corner. An array of colour, tropical plants in abundance, red, blues, yellows and purples embroidered on a lush green cloth. Fan-shaped palms waved in the breeze, looking as if a vain attempt was being made to cool us down.

Advantage was taken of the excellent facilities to do our washing and have a long-overdue shower. An excellent meal was had at a nearby restaurant, far more than we could manage and at a price to suit our pockets.

Tim caused a few turned heads as he walked through the streets in leather boots, shorts and a purple shirt which stood out amongst the more conservative dress of the Ceylonese. Dick's comment was, "I am not with him, I am staying well behind," and from Ron, "You've gotta laugh."

Pleasure indeed it was to snuggle into our well-sprung beds and to be lulled to sleep by a chorus of croaking from the lakeside frogs.

With intentions of visiting Thailand, advantage was taken of the close proximity of the Thai Embassy to obtain visas. If the Consul's secretary was anything to go by then we were in for a very pleasant time in Thailand. "Could you come back this afternoon to collect your passport?" she asked. It would indeed be a pleasure – such beautiful legs!

A red Leyland double-decker bus (ex-London Transport?) conveyed Dick and myself to the city centre, alighting us just outside the railway station where we made enquiries on trains to India.

How friendly the Ceylonese are, and so scrupulously clean. Small children in Persil-white shirts and razor-creased shorts, whilst the women, so feminine and graceful, add the colour with their Neapolitan cottons. Poverty can still be found, though not nearly so widespread as in Pakistan. Here everyone seems oh, so much happier.

Two-thirds of Ceylon's population are Buddhist Sinhalese along with Tamils, mainly in the north, and a few Arabs and Malays.

Whilst walking through Colombo an elderly man attached himself to Dick and myself, offering his services as our personal guide. He was a friendly chap: we did not spurn his attentions but allowed ourselves to be taken on one of his tours.

We shadowed him through a maze of backstreets until coming to a flight of stairs. Beckoning us to follow him, we were led to a small apartment where we were greeted by a friendly smile. "Welcome to my emerald factory."

Once again we found ourselves politely admiring jewellery over numerous cups of tea and listening to all the advantages of purchasing these stones and reselling elsewhere.

Next on our guide's syllabus was a visit to the nearby Hindu Temple. Leaving our shoes at the doorway, we walked through the foyer where we were introduced to the high priest. The priest showed us around the sparsely furnished building where the only extravagance was the thick, red carpet. Occasionally people would wander in to pay their respects. A quick kneel, a few head bangs on the floor (I now see the reason for the thick carpet), a natter, and off they would go. The priest did not try to convert us, but said how pleased he was that people of different faiths were interested enough to pay him a visit, and stressed that this religion was not dissimilar to Christianity. His explanation seemed reasonable enough.

Leaving our ecclesiastical friend to his devotions, we departed from the coolness of the temple, donned our shoes and walked out into the tropical heat. It was time to return to the Thai Embassy to pick up our passports. The memory of those legs spurred us on!

Our guide directed us to the bus stop: we thanked him and offered payment, but he refused. "It was a pleasure, and if you meet me tomorrow I shall show you much more of Colombo." The bus passed close to the docks. Over the tops of large warehouses peeped cranes, a regiment of 'praying mantis' busy feeding Ceylon's vital exports, tea, rubber, coconut and rice to hungry cargo ships.

Whilst Dick and myself had been doing the sights, Tim, Dorte and Bo had been looking for other pastures. They returned with rave reports of an idealistic site with a fishing community a few miles down the coast at Mt. Lavinia. Meanwhile, Bo and Peggy had been making enquiries on shipping our excess gear to Australia.

With the prospect of much footslogging before us, we wanted to rid ourselves of as much gear as possible, leaving only the bare essentials. A tea chest was obtained and soon filled with our unrequired gear, mostly Afghan costs, leathers and other such items that now we were in warmer climes would not be needed.

Tim, Dorte and Bo made an early start the following day to travel down to their utopia on the beach. Dick, Mike and I promised to meet them later that day.

Having packed our bags we spent a pleasant hour chatting, over more cups of tea, with our amiable hosts. Their friendliness could have few rivals. They allowed us to leave the bulk of the gear at the lodge, to be collected on our return in a few days' time.

Dick, Mike and myself left to meet up with Tim, Dorte and Bow whilst Bo, Peggy and Tony would be following later, having dispensed with the tea chest at the docks. Ron opted for the comfort of the lodge until our return.

At a nearby suburban station we caught the train for Mt. Lavinia. The train never left the beach out of its sight on the 30-minute journey. Stepping off the platform we found ourselves on the beach. Now where did Tim say the fisherman's hut was?

Backing onto the station was an affluent monstrosity of a hotel, the start of a tidal wave of tourism? I hoped not. Ignoring this slab of concrete, our eyes feasted on a tropical extravaganza. Deep blue waters teased playfully with golden sands which stretched as far as the eye could see. A dense army of tall coconut palms swayed searchingly in the breeze as if guarding the coastline from uninvited guests. In the bosoms of these palms nestled a handful of small, whitewashed mud and straw houses. "These must be the fisherman's huts that Tim mentioned," said Dick.

We approached the first hut. Two naked children peeped between the legs of an elderly gentleman. "Have you seen three Europeans?" I asked. He did not comprehend, but indicated that we follow him. "You can sleep in here, I shall clean it out for you," he said, pointing at a small stone building whose bare cement floor was covered with chicken manure. "Thank you very much, but first we must find our friends: we shall come back."

Walking along the beach we heard a familiar voice. Nearby was Tim leaning against an upturned boat. "What kept you? Come and meet the gang." Tim led us to a nearby hut. We did not quite reach it before a crowd of people emerged to greet us.

The whole family lived there, from grandfather downwards. I never did manage to find out just how many people lived in that small mud and straw house. I kept seeing a fresh face, mostly small children. Cashion, the father, offered to accommodate Dick, Mike and me: "You can sleep in the small straw hut where we keep our sails." We readily accepted.

"This has been my home all my life," said Cashion. "I am a fisherman, come, see my boat." It was a kind of trimaran, a crude affair but very sturdy. The centre hull was hewn from the trunk of a tree, whilst the two riggers were solid timber runners. Under full sail the boat took on the look of someone doing the splits whilst water-skiing. "You can come out fishing with me in the morning," said Cashion.

The cool sea breeze kept the temperature comfortable. I was in no mood to be energetic. Suffice enough to laze on the beach and have the occasional swim. This is the life. Oh! How easy it is to have an affair with Ceylon. A perfect tropical island. How contented those fishermen seem, their simple way of life, far from the bustling rat race. One wonders who is richer, the millionaires in their concrete jungle or these happy-go-lucky fishermen. Apart from the occupants of the fisherman's hut, the beach was deserted. I was at peace with the world. Cashion brought me back to life.

"Have you been to the zoo?" he asked. "No." "Then I shall take you before it gets dark." The zoo was a twenty-minute bus journey away.

"You are lucky," said Cashion. "We are just in time to see the dancing elephants." It was indeed an impressive exhibition of man's control over beast. A zoo attendant took us inside a cage to see a chimpanzee that smoked cigarettes. "Unfortunately he is not well, we believe he has lung cancer."

Dusk was falling: it was time to leave. Cashion took us to a Chinese restaurant where we gorged ourselves on a bowl of chow mein whilst our host waited outside.

It was dark by the time we reached the fisherman's quarters. During our absence our family had grown. Bo, Peggy and Tony had joined us.

Our hotel at Mount Lavinia,
Ceylon.

Our fisherman and family,
Mount Lavinia, Ceylon.

The Bagoda, Anuradhapura, Ceylon.

The smaller children were bedded down on matting on the floor; they were soon asleep. It was a clear, warm night and we sat outside under the palms. A hurricane lamp lit our way, though the moon would have been sufficient. I listened to the jungle chatterings and the bony rattle of the palms in the sea breeze. It was oh so peaceful. The last of my bottle of duty-free whisky was shared with the grandfather. It was a rare treat for him.

"Would you like some crab soup?" asked Bori, one of Cashion's boys. "First of all we shall have to catch some crabs." Grabbing a stick, Bori led us onto the beach. "Look for holes in the sand, they will be in there." It was like playing hide-and-seek: we would see a crab in the moonlight, chase it across the beach only to see it vanish down a hole, never to be seen again. There must be a knack in it. Bori returned with a bag full of kicking crabs. "I have enough," he said. "It shall take us about an hour to cook them, wait on the beach. I shall bring the soup down to you."

All I needed now to complete this jigsaw would be one of those beautiful Ceylonese girls and a crate of beer. Ah well, one cannot expect everything at once: patience is a virtue. Satisfaction enough to laze at midnight under the bow of Cashion's boat studying the moon and the haze of stars. A shout from the hut: "Your soup is ready!" Bori brought out the steaming cauldron of crab soup. It was delicious.

"It is time to sleep," said Cashion. "Come, I will show you where you can bed down." Dick's, Mike's and my bedroom was a small straw hut on the beach; our bedding was a large sail which covered the sandy floor. We were not alone: three children and an elder also slept there. The gentle lapping of the sea soon soothed me to sleep.

I was woken by the glint of the sun seeping through the roof. Dick, Mike and I were the only occupants. The others had already risen and were busy working on the boats. Water was brought up from the well for us to wash. The coldness of the water soon brought us back to life.

Down on the beach I could see the fishing boats returning after a night's fishing. They had had a good catch and were happy.

There comes a time when all good things must come to an end. Dick was impatient to move on. I, along with Mike, agreed to accompany him. Tim and Tony wanted to stay a little longer at Mt. Lavinia before moving up through India and on to Nepal. Bo and Peggy wanted to see the Taj Mahal at Agra, whilst Dorte and Bow planned to spend a few weeks in Ceylon before touring India and heading back to Denmark. I wanted to spend as little time as possible in India, preferring to spend my time satisfying my curiosity on the legendary beauty of the girls of Thailand. It looked as if this would be the parting of the ways.

The whole family came out to see us off, together with the remnants of our gang: it was quite a formidable crowd. I am not one for farewells, but having travelled so far with Tim it seemed strange saying goodbye on such an isolated spot as this beach in Ceylon. We were now down to three, though we suspected Ron would join us when we returned to Lake Lodge.

A half-mile walk along the beach brought us to the station: a train was waiting to convey us to Colombo.

Back at Lake Lodge we found Ron preparing to leave. A shower and a shave followed by yet more cups of tea with the management, and once again we were back on the road.

Any cooling the shower had done was soon cancelled as we walked through Colombo in the sweltering heat with our heavy rucksacks. We were grateful to a friendly information officer who allowed us to leave our bags in his office at the station.

As we were running short of rupees we went in search of a black market tout. It did not take long to find one and we were soon following him through the backstreets to his 'shop'.

A miniature Wall Street. "What have you got, pounds, dollars or marks?" I had a mixture of dollars and pounds. He calculated, we calculated. Of course his answer did not tally with ours. We arrived at a happy medium: he gained, we gained, all sides happy. "While you are here, how about buying some batiks?" "No." "Hand-carved elephants?" "No." "Wooden masks?" "No thanks, our bags are heavy enough as it is."

Sufficient time was left before the departure of the north-bound train to Anuradhapura for us to snatch a quick curry from an Indian restaurant.

Collecting our bags we rushed into the station, and not too soon, as the train was just about to leave. It was fairly crowded, though not by Pakistani standards. People willingly squeezed up to allow us room to sit. They seemed keen to converse.

Much of the five-hour journey was through fertile, tropical terrain. Occasional dense undergrowth, but on the whole well cultivated. The occasional village slipped peacefully by. In these rural parts of Ceylon the houses are made of wattle and daub and thatched with straw or coconut palm. At Polgahawela there is a branch line that swings eastward to Kandy, a hillside city of legendary beauty, home of many tea plantations and reputedly with a climate not unlike an English summer. We were in two minds whether to give Kandy a visit, but no, we would press on.

"What was that?" I was caught unawares. "Girls bathing in the river, weren't they naked?" "I don't know," said Dick. "The train was going too fast." My hand reached for the communication cord .....!

I had seen very little begging in Ceylon. It is not encouraged. Many times we were told by the Ceylonese not to patronise a beggar. "It would only encourage his laziness," they would say. We could not fail but be sympathetic to one unfortunate who boarded the train. He was entwined around a stout staff, one deformed leg wrapped itself rather like an ivy; he used his staff as one would a pogo stick. Regardless of his liabilities he seemed happy enough as he sang whilst hopping between the seats.

It was almost 1700 by the time we pulled into Anuradhapura, the second and most famous capital of the ancient Sinhalese Kings, and now the administrative capital of the north central province of Ceylon. A city with a population of little over 18,000 and a resort of many Buddhist pilgrims.

"What have we landed ourselves into this time?" said Mike. I, too, was having misgivings: the place seemed practically deserted. Outside the station, the yard was empty apart from a small boy and a bullock and cart. "Is there anywhere we can stay?" we asked the boy. "Hotel? I shall show you." With that, he threw our bags into the cart which looked like a remnant from *Wagon Train*. Dick, Mike and myself clambered on top of the bags. Ron preferred to walk alongside. "You won't get me up on that thing," he said.

The boy walked alongside the bullock, giving the poor, lumbering beast occasional slaps with his stick, necessary to propel the animal along. A cortège of laughing children followed us through the streets of Anuradhapura. People stopped and stared. "Who are these strange white men riding through our city on a bullock cart?"

Passing market stalls and through narrow streets, where mud and straw huts mingled with affluent houses, slowly we wound our way until coming to a sedate-looking hotel. "Sorry, full up, we are expecting the Australian youth cricket team today." "I know another good place," said the boy. Like a light-hearted funeral procession we proceeded through palm-fringed lanes until finally arriving at the Hotel Paramount. "Here you will get a good room."

The hotel staff came on the scene. "Yes, we have rooms for you, you have come at a good time, we are holding a wedding reception." Our room was up to our usual standard and price. "Come downstairs and join us when you are ready," said Rex, the hotel manager. "The bride and groom have invited you."

Downstairs the dining room was packed, with the reception in full swing. We were introduced as "those Englishmen who arrived on a bullock cart". "The girls want you to dance with them," said Rex. It was not quite the sort of dance we were accustomed to, but nevertheless their persuasions had us 'floored'.

How beautiful the Sinhalese girls looked, their delicate shoulders covered by fine, semi-transparent silken blouses. Some wore saris, which added to their somewhat reserved charm, or would one call it shyness?

Dick produced his banjo and offered a few tunes. His excuse that he was tone-deaf satisfied the crowd. There was food in abundance: on orders we tucked in ravenously.

I was hoping it was the custom that all guests kissed the bride. Unfortunately, this was not so and we had to be content with a handshake as we bade the couple farewell. The guests faded away, leaving us with Rex and his two comical aides, Bill and Ben.

The following day we were up early, allowing maximum time for seeing the sights of this fascinating city. A city that was established as long ago as the 5th century BC. How far we walked that day I do not know, I think it must have been over ten miles. Ron did not stay the course, returning to the hotel.

The city is completely surrounded by jungle. It had been abandoned to nature until rediscovered and opened by the British in the mid-19th century.

Walking through Anuradhapura one never gets the impression of ever having left the jungle. Thick foliage and dense tropical undergrowth flourish. It was hard to imagine that we were actually walking through a small city. On the outskirts there is a huge reservoir, Tissa Wewa (there is also another nearby, Nuwara Wewa). It was here that I got caught in one of those sudden tropical storms that seem to switch themselves on at the most inconvenient times.

Whilst sheltering inside a large, hollow tree alongside the reservoir, I heard a shout coming from a nearby pump house. "Come over here!" a man yelled, and I did. "Shelter here in the pump house," he said. "Never shelter inside those trees, they house deadly spiders!" The rain switched itself off and the sun came out as if nothing had happened apart from the steam that it was sucking out of the ground.

Encircling the city we arrived at the cause of Anuradhapura's claim to fame, its archaeological remains, the most remarkable being the huge pyramidal 'dagobas', constructed of small, sun-dried bricks, many of which are hidden beneath foliage. There are also many foundations of monastic buildings, palaces and 'pokunas' (bathing pools).

This was hallowed ground we were treading on, Anuradhapura being one of the main centres of Buddhism. It was here that the Buddhists built monasteries (viharas) and erected high stupas (dagobas) which commemorate the founder's attainment of nirvana or enlightenment. His followers are dedicated, saffron-robed Buddhist monks with hair shaved off, wandered slowly along, their serious gaze fixed five or six steps ahead.

The centre of attraction for the multitude of pilgrims to Anuradhapura is the famous Bo Tree, believed to be originally a branch of the very tree under which Gautama attained Buddhahood. It was reputed to have been transported from India in 245 BC and is the oldest tree in existence, of which there is no historical record. To a non-believer its attraction leaves much to be desired. Its fresh leaves bely its age, though its gnarled trunk hints at having seen better days. More attractive is the colourful shrine at its base, where a constant stream of people come to scatter flower-petal offerings (conveniently on sale at the entrance) before a pint-size Buddha and flickering candles.

Dominating the ancient capital is the enormous 'Gold Dust' stupa, a dome-shaped shrine. This immense hemispherical structure is sustained by a huge square which is supported by 500 elephants modelled in brick and placed less than two feet apart. Crowning the dome is a square block of masonry topped by a conical spire. Inside these stupas are richly gilded chambers in which relics are enshrined.

Anuradhapura has many other links with the past. There is the Lohapasada, or Brazen Palace, a vast monastery nine storeys high, built about 150 BC. The whole outer façade was covered with copper plates, whilst the interior consisted of 1,000 chambers richly ornamented with gold and silver. Unfortunately all that remains of this marvellous edifice is its foundations of 1,600 stone monoliths arranged in 40 parallel lines with 40 columns each.

Adding to this lost city in the jungle atmosphere is the abundance of wildlife. Monkeys swing through trees teasing groups of long-haired goats. Timid deer scampered before a bullock, or was it a wild buffalo?

The hot sun sapped our strength: we were relieved to come across a vendor selling king coconuts. A swift incision from his parang produced a diamond-shaped hole from which we quenched our thirst from the rich, milky liquid.

Our archaeological appetites sated plus fatigue returned us to our hotel. A cool drink and a wash soon had us revived. Ron amused the hotel staff by walking around in his suit. "This has not been seen here since the British left," laughed Rex.

A congenial evening was spent with the hotel staff. Rex reminisced on his wartime experiences and stories of Ceylon. Bill and Ben were more light-hearted, being practical jokers and comics. "You must join us for supper," said Rex. We did and enjoyed an excellent Ceylonese meal.

Our train was due to leave at midnight. Rex offered to drive us to the station. Along with Bill and Ben we piled into Rex's car and trundled off to the station to await the train north to Talaimannar where we would catch the boat to India.

Any hopes of getting any sleep on the train were soon shattered by the invasion of young students returning to college. Along with Dick's banjo and bongo drums from the students, most of the night was passed in an uproar, intercepted only with occasional visits to the bar.

During the journey an elderly man, fascinated by Dick's banjo, offered to buy it. "My son would like that," he said. "For 100 rupees, it's yours," replied Dick. "I have no idea of its worth but I shall buy it." He did, much to the delight of Dick who had been trying to rid himself of the cumbersome item.

The students left the train at Mannar, leaving us in comparative peace for the final twenty miles along the narrow peninsula to Talaimannar.

Tiredness overcame us and we dozed off. Our sleep was interrupted the sound of the guard. "Wake up, you have arrived at your destination, this is Talaimannar, the train has been here for over an hour." Luckily it was the end of the line. "Where do we catch the ferry?" we enquired. "The pier is about four miles further on, you will have to catch a bus."

It was 7 am already. The sun was up to its tricks as we sweated with our heavy rucksacks to the bus stop. A bus arrived within an hour and took us through sparsely populated countryside to Talaimannar pier. Apart from a few shacks about 200 yards from the pier and the odd house or two, nature held the upper hand.

The ferry to India was not due to leave for another 24 hours. Ron and Dick went in search of somewhere to spend the day, whilst Mike and I went along the beach in search of a quiet corner to spend the day in oblivion. I found my peace underneath a tall palm tree which at least offered some shade, though I had to consistently shift my berth to keep one step ahead of the sun.

It was midday by the time I awoke; there was no one in sight. I returned to the pier in the hope of seeing a familiar face. There was no one. Not having eaten since the previous day, I felt hungry. The nearby shacks looked promising. I went over. For a couple of rupees, I was able to procure a plate of rice and some meat.

The familiar voice of Dick came as some relief. "There is a rest house about a mile down the road, Ron is staying there." I went with Dick to the rest house where we found a handful of Europeans also on their way to India.

Mike had not been sighted since early morning. Dick and I returned to the beach to look for him. After a fruitless search, we finally found him on the pier. He had been sleeping on the beach when he was woken by a customs officer who invited him back to his office-cum-house near the pier. "He has offered to put us up for the night," said Mike. We returned to the rest house to pick up our rucksacks. Ron said he would spend the night there.

The customs officer made us welcome. A bottle of coconut wine worked wonders with any language barrier and we were soon conversing amiably in Ceylon English. Mattresses were provided for us to sleep on and it was not long before the snores took over from the jungle sounds.

I was about to have my way with a beautiful Ceylonese girl when a voice woke me. "You have an hour before the boat is due, here is a cup of tea." It was the customs officer: how I could have cursed him, he could have left me for a further five minutes!

Water was provided from an ancient storage tank for us to wash. "I must leave you now," said the customs officer. "I have to get ready for the boat's arrival, see you on the pier."

Barely had he left when a small boy brought in a tray of food. "This is for you from the customs man: it is your breakfast." There was a bunch of bananas, a pile of chapattis and bowls of 'All-Bran'-looking cereal plus more cups of tea. It was more than we could manage and typical of the friendliness we had received whilst in Ceylon.

Having had our fill, we made our way to the pier, where already crowds of people, mostly Tamils, were queueing. The boat was in and there was much activity, loading and unloading. Ron arrived and we settled down on a bench for what looked likely to be a long wait.

Our customs officer friend caught our eye, he beckoned us to the front of the queue, stamped our passports, shook hands and directed us to the boat, much to the annoyance of the impatient Indians.

We boarded the 'Irwin' and claimed our patch on the upper deck. It was midday by the time the 'Irwin' finally cast off from the jetty.

It was amusing to watch the emotional actions of the parting relatives and friends. There was much weeping, wailing and gnashing of teeth, both on the jetty and on-board. Hair-pulling and clothes-rending were not excluded. As actors, they all deserved Oscars. No sooner were the nearest and dearest out of sight than the weeping stopped and the participants returned to their normal selves.

The boat was crowded: there was barely an unclaimed patch. Families of Indians huddled with their bundles of wealth in corners forming their own miniature ghettoes. Most looked poor and were perhaps the result of a purge to Ceylonese Ceylon, and had only the prospect of a gloomy future in their homeland ahead of them.

A slight swell caused many to rush to the ship's side to vomit: most did not make it or did not even bother to make it. Perhaps they preferred not to waste their precious rice.

The 'Irwin' followed closely to the course of Adam's Bridge – a string of coral reefs and sandy islets which stretch from Ceylon to India. In little under four hours the flat shorelines of Southern India came into view.

CHAPTER 13

Into India

The staccato rumblings of the anchor chain racing through the hosepipe announced our arrival in India. A fleet of barges came out from Rameswaram to meet the 'Irwin'. There was a scramble as people jostled to disembark. Tempers were frayed, it was a question of the fittest off first. Fortunately we managed to get on one of the initial barges and were soon being towed ashore. The tug released the barge, allowing it to drift into the jetty.

Any hopes we had of a swift exodus from Rameswaram were soon jettisoned as we were herded by officials into a large, barn-like reception centre.

Officialdom at its bureaucratic worst. Numerous officials, puffed with importance, stood behind a haphazard array of desks. Forms and yet more forms. "How much money have you?" (We always claimed to have less than we actually had to allow us some for changing on the black market.) And so it went on. I was waiting to be asked what colour underpants I had on, but they did not.

"You must have an injection." What it was for I do not know, probably malnutrition. I reluctantly allowed a rusty-looking needle to be thrust in me, in exchange for which I received a stamp on one of my many forms.

Two hours had elapsed since arriving at Rameswaram: we were impatient to leave as the last train to Madras that day would shortly be leaving.

Eventually the formalities were over and we were allowed to proceed. There was no time to lose. We ran to the nearby station in time to see the Madras train, hauled by a vintage steam engine, about to depart.

Disregarding shouts from the ticket collector, we ran onto the platform and jumped onto the moving train. The guard issued us with tickets and allocated us wooden bunks for the 22-hour train journey.

Rameswaram is practically an island. To get to the mainland we had to cross the Pamban Channel. Here the single track ran almost three miles on stilts, barely feet above the water.

Darkness approached, removing our ocular privileges, and we jolted off through the sticky night, stopping at one crowded halt after another.

To compensate for our hard beds, we inflated our lilos and resigned ourselves to an intermittent night's slumber. I was woken by the bedlam that accompanies a large station: we were at Tiruchirappalli. The sun was stretching itself like a half-submerged bloody octopus over the horizon.

Shortly after leaving Tiruchirappalli we crossed the Cauvery River, introducing us to a landscape of rice fields. Although it was only 7 am already the fields were alive with workers. Near-naked men with little more than a handkerchief to cover themselves whilst others, naked to the waist, rolled their dhotis up to their knees. Quite contentedly they were going about their daily tasks, working up the mud with a wooden plough drawn by big, groaning water buffalo. Machinery was primitive, human treadmills a common sight, poverty abounded.

As we pulled into stations, tiny, ragged children would scramble up at the window from the track, begging. They would squeeze between two trains and even climb underneath the carriage. They were everywhere. Sometimes a turbaned porter might drive them away, but they would return as soon as his back was turned. Dick gave one small boy some laxative tablets which were promptly scoffed. Luckily the train did not stay long: the results we could only imagine. On the platforms, men pushed little carts piled high with uninviting spicy Indian foods, nuts and fruits; others carried brass water bottles and tea urns, walking along filling cups which were being held out from the windows. On arrival at these stations there was always a manic rush to obtain food. We kept our platform purchases to a minimum. Even our cast-iron stomachs would turn a little rusty in overindulgence of these dubious railway offerings. However, we kept ourselves alive on peanuts and the odd cake or two.

The journey passed pleasantly enough: the ever-changing landscape of rice fields, palm groves and primitive villages ensured our interest, though the hard, wooden bunk seats were not conducive to comfort.

The simple life of the railside villages with their makeshift shacks and where women walk about with pots and tins on their heads. Water buffaloes appeared to be the workhorses, always seemingly shackled onto something, a wooden plough, water cart or a cartload of people. Always a small boy would run alongside the beast, urging it forward with constant lashes from a stick. Pigs roamed wild, fossicking for edibles, including human excreta. Perhaps the latter was nature's way of counteracting the lack of sanitation in much of India. Cows ambled along showing their ribs. A dog yawned and collapsed in a heap.

Having journeyed well inland, we were now once again nearing the coast as we pulled into Villupuram, the junction for the former French territory of Pondicherry.

It was late afternoon by the time we arrived at the southern terminus and headquarters of the Indian railway – Madras. Outside the station we bartered with taxi and trishaw drivers. On recommendation, we had decided to stay at the YMCA. Ron could never get accustomed to bartering and was always averse to doing so. He hailed a taxi and sped off, leaving Dick, Mike and myself to argue it out with the remaining drivers. A price was agreed upon and we moved off, Dick and Mike in one trishaw and me in another. With sinews straining, our drivers stood on their pedals gathering speed as we raced through the streets skilfully dodging the traffic with hair-raising closeness.

Whilst booking in at the YMCA we had a phone call. It was from Ron. He had been taken to the YWCA and was about to get another taxi to the YMCA. Such was the price of his impatience.

Madras does not 'die' at night, though many of its residents look as if they would not see another day. Walking through the streets in the early hours, one gets the impression that there are more people out than in. The pavements are full of bodies prostrated on rags and old newspapers. These are the homeless millions, forming their family ghettoes, so dense at times that you are forced to leave the pavements and walk in the road. Some have barely the strength or will to move their legs, and are quite content to let their offspring do the begging. Ragged children come running, patting their bellies with one hand whilst holding out the other for a rupee or two. Some of them look lovely in a cute sort of way, and all look hungry.

The priority during our stay in Madras was to find the cheapest way out of India. A tour of the shipping and travel agencies left us with two options. Either by flying from Calcutta to Bangkok, or by ship from Madras to Penang. Pricewise there was not a lot of difference, though the thought of the long haul up to Calcutta swung the vote in the latter's favour.

A steamship, the SS *Rajula*, was leaving Madras in five days' time for Penang. Our request to travel as deck-class passengers was refused, the company having recently stopped Europeans travelling in this way (for reasons we were to discover later). In lieu we were offered accommodation in an 8-berth cabin. This we accepted and promptly handed over the £52 fare in return for the passage tickets.

With four days remaining in Madras we had ample time to see the sights. Madras is India's fourth city, created by the East India Company as a trading post. The city is cut into two almost equal parts by the Cooum River, and is graced by many fine trees, gardens and parks, though poverty amongst its predominately Hindu population is forever prevalent. Madras's large, artificial harbour is the export hub of hides and skins as well as tobacco and raw cotton. Tanning, leather and cotton are its premier industries.

Along the seafront, running for more than two miles, from San Thome to Fort St. George is the broad marina, which must be one of the most beautiful promenades in the world, a promenade of palm trees and golden sands. Opposite the marina are most of the government offices and college buildings. Here, too, is Madras's well-publicised aquarium, interesting though not impressive, worth a visit if one has time on one's hands.

One evening we were fortunate enough to see a colourful wedding reception. In a way, not unlike a West Country carnival procession with floats, fancy dress and much gaiety, though the din was overpowering, rather like the sounds of two cats fighting on a piano keyboard. Pedestrians dashed to and fro across the road as if tired of life.

During one of our evening excursions we discovered an excellent restaurant where for 2.5 rupees (10p) you could eat as much as you liked. Waiters hovered, ready to fill an empty plate with a variety of strange foods, most of which were of a garlic or curry flavour.

We had little difficulty in changing our money on the black market. Small boys would approach us: "Sir, would you like to change your dollars or pounds on the black market? You get twice the normal price." Incentive indeed. We were led through backstreet stalls where the unofficial banks had their offices. Maybe we did not get twice the normal price, but it was well above the normal bank rate.

The day for our departure from Madras arrived and we could now look forward to seven days of relaxation on the boat to Penang. In the hot midday sun, we trudged the mile or so to the docks where we had little difficulty in seeking out the *Rajula*, standing surprisingly white and virginal between the rusty bulks of large tankers. A human, ant-like army of workers fussed around the ship, busy with last-minute preparations.

In the large quayside hangar, we fought our way through a battleground of immigration and custom officials who gamely battled with the impatient hordes of intending passengers. At last, after queueing for an hour, I had reached the elusive table, "Sorry, Sahib, you should be in the other queue." That is all I needed (for obvious reasons a few words have been omitted here!). I turned to the other queue: it seemed to be endless. Pushing in front of some inoffensive-looking Indian, I was able to get my credentials cleared fairly quickly and was at last allowed to proceed aboard.

A steward directed us to our 8-berth cabin which we were to share with four other Europeans. Showing little sign of its fifty years at sea, the *Rajula* was surprisingly clean. Owned by the British India Steam Navigation Company, it had been used as a hospital ship during the war and has since spent most of its life in the Far East waters, being now one of the few steamships still operating.

It was late afternoon before all the passengers were aboard. The gangways were lifted and the spring-head and stern ropes released their grip on the bollards, leaving the ship to slowly drift away from the quay. On the starboard side tiny tugs busied themselves as they hauled 8,000 tons of steel away from the quayside. A couple of blasts from the *Rajula* and the tugs relaxed their hold. The ship stirred into life as deep rumblings from its bowels and frantic threshing astern suggested that at last the *Rajula* was on her own – though as if having little faith in the old lady, the tugs still fussed around, offering a nudge here and there. Once clear of the harbour entrance the tugs about-turned and with little toots scurried back to their berths.

It had been exactly three months ago that we had our last sea journey, the beginning of our trip, from Southampton to Le Havre.

Madras slowly drifted astern, we set about the task of acquainting ourselves with the ship. Apart from a few Malays, the majority of the cabin-class passengers were Europeans. Completely segregated from the cabin-class passengers were the deck-class passengers, mostly

Indians who were packed into the holds and lower decks. Very rarely would they budge from their chosen spot, no doubt frightened of it being claimed by someone in a less comfortable position. Their meals were brought in a communal bowl and were quickly devoured. I began to appreciate the wisdom of refusing to allow us to travel as deck-class passengers. The extra cost was well worth a comfortable bunk and excellent food. Three meals a day were served by friendly Malay waiters in the clean and comfortable dining room: as much as we could eat and more if we wanted. Tea would be brought to us in the mornings, but this was a luxury we soon did without: 7 o'clock was just too early to be woken up.

Most of the ship's officers were British, ably supported by a predominantly Malay crew. A small bar supplied our liquid requirements with the majority of entertainment being courtesy of the passengers, all of whom appeared to be in the 20-30 age group. Amongst this happy band of travellers were guitarists and pianists, backed by a very willing band of vocalists who performed most nights at the bar. Apart from home-grown entertainment we had evening film shows and horse racing, plus the usual shipboard games of deck quoits etc.

We had not seen the last of India. During the night the ship had been steaming southwards and by early morning had anchored off Nagapattinam, where a cargo of onions and yet more deck passengers would be embarked.

Large, cumbersome barges, propelled by a combination of oars and sails, plied to and fro all day, bringing out their cargo of humans and onions. The onions seemed to be handled with more respect than the humans. Whilst the onions were gently lowered into the holds, the insurgent masses of deck passengers were roughly pushed through a small hatchway in the ship's side. I could imagine the chaos there would be if the sea was anything but calm. Men literally walked over old women in the mad rush to board the *Rajula*. Tempers flared and twice I saw an uppercut send someone swimming. At least it provided us with a good day's entertainment! Most of the new arrivals were in rags, their worldly possessions but a small bundle of cloth. Hoping to find a better life in Malaya?

The newcomers filled up the vacant spaces in the holds and lower decks whilst the barges returned to Nagapattinam. By late-afternoon the *Rajula* had weighted anchor, nosing her way to the east and out to sea.

Five days of relaxation ensured, a good opportunity to catch up on belated letters, washing, and revelling in the luxury of a real bath, our first for three months. Conducted tours of the ship were provided by the officers.

Although archaic, the *Rajula* held an impressive record of service which was a source of pride amongst the crew, all of whom seemed very attached to the old lady.

The days passed lazily enough. Sunbathing sessions were disturbed only by the call for meals or the opening of the bar. On the fourth day out we had our first sight of land as we passed close to the low-lying, palm-fringed Nicobar Islands.

Many of the Europeans on-board were on a similar 'shoestring' budget as ourselves, and having travelled along diverse routes there were many interesting items of news to be exchanged. Steve, a Londoner who had started out on an organised overland tour which he had abandoned because of frequent breakdowns of the bus, asked if he might join up with Dick, Mike and myself. We readily agreed, especially as Ron had decided to travel post-haste to Singapore as soon as the *Rajula* arrived at Penang.

Early on February 11th the *Rajula* anchored off Penang where we were besieged by a multitude of customs and immigration officials.

Formalities were brief, but until the multitude of deck passengers, most of whom were immigrants, had been cleared, the ship could not berth alongside.

By midday the officials had departed, leaving the *Rajula* to slowly steam to her berth in Penang's main town, George Town, an entrepôt for the northern coastal plain and the Kinta Valley. It is also a free port. Dodging junks and sampans, the *Rajula* handed herself over to the fussy tugs who nudged her to her berth.

CHAPTER 14

Into Penang

Ron wasted little time in getting ashore once the ship had tied up. He intended leaving for Singapore as soon as possible. Farewells were brief, with a "See you in Australia", and he was gone. Dick, Mike, Steve and myself were in no hurry and stayed on-board for a final slap-up meal. When the disembarkation chaos had subsided, we proceeded ashore.

There was little need for us to concern ourselves as to where we could find somewhere to stay. No sooner had we stepped through the dock gates when we were besieged by hordes of trishaw drivers with their three-wheeled sidecar cycles. Those small jackals had been lying in wait like tigers, offering us everything and anything from money changing, nice girl or cheap hotel. For the time being we settled for the latter. "$3 to take you to a very good cheap hotel," said one boy. "Too much, we have already had an offer at only $1," we lied. "Okay, okay, get in," he submitted with a broad grin. There were no hard feelings.

The boy stood on the pedals with his bare feet, the sinews of his thin legs quivered and the veins stood out. Slowly the vehicle gathered momentum and we were soon in the thick of the suicidal Oriental traffic. This mode of transport is an ideal way to get acclimatised to the slow tempo and the tortuous business methods of the Orient.

Through the confusion of Penang's Chinatown we trundled until coming to rest at a shabby building. A facia blotched with flaking paint. Above the door a sign proclaimed that here stood the Hotel Paradise.

There was little ceremony on our being handed over to the Chinese manager. $2 (28p) for a room, take it or leave it: we took it. Not of the highest standards, but you get what you pay for. The small room's solitary furniture was two beds. I was quite content to sleep on the floor until I saw a rat scuttle across it. As long as he does not try and get in my sleeping bag with me, I will put up with the furry rodent.

During the night, Mike's rucksack had been raided in the rat's successful attempt to get at an apple. Dick in his naivety wondered why there were a lot of young Chinese ladies with towels wrapped around them queueing up to go in the shower. I had to enlighten him that I thought we were staying at a brothel. Comings and goings of the ground-floor bar girls during the night confirmed our suspicions that we had landed at a house of ill repute.

I had previously visited Penang about four years ago: it had changed. The ugly scars of tourism were beginning to show. Gone was the feeling of being one of the fortunate few to have visited this tropical paradise; instead I felt as if being caught in a tidal wave of package tours and instant holidays. Personally I still regard Penang as one of the most pleasant islands in this tropical region of Southeast Asia. Along its sixty miles or so of coastline, hotels are mushrooming, although it still has a long way to go before catching up with the stereotyped tourist resorts of the continent.

Penang, its 110 square miles shaped like a skin rug, was founded in 1786, the area having been ceded to the East India Company by the Malay Sultan of Kedah by an agreement with Captain Francis Light. Now part of the Federation of Malaysia, it contributes handsomely with its exports of rubber, tin, coconut oil, copra, betel nuts, spices and reptile skins. Rice is also cultivated. The island's centre provides a picture of mountain and dense jungle, whilst coconut and rubber plantations supply the frame. Its population is predominantly Chinese and Tamil, though Malays are well represented. The climate, although hot and humid, is not unpleasant, with natural air conditioning from the sea breezes, and various little else apart from the seasonal allocation of rain.

We allowed ourselves four days in which to see Penang. A visit to the tourist office where the attractive Malay receptionist, slim and small-waisted, spoke to us on the beauty of her island, what to see and how to get there. In her Malay blouse and tight sarong, she was, to my mind, Penang. Armed with maps and literature, by courtesy of 'Penang', we set out to tour the island.

Ridding ourselves of the bustle of George Town, with its distinguished public buildings, tree-lined streets and pulsating life of its Chinatown, a bus took us to Ayer Itam, where the Buddhist temple of supreme bliss, Kek Lok Si, stands guard over the makeshift shanty homes of the villagers. Reminiscing, it was here four years ago that a car I had hired had broken down right in the middle of a Chinese wedding procession. To reach the temple we had to negotiate nearly a quarter of a mile of steps which carried us through a covered cascade of souvenirs, candles, joss sticks and other Oriental knick-knacks, and a gauntlet of gibbering salesmen. Fortunately we did not look the part of the affluent tourist whom they relied upon to fill their bellies, so we were allowed to pass practically unmolested. Short of breath and our clothes clinging in the morning heat, we reached the temple: it seemed like the end of a pilgrimage, surely enough to discourage all but the most devout followers to regular attendance. The long climb proved well worth the effort. The huge, tiered temple is the ultimate in Oriental fantasy, beautifully decorated both inside and out. It was rich in figurines, rotund Buddhas and mystical symbols. Incense burns with gay abandon, joss sticks abounded; the smell is sweet but not unpleasant, almost sleepy. Collection boxes appealed to visitors in five languages, contribution towards the purchase of yet another Buddha statue. Colours were rich and lavish, and red was dominant. Under the shadow of the temple was a turtle pool, where a mobile mass of shell held the young ones' interest, whilst their elders concentrated on the temple.

Nearby is Penang Hill from the base of which a funicular railway will haul you to the summit, which at 2,428 feet offers a commanding view of Penang. Nestling at its feet is George Town, a grey splurge three sides of which are surrounded by rich, green jungle. Closing the gap were the deep blue waters where large tankers and cargo vessels rested like stepping stones to the Malaysian mainland. Behind us the jungle-clad hills rolled gently along Penang's backbone, sloping gradually to the distant waters of the Malacca Straits. There is a restaurant at the summit, though the prices are as steep as the hill. I settled for a glass of water. It was not begrudged. An alternative to the railway is a road which winds its way down from the summit. The abundance of tropical flora and breathtaking views ensure a pleasant if not tiring walk.

Enough sightseeing for one day: we returned to our hotel for a clean-up, a term to be used loosely. A clean-up consisted of splashing oneself with stagnant water from a filthy ceramic sink. The toilets were raised platforms with a convenient hole; underneath was a dustbin which was emptied daily.

Meals were no problem. In George Town there is an excellent open-air community eating centre. A circle of stalls serve a host of tasty Chinese, Indian and Malayan foods. Each stall had its own speciality; we would circulate from stall to stall in an effort to vary our diet. For 80 cents (12p) you could be well sated. A couple of meatballs here, some beanshoots there, prawns, mee, or whatever unknown delight took our fancy. We endeavoured to have something different each night. Sometimes we were greedy and had breakfast which usually consisted of a bowl of beanshoots, which at 20 cents was not really extravagant.

Most of the shops in George Town remain open until late in the evening and the streets are crowded until the early hours. The main streets with their modern shops and bright lights hide the poverty and squalor of Chinatown to the casual visitor. When business is over for the night the trishaw drivers curl up in their vehicles, pull a canvas, newspaper or sacking over their heads, and go to sleep, though still alert for custom.

For $2 (30p) we were able to travel by bus the complete circuit of the island, breaking the journey at places of interest. The road around the island is 46 miles long and passes many inlets and beautiful sandy beaches. Also rubber plantations where you can watch rubber tappers at work, and deep valleys where cloves and nutmegs grow. Occasionally a village or kampong of thatched wooden houses would cower for protection beneath tall palms.

The recently opened aquarium is worthy of a visit, harbouring nigh on every form of tropical fish in large, clean tanks. Sharks, piranhas, angelfish, sea horses – just to mention a few, plus a multitude of other aquanauts.

We boarded another bus for the next leg of our journey, requesting the Chinese driver to drop us off at the botanical gardens. Doubting whether he had understood us, we rose when he indicated that we had arrived at our stop, which seemingly was in the middle of nowhere. An old man carrying food in two cane baskets hanging from a long pole supported across the shoulders, staggered towards us. He stared at us. Dick pointed to a picture of a waterfall on our map. He grunted and pointed ahead. Following his direction, we could hear the sound of rushing water. The road turned sharply over a bridge revealing a waterfall cascading from, according to our map, 1200 feet and completely surrounded by evergreen, jungle-clad hills. Our efforts to climb to the freshwater pool at the top met with little success. Thick undergrowth barred our way and the steep climb in the hot afternoon sun drained our resources and soon discouraged our enthusiasm to reach the summit. "I am sure there must be an easier route," said Mike. We found none, so retreated to the road. Some consolation for our efforts could be had in the unusual wealth of flora, shrubs and trees.

Over an hour passed before a bus arrived. On the outskirts of George Town we stopped at the Thai Buddhist temple. A remarkable building. Colourful concrete dragons and resplendent Thai symbolic figures try to convince those who pass that they are guarding the temple. Dominating the interior is a huge, reclining Buddha sprawled practically the length of the building. His right arm supports his head which contained... was it a malicious smile? No, I do not think so, but more, shall we say, gentle with perhaps a hint of fatherly amusement in the corners of his eyes. He may well smile, for he is reputably the third-largest reclining Buddha in the world. Keeping him company are a multitude of smaller Buddhas standing out against a background of red or blue. Behind the reclining Buddha are thousands of small lockers where devotees preserve ashes of their departed relatives. A photograph informs one who is inside. In front of the Buddha, in the glow of dozens of red candles, was a rotund priest sitting cross-legged, receiving and administering to his devotees. He looked not unlike a Buddha himself.

There certainly seem to be enough temples in Penang to satisfy anyone's lust for the arts. By the time we left the island we were punch-drunk with temples.

Whilst the weather was in our favour, our final day in Penang was spent on one of the island's many splendid beaches. Any hopes of cooling off were extinguished by the centrally heated waters. Suffice to relax beneath palms and watch sampans and junks glide leisurely past.

We departed from our hotel in the early evening, depositing our rucksacks at a police station near the ferry terminal, thus relieving us of a burden for the few hours prior to the early morning ferry to the mainland.

Whilst Dick, Mike and Steve went to the cinema, I spent the evening wandering around George Town.

It was the start of the Chinese New Year. The streets and shops were gaily decorated with liberal splashings of red and gold. Red candles flickered on red and gold holders painted with Chinese characters, and attached to doors and walls. Broad, red banners with gold lettering wished everyone a "Kong Hee Fat Choy" (Happy New Year). Chinese firecrackers exploded almost continuously. Festivities with noisy parades and lion dances to celebrate the birth of the year of the rat would continue for fifteen days.

It had started to rain by the time I met Dick, Mike and Steve from the cinema. A nearby bar offered us shelter where we spent the rest of the evening with the more than friendly barmaids.

After collecting our bags from the police station, we made our way to the ferry port to await the 1300 departure.

CHAPTER 15

Into Malaya and Thailand

It was still raining by the time we reached Butterworth, the Malayan mainland terminus. Fortunately there is no need to leave the covered way to reach the railway station where we would have six hours to wait before the 0700 train north to Thailand.

The station was locked, necessitating a scaling of a six-foot-high fence to let ourselves in. Except for a solitary policeman who, apart from affording us a cursory once-over, ignored us, the station was deserted.

Tiredness gave the benches the look of a 'four-poster' bed with a Dunlopillo mattress. We staked our claim and awaited the dawn. Sleep did not come easily. Much of the night was spent shadow-boxing in the dark trying to catch mosquitoes and slapping oneself in an attempt to squash those humming near one's ears. No alarm was needed: the day starts early in these parts. It was not yet 0600, and already the station was coming alive.

The smell of cooking and increasing activity stirred me into life. Feeling rather wretched, I staggered from the bench. Dick, Mike and Steve were already awake. Rumbling stomachs led us to the station restaurant. An Indian was busy 'flapping' chapattis, and a cup of tea did little to settle the difference with my rumbling belly. However, a swill in the station wash house did help revive us in time to hear the tannoy announce the imminent departure of our train to Thailand.

A sleek, silver railcar was revving up: we boarded, relieved to see there was ample room to stretch out. An aggressive blast from the engine's horn hinted at its impatience to leave. Permission was given. Shuddering itself, it slowly purred its way southwards to the old ferry terminal for Prai before swinging round to the desired direction, north.

The train clattered through an almost endless tunnel of jungle. Four-fifths of Malaya is under jungle, including its central mountain backbone which rises to 7,000 feet. Industry is gradually gnawing into the undergrowth and transforming the semi-feudalistic existence of many Malays.

Occasionally we would halt at a little station. They seemed almost suburban – neat, gay with flowers and potted plants and neatly trimmed hibiscus hedges. Alor Setar, capital of Kedah state, was the first station of any size, but the train seemed reluctant to stay for long, perhaps embarrassed at being caught out in the open and only too glad to be back in the thick of the jungle where kampongs peep shyly from behind tall palms which shake their heads as if we should not be there. Monkeys swing through the trees, chattering excitedly, annoyed at this disturbance from the silver monster. Oversized butterflies, dressed for the occasion, flit through the windows intent on having a flirt with some of the passengers.

With so many attractions the journey passed quickly and we were surprised to find that it had taken four hours to reach Padang Besar on the Thailand border. Here we alighted from the train to participate in the ritual custom of the immigration formalities.

The border town of Padang Besar is a rather remote outpost, surrounded by jungle and in an area of smouldering political activities, a playground for guerrillas and insurgents.

Formalities were reasonably brief and within an hour we were again on our way. The train slipped its way into the oldest independent nation of Southeast Asia, formerly Siam, now Thailand or Muang Thai, 'Land of the Free'.

Southern Thailand lies in the long, slender neck of the Malay Peninsula. A beautiful region of palm-lined beaches, offshore islands, verdant mountains and tropical jungle. Stations were few and as we travelled north the jungle eased, giving way to evergreen forests which thickly clothe the hills. Rubber trees were plentiful: these, along with tin and rice, represent Thailand's lifeblood.

A guard came round and collected all foreigners' passports. "Just for checking," he said. "They will be returned to you at Hat Yai." Reluctant as we were to hand over our passports, we had little choice. The train arrived at Hat Yai, the end of the line for the Malayan railcar. On the platform a crowd had gathered around the Thai official who was distributing the recently collected passports. We joined the melee to await the call of our names.

"Where do we go from here?" asked Steve. I shrugged my shoulders. "Let's look at the timetable and find out where we can go." It was of no help, it was written in Thai, a writing of scribbles like Pitman shorthand. A notice in English informed us of the presence of an information office. Here we acquired a railway timetable in English. It contained many magical-sounding names, and one especially attracted us: Songkhla. Our map informed us that it was a coastal town only about 40 miles from Hat Yai. There were no objections to Dick's suggestion of "Let's go to Songkhla!" A train was due to leave in two hours, giving us time to have a quick tour of Hat Yai.

Compared with its modern station, Hat Yai seems almost medieval. Although its almost geometrically well-laid-out streets give a hint of a modern yesteryear, its houses and shops indicate that money is not easily obtainable. Time did not permit an extensive tour, our first objective being to obtain a meal. Usually a simple operation, but not in Thailand. In most places we had visited, English could nearly always be understood, here nobody seemed to comprehend. Sign language got us through. A rubbing belly and a point at the mouth indicated food was required. The pretty waitress giggled and handed us a menu. It was in 'shorthand'. We waited until someone was served with something that looked palatable, then ordered four. It turned out to be mee grob, a meal of fried noodles which at two bahts (6p) was reasonable.

Time expired, we returned to the station to purchase our tickets which, much to our surprise, only cost 1.8 bahts, about 5p. An ancient steam engine headed the train. Shrieks from its whistle added a touch of nostalgia as we jerked away from Hat Yai.

Here and there, flat plains of paddy fields yielded their vital crops of rice. Farming methods looked primitive. Waterwheels lifted water from the rivers to ditches; these in turn carry the water to the rice fields. Water buffaloes turn the earth with wooden ploughs, efficient but slow. But there again, who cares? No one's in a hurry in these parts of the world.

Increased activity indicated that we were nearing Songkhla. The train stopped, had a brief argument with the carriages, then slowly tugged us into Songkhla's station, the end of the line.

That sadist, the sun, was up to its tricks as we sweated under the weight of our rucksacks. An American aid office afforded us temporary relief. Here we were able to glean some information on Songkhla and were recommended a hotel. The hotel just off the main street turned out to be down to our usual standard, about 15p a room. Having offloaded our burdens and cleansed ourselves, we set out to explore the town.

Songkhla is a fascinating place: it gives the impression of a film set of a Wild West town. Many of the streets are unsealed. Bullock and buffalo carts are the main form of goods transport. Bicycles are popular, trishaws are plentiful. Small shops sell silks, silver, basketware and bronzeware for a song compared with the boutique prices of Bangkok. Street stalls vend fruit, vegetables, spices, and nuts to barefooted housewives, many of whom wear their ragged pasin (a kind of sarong skirt) and their lampshade hats. Some wear the panung, a piece of colourful cloth worn so that it looks like baggy, knee-length trousers. The younger generation are leaning towards Western fashions, and the miniskirt fortunately is not uncommon.

The beauty of Thai girls is legendary: the aristocracy of femininity. Their cute, doll-like features, captivating smile and elegance give them some advantage over the rather stereotyped features of Western girls. Many of the older women do themselves a disservice by chewing betel which reddens their lips and gums and blackens their teeth. Muslim Malays predominate in the south of Thailand, though this does not mean that glamour is watered down. Malays, too, rank high in the beauty stakes. They differ somewhat from the Thai girls. Their skin is an octave darker, their lips and face a shade fuller, they have perfectly rounded hips, small waists, and small, firm breasts. Perhaps a little less of the Oriental beauty of the Thais, but to my mind the edge in sex appeal.

Most Thais are Buddhists, whose philosophy is that, by performing acts of merit, they hope to gain everlasting extinction which will prevent his having to return to earth in another form. They believe that if they fail to attain a sufficient standard, they will be reborn as lowly beasts. Many works performed by pious individuals as acts of merit enrich the country. The saffron-robed Buddhist monks live on charity, and many employ themselves as village school teachers.

Songkhla is graced with a beautiful wat (Buddhist temple) which has a spectacular ornamental entrance crowned with a miniature prang (spire). Carved serpents' tails decorate the eaves of the steeply sloping red and green, three-tiered, overhanging roof. Many of the houses are of wooden structure: most of those off the main street were raised on stilts in typical Thai fashion. Restaurants were plentiful: most comprised of little more than a few tables and stools clustered behind a charcoal-burning stove. Meals were extremely cheap and tasty. Apart from the basic beanshoots, rice or noodles, it remained a mystery to me as to what ingredients were used; anyway, we survived. The sexy gaiety of the waitresses in their light dresses offering a wink and nod of brown flesh was enough to ensure we would not starve. The equivalent of 10p would provide us with ample food for the day.

Arriving at Penang on the 'Rajula', Steve, Dick and Mike (back turned).

Buddhist temple, Songhla, Thailand.

Hitchhiking through Malaya between Ipoh and Kuala Lumpur.

In the evenings, the pavements were transformed by settlements of stalls. These stalls seemed to be the focal point for young and old alike who would gather to while away the evenings. Food and a concoction of coloured drinks ladled from glass bowls were sold. One particular drink I tried was green and had a very unusual sweet taste; having drunk the liquid I ended up with half a glass of soggy noodles. Our presence created quite an interest amongst the locals. Students approached us in an effort to experiment with their English. They were friendly enough and talked not of wars, religion or politics, but mostly about the opposite sex. Glancing around, I understood why.

During our first evening in Songkhla we were fortunate enough to witness an open-air concert which was being staged outside the local cinema. A rather amateurish group plucked away at electric guitars, encouraged by the enthusiastic response from the large crowd of youngsters. The group were followed by a couple in smart, Western-style suits, who I believe were comedians or politicians, judging by the way everyone laughed. Unable to comprehend, we left.

About one mile from our hotel was the beach where mile after mile of golden sands looked out over the Gulf of Siam. Edging the beach were acres of wooded parkland offering refuge from the hot sun. Across the waters is war-torn Vietnam, seeming so far away from the peace and solitude of these beaches. We practically had the beach to ourselves, a few isolated pockets of activity and the occasional tinkling as an ice cream vendor on a trishaw tried to attract our attention, confirming that life still existed. In the distance a couple of boys could be seen having an aerial battle with their kites.

Close to the beach was a hill at the bottom of which a notice told of the existence of a Buddhist temple at the peak; we took one look at the thousand or so steps leading up the hill – we did not dispute the notice.

Whilst in Songkhla I contracted the scourge of travellers, the 'runs'. A dose of Entero-Vioform soon cured me. Unfortunately, they worked too well and it was to be eight days before I broke my fast!

It had been hard keeping away from the Thai girls: they had been offered us in every shape, form and size by trishaw drivers, shopkeepers and our hotel manager. So far the will had been strong but the flesh weakened. A small boy offered to sell his sister. "Well, not actually sell, just on loan," he said. Mike and I succumbed. The boy made the arrangements in consultation with a trishaw driver and into the night we disappeared. I did not realise the boy had so many sisters!

It was time to leave Songkhla: our brief diversion to Thailand had been more than justified. One day, I vowed, I would return for a more extensive visit.

The early morning train chugged its way out of Songkhla. Wooden seats and constant jerks caused insomnia. Again we had a two-hour wait at Hat Yai before catching the crowded railcar to the Malay border.

Our passports were again taken off us for inspection, being returned prior to our arrival at Padang Besar on the border where we were put through the usual custom and immigration rituals.

Returning to the train, I lost the fight to regain my seat and stood for the remainder of the journey. But I did not mind: I shared the hanging safety strap with a luscious piece of Malay whose tiny frame pulsated sex. Her fine, semi-transparent blouse and gay, flower-designed, ankle-length sarong wrapped round her slim waist ensured the passing jungle received little of my attention. I hope she did not notice my exaggerated swaying.

As an economy measure and also for the experience we agreed to hitch-hike through Malaya to Singapore starting from Alor Setar, the first major town over the border. To enable a better chance of a lift we decided to travel in pairs, arranging to regroup in Singapore.

The heat hit us as we stumbled off the train at Alor Setar. I looked back fondly as the train moved out of the station. "There goes the easy way out," I thought to myself. These past few months travelling had made masochists out of us.

Dick and Steve moved off. Mike and myself would follow, having hopefully given them enough time to have got a lift. We bided our time in a small shack across from the station, refreshed ourselves with a drink, and proceeded on our way.

Unfortunately, the planners of Alor Setar were most inconsiderate: they had built the town on the wrong side of the station, or vice versa. With little hope of obtaining a lift whilst in the town, we were subjected to a long walk through Alor Setar. The wide streets and modern buildings seemed out of place amongst the surrounding jungle.

Success came soon: barely had we reached the outskirts when a young Malay in an Austin Mini pulled up. He was going as far as Garum, about twenty miles on. Little time was wasted as we sped along the good bitumen road through a corridor of thick vegetation. Our driver overstepped Garum. "You will have a better chance this side of the town," he said. Before leaving he gave Mike and me a bag of rice each. "You may need this, it is a long journey." We protested, he insisted, we accepted. With a friendly wave he turned around and returned to Garum.

Within ten minutes another car pulled up. "Yes, I can take you as far as Sungai Petani, it is about twelve miles further on." He was a police inspector returning to his unit. So far we had had no sign of Dick or Steve, so presumed that they, too, had met with success. The police inspector dropped us off at a garage on the outskirts of Sungai Petani. "You should have no trouble getting a lift from here," he said as he waved goodbye.

After waiting for about fifteen minutes we started walking; within 100 yards a battered Hillman rattled to a halt. Its brakes were not too good, causing us to run twenty yards or so to catch him up, a small price to pay. The two young Malays were on their way to Kroh. "We turn off about ten miles this side of Butterworth." "That will do." We scrambled in. "This is just going too easily," I said to Mike. We were put down near a small village about nine miles from Butterworth.

An hour elapsed. With the approach of darkness the chance of getting a lift that night lessened. The light of the rising moon began to filter through the foliage, coinciding with the awakening of the jungle which stirred with a myriad of rustlings, rising and falling like waves on a seashore to a background chorus of incessant chattering from the crickets.

Perhaps flushed with the ease of previous lifts, we began to get impatient. A small army of workers returning from a day's toil in the nearby paddy fields passed us. A young boy stopped, pointed to the distant lights of the village. "Bus to Butterworth come soon, no stop here, you have to go to village." Preferring not to risk spending the night in the jungle, we took his advice and followed him the mile or so to the village. Within an hour an ancient Leyland bus arrived. We got on and rattled away into the night, arriving at Butterworth at 2100.

Food was uppermost in our minds as we got off the bus near Butterworth railway station, it having been well over 24 hours since eating. A scruffy Indian restaurant supplied our needs in the form of a curry.

The proximity of the station decided our hotel for the night. After a wash and brush-up in the station's toilets we claimed our bench for the night. Fatigue knocked us out until 0530 when we were woken by the bustle of the early morning travellers. Deciding to take advantage of our early call, we set off in semi-darkness to the outskirts of Butterworth.

Apart from being a main rail and ferry terminal, Butterworth is also a centre of tin smelting and rubber, and houses an Australian Air Force base.

It's a long road out of Butterworth and it was two hours before we received the sympathy of a 'Samaritan'. Gratefully accepting his offer to take us a further twenty miles, we jumped in and were soon speeding through an endless silver regiment of rubber trees misted by the steam of the early morning. This was the start of the tin and rubber belt, which extends from Singapore to Butterworth.

We were dropped off at Bagan Serai, a small village of timber and thatched shacks and very little else, apart from a small stall where we were able to quench our thirst with a carton of chocolate milk.

Back on the road we met with little success. Our pace slowed as the temperatures rose toward the nineties. Our rucksacks and bags of rice were growing continually heavier as the day wore on, a curious property that Newton failed to notice. Mike and I surrendered to the heat and our impatience. Short of lying in the road, nobody seemed keen to entertain us. A bus came along, we thumbed it down, it stopped, we got in: capitulation! The bus took us as far as Taiping, the centre for one of Malaya's main tin fields.

There was a coach leaving for Ipoh in an hour's time; we booked our seats then retired to a nearby stall for a drink. With so little time to explore Taiping I had to be content with a first impression of it as a fairly large, bustling industrial/agricultural town in dire need of a facelift. Apologies if I missed the buttered side!

The full coach pulled away from Taiping's battered bus station and was soon racing through lush, tropical countryside stopping for no one. It was 1730 by the time we arrived at Ipoh's modern bus depot. Time for us to call it a day: we would spend the night in Ipoh.

A trishaw driver peddled us to a 60c (10p) 'doss' house near the centre of town. We lost no time in cleansing ourselves, an operation on its own. The 'shower' consisted of a large sink of water with an old peach tin provided to scoop water to pour over oneself, simple but effective.

Ipoh is another tin centre. It seems to have spent its profits wisely. It has wide, well-lit streets and modern buildings which harmonise well with its older counterparts. Impressive is the three-tiered, spiralling shopping precinct where Tom Jones yells about the "Green, green grass of home" from one of the many music shops challenging for audible supremacy. Entertainment seems to be well catered for with cinemas, bars and many restaurants and stalls. With our limited budget we had to be satisfied with a 50c (7p) bowl of mee (noodles) and the extravagance of a bottle of beer which we took back to our hotel to drink. Insomnia never had a look in that night, despite the unsprung bed and straw mattress, ten hours on the road ensured that. I was woken by coughing and spitting from the next room. A cock crowed: it was 0630, time to get back on the road.

A breakfast of a bowl of soup fuelled us for the journey. The road was busy with people on their way to work at the factories on Ipoh's outskirts, bringing little hope of a lift until we were clear of the town. Fortunately the sun was only just beginning to stretch itself and the early morning air lent itself to a bracing pace. Two miles of thick foliage and the occasional patch of rice fields slipped pleasantly by when a young Chinese pulled up. We gladly accepted his offer of a lift to Kangar another 20-mile bite off our journey to Singapore.

Having been dropped off just before Kangar we waited fruitlessly for over an hour. Mike had disappeared into some bushes to relieve himself when an SWB Land Rover drew up. I shouted to Mike. He came running from the undergrowth, adjusting his trousers. Already four Malays were crowded into the front of the vehicle, and the back was full of tools and other bits and pieces. They did not seem to mind the extra burden. "Jump in if you can find room!" they yelled. We did not need a second bidding, we made room. "I can take you about 70 miles towards Kuala Lumpur," said the driver. "We are going to do some repairs at a rubber plantation." Despite the bumpy ride and our cramped position, the journey passed pleasantly enough with a constant flow of chatter between us and the Malays.

With the village of Tapah behind us, we could see the jungle-clad hills of the Cameron Highlands rising in the distance to our left. Nearer, dense undergrowth shared the terrain with regimented plantations of rubber trees.

The driver turned to us. "We are nearing Kuala Kubu Baru: here we shall be stopping for a meal, you are welcome to join us." At Kuala Baru we pulled up outside a small restaurant. Inside it was crowded, but we were ushered to a back room where seats were made available. Not wishing to impose too readily on our generous Malay friends, Mike and I refused their offers to buy a meal, feigning full stomachs, but readily downed a couple of bottles of chocolate milk which they insisted on paying for. Our short break over, we returned to the Land Rover. The driver came out from the restaurant and thrust two giant packets of peanuts at Mike and me. "If you are not hungry now, you will be later on," he said. Mike and I, somewhat overcome by his generosity and warm-heartedness, stuttered our thanks.

Back on the road we sped southwards for about half an hour before stopping. "We turn off here," said the driver, pointing to a track leading through a rubber plantation. Mike and I threw our bags and ourselves out of the vehicle. A cursory wave and the wheels sped from us, leaving us once again to our own devices.

We stood on the verge waving self-conscious thumbs at the occasional southbound traffic. Our recent successes were soon forgotten as the traffic whizzed unheedingly past. As the heat rose we became more lethargic and bad-tempered. Nobody seemed to notice us until, surprise, surprise, an Indian stopped "I am only going about six miles before I turn off, if it's any help, jump in." Our new Samaritan was a government official and had spent most of his life in Malaya. Before dropping us off he invited us to his house for a meal. "It is not far away, and my wife would welcome you." We thanked him, but regrettably had to refuse his kind offer as we wanted to be in Kuala Lumpur before nightfall.

With all the natives offering us food we must have looked half-starved, though we still had our survival packs of rice and peanuts, so they need not have worried.

The minutes passed by, so did the cars; we excused the ones that were full but cursed the ones with spare seats. It was too hot for walking like mules under the weight of our packs, so we stopped and held our ground like one-armed scarecrows looking pleadingly at the drivers of passing vehicles. What right have they to ignore us? We were being unfair, but frustration provoked us.

We had almost given up hope when a brand new Alfa Romeo, complete with decorations and trimmings advertising the government lottery, screeched to a halt. Grabbing our bags we ran to the car – already it had three occupants. "If you do not mind squeezing in, we can take you to Kuala Lumpur, though we have some business in a village to do first," said the young Malay driver. There was no hesitation, we squeezed in. Their car was on an advertising tour, being first prize in the government lottery.

The three young Malays listened intently whilst Mike and I described our travels. They were envious that the lack of finance and perhaps initiative kept them hemmed in their own country. "One day," said Chu Han Bin. "I am going to leave Malaya and travel to Europe."

We arrived at a small village, the name of which escapes me, where our friends had to collect some lottery tickets. Mike and I retired to a small restaurant where we were shortly joined by the three Malays. Having refreshed ourselves with a bottle of Coke we returned to the Alfa Romeo. In less than fifteen minutes we were on the outskirts of Malaysia's capital, Kuala Lumpur. "I shall drop you off at the railway station," said Chu Han Bin. "It is fairly central."

It had started to rain as we neared the station, that hot, clammy rain typical of these tropical climes. Though the temperature in Malaya remains fairly constant, between 77 and 90 degrees Fahrenheit, the humidity is high. Even the minimum effort causes a profusion of sweat. By the time we reached the station we were smelling a little 'high', but nature did its best to wash us down. We thanked our Malay friends and on the promise of a postcard from Australia, they departed.

From the outside Kuala Lumpur station could easily be mistaken for a rajah's palace, an overdecorated fort or even a mosque. It harbours a marvellous collection of domes, arches, towers, minarets and columns, and has an architecture that is Victorian Moorish. To my mind it seems far too large for its status, serving only a few daily trains which meander into the vast, vaulted interior seemingly never to emerge. The station contrasts sharply with nearby constructions of office blocks, cubed buildings and areas of steel and glass, all of which seem intent on gobbling up this quaint museum piece.

Mike and I decided to take the easy way out by catching the night train south to Singapore. Having had a clean-up and purchased our third-class tickets, we set out to make the most of our four hours before the train's departure.

The weather was not conducive to an overindulgence of sightseeing. Nevertheless, my memory serves me well from previous visits to the city. Kuala Lumpur is a city of fine buildings, combining the best in European and Asiatic architecture; it also has many splendid gardens. We crossed one of the rivers from which Kuala Lumpur receives its name, the rivers Klang and Gombak. Kuala means mouth, Lumpur muddy. By the look of the river it must have been the latter. "I know of a good bar," I said to Mike. We went to where it had been, it had gone, and in its place stood a 30-storey office block. Much of the Chinatown I had known had disappeared, having made way for concrete cubes. Maybe in the name of progress but I still prefer the mystery and shambles of the former. There was time for us to have our 'daily bread', a 50c (7p) plate of fried mee (a noodle dish) from one of the many street stalls.

It was still raining as we walked back to the station. The train was already in. Collecting our packs we crossed over to the appropriate platform. Just our luck, the train was packed with Indians returning from a pilgrimage to Mecca. Not a vacant seat could be found; it looked as if we were about to spend an uncomfortable night. A tour of the train proved fruitless: there was nowhere, the corridors were full of bodies, luggage, bedrolls and what have you. Eventually we came across a clearing, a small space adjacent to a lavatory. We wedged ourselves in and awaited the coming ordeal.

At about 2300 the train pulled away from Kuala Lumpur and was soon racing into the blackness, its dung-painted carriages twisting and straightening as it ploughed through the jungle hills. With the continual procession of people stepping over and onto our prostrate bodies, sleeping was out of the question. To choose a site alongside a toilet had been unwise but we were both unwilling to risk losing our 'patch' whilst searching for greener pastures. Nevertheless, our fellow occupants were friendly enough and we chatted amiably through the night. Intermittent stops would break the monotony. Kajang, Seremban, Tampin – change here for Malacca. We were sorely tempted but by the time we had made up our minds the train was on the move again. Gemas, Segamat, Labis and Kluang, we had now entered Johore state – pineapple country. Dawn was breaking as we pulled into Johore Bahru, Malaya's gateway. Officials boarded the train distributing various forms which were to be completed and handed in on arrival at Singapore.

CHAPTER 16

Into Singapore

A thick mist hung over Singapore as the train crawled across the mile-long causeway which links the mainland to Singapore Island. To the left I could see the sprawling naval base at Sembawang, much of which is now converted to commercial use. We had reached the crossroads of the East, 26 by 14 miles of bustling commercialism that is Singapore. The train crept shyly into the rapidly diminishing core of jungle and palm, past peaceful huddles of kampongs (hamlets), completing its short honeymoon with a whistle as it entered the concrete entrepôt of Singapore City.

The train came to rest against the buffers. Doors were flung open, spewing out their human cargo. Mike and I waited until the dust had settled before challenging the gauntlet of custom and immigration officials.

We were permitted to stay in Singapore for two weeks after which time we would have to apply for an extension. Some not so fortunate had their passports withheld until such time as they had had their hair cut to an acceptable length, a new ruling from Lee Kuan Yew, who considers the best way to stem the tide of drug trafficking and adverse influence on Singapore's youth is to threaten to take from the hippie his most valued possession, his hair. A ruling Dick had to comply with, much to his consternation!

From the barrier, we stepped into the artistically muraled station hall, a vast interior resembling the entrance to some large hotel. Whilst at the station we unsuccessfully attempted to phone Dick, who had made arrangements to stay with some friends whilst in Singapore.

Outside the station, we fought our way through the profusion of trishaw coolies who attempted to block our path. The sun beat down relentlessly, trying to persuade us to take the local transport. We were adamant we would walk, to where we did not know. Travel and tiredness had its usual intoxicating effect and we did not really care. Respite was near at hand as we approached the shaded recluse of Queen Elizabeth Park. We collapsed onto a bench overlooking Keppel Harbour, watching large, ocean-going vessels mingling with junks and tiny sampans which rocked in propeller wash as heavily loaded tongkangs from anchored ships moved in towards Singapore's waterways like weary animals.

Nearby, kneeling before a basket, a snake charmer was playing his bulbous flute. Its clear tones incited the greenish beast to rear itself out of the basket, swaying on its tail and seemingly listening with ecstatic enjoyment to the melancholy thread of music.

Whilst contemplating our next move we heard familiar voices. It was Jim and Roamer, a couple who had travelled with us from Madras to Penang on the *Rajula*. "We are fixed up in a sleazy but cheap pad in Race Course Road. I believe there are some spare rooms, why not join us?" said Jim. It seemed a good idea, at least it would solve our accommodation problem. "It's quite a distance, we shall have to grab a couple of trishaws," said Jim.

A wave of a hand brought half a dozen trishaws plus two taxis. Having commissioned two trishaws we weaved through the crowded streets towards the north of the city, skilfully evading the black and yellow flotilla of diesel taxis. Past the large neon tiger which limps along a rooftop to advertise Tiger Balm, an embrocation that claims to cure everything and anything, and on into that splatter of streets where Serangoon Road rises and Little India begins. The smell of India – curry, rose water, oil, hot ghee and dal – merging with cooking smoke and incense. A turn to the left brought us to Race Course Road.

"Wait here," said Jim as he stopped his trishaw and disappeared through a doorway. He returned shortly with a middle-aged Chinese.

"This is the manager: he has a spare room $1 (14p) each, though you can have a discount if you pay weekly."

Our room was in the centre of the house on the second floor, completely windowless, and resembled more a cage than a room. Nevertheless, it contained the main ingredient, a large double bed. Bedding, in Singapore's sweat of endless summers, is not required, though sleeping bag inserts proved useful for keeping mosquitoes at bay. The room was crawling with copulating geckos, small, pink-tongued house lizards who earn their keep by keeping down the flies. The only source of light filtered through a solitary filth-stained window at the end of the corridor. This looked out onto a dirty backyard, impaled washing on a battalion of bamboo arms and tiny, corrugated shacks overcrowded with segments of humanity. Many of the occupants of the house were European hippies, though a large percentage were Chinese. Some Oriental ladies occupied some of the rooms during the day – I never did get round to finding out what they did at night! Jim and Roamer were in rooms in the house next door; they, too, would eventually be heading for Australia.

Another attempt at phoning Dick proved successful. He was staying at his friend's house and had arrived in Singapore a day ahead of Mike and myself. Dick also cheated by journeying by train from Kuala Lumpur. Steve had been taken ill with severe toothache and was last seen heading for a dentist in Taiping. Arrangements were made to meet Dick at his friends' garage the following morning.

Whether it was fatigue or the fact that no natural light penetrated our room, but it was midday by the time Mike and myself awoke. Following Dick's rather vague directions we eventually arrived at his friend's garage, but not before a two-mile walk, three bus changes and an SOS telephone call which resulted in Dick's friend coming to the rescue in his car.

Dick introduced Mike and myself to Loxley, a Malay he had colleged with in England. At the garage cups of tea were brought to us whilst we exchanged news and met the manager, Brian, who was busy preparing his Holden for the coming Singapore Grand Prix. Loxley informed us that Ron had contacted him and had sailed for Australia two days previously.

During the day we did a tour of the travel and shipping agencies, making enquiries on berths to Australia. So far they seemed either out of our price range or fully booked. Loxley drove Mike and me back to Race Course Road, whilst Dick returned with him to his house in Changi, which Mike and I would be visiting tomorrow.

A number 20 bus took us the ten miles or so to Changi, on Singapore's east coast. Dick met Mike and me off the bus and took us to Loxley's house where we met Loxley's attractive English wife, Janet.

Since its days as a thriving RAF base, Changi has quietened down to an almost suburban peacefulness. The rows of shops are still full of duty-free goods, but the customers are few. The village's long, golden beach was practically deserted apart from a group of boys and the odd dog or two. A few shells of military and NAAFI club buildings suggested that once the sounds of barrack ribaldry echoed across the South China Sea. It was hoped to have been able to find a beach hut where Mike and I could stay during our duration in Singapore. There was none: we resigned ourselves to Race Course Road.

On our return to Loxley's house, Janet showed us an advert in *The Straits Times* referring to a charter boat sailing from Singapore to Perth. A phone call secured a tentative booking. A visit to the travel agents and $S445 (£61) confirmed Mike's and my passage on the *Kota Singapura*, departing from Singapore in three weeks' time. Dick intended staying in Singapore until at least the completion of the Singapore Grand Prix.

The following three weeks were spent idling away the days as leisurely as possible, though during that period we did manage to see practically all of Singapore. During my period in the services I had spent almost eighteen months in Singapore, so to me it was familiar ground, ground that I never tired of seeing.

Singapore is a cosmopolitan island of many races and creeds, three-quarters of which are Chinese, and the rest made up of Malays, Indians and Europeans, a racial spectrum of over two million people. A country where summer and winter are non-existent, the seasonal contrast lies in the wind direction. Throughout the year the length of day and night varies by only nine minutes. Fruits, vegetables, rice, coconuts and rubber are grown, but surely the greatest source of income must be from the pockets of the ever-increasing influx of tourists.

The days passed slowly. Occasionally Mike and I made trips to Changi, where together with Dick we would borrow Loxley's small boat and while away the time with a fishing rod, though all we ever caught was sunburn. On other days Dick would venture into the city, usually arriving at Race Course Road at some unearthly hour of the morning which resulted in him being the recipient of much abuse from Mike and myself. Fortunately, Dick soon got into the routine of sleeping on the floor until Mike and I awoke at the more earthly hour of about 1100.

Our daily itinerary usually commenced with a 'brunch' of a banana and a cup of coffee from a small stall off Serangoon Road.

Serangoon Road is one of the main arteries out of the city. You pass restaurants where tables and stools spill onto the pavements. Shops of the goldsmiths where rings, bangles and necklaces wink from glass cases. Where shops sell endless reams of colourful silks and cottons waiting to be transformed into sarongs, saris and other exquisite Eastern garb. Shops of jewellers and shops where birds call melancholily from gilt cages, all contributing to making this corner of Singapore a little Indian suburb.

Our 'hotel' faced onto a park where most afternoons football matches would be played. I spent many an afternoon enjoying a 'kick around' with the locals. A short distance away was the Temple of One Thousand Lights. From the outside a rather unimposing building, but the interior is decorated in typical Buddhist lavishness. A large Buddha statue claimed its usual prominence amongst the smoke haze of burning incense.

Singapore is a gourmet's paradise: myriads of tiny food shops and stalls are enough to satisfy any gastronomic lust. It's not just simply eating Chinese, there is a choice of Hokkien, Cantonese, Peking, Teochew, Hakka or Hainanese, and there are others, each a province of China and each supplying its own peculiar cooking techniques. If these do not satisfy you then you can try Malay, India or Indonesian dishes, and for the unenlightened there are always European menus.

We always ate out at the night stalls, alternating between Orchard Road, Albert Street, Bugis Street or the Satay Club. Each area had its own specialities. My favourite was the Orchard Road food stalls.

Situated halfway up the bustling Orchard Road – a car park by day, but as dusk falls the cars disappear, being replaced by portable food stalls, complete with tables and stools. Each stall has its own individual gastronomic speciality, it might be oyster foo yung, duck porridge, Satay, Nasi Goreng, chow mein, hokkien prawn mee and so on, the menus are endless. At about 50c (7p) a serve, who could grumble? We usually allowed ourselves $1 per night and with that we were well sated. Bright lights dangle between stalls, mostly electric but still there were many hurricane lamps. The food is cooked over charcoal stoves in huge saucer-shaped pans. Cutlery is chopsticks. Preparation for the meals is minimal. Even the most nauseating concoction, once chopped, beaten and expertly thrown about is soon transferred into a mouth-watering dish. From dusk till dawn a constant procession of customers wander in and out. At dawn the site quickly reverts to its intended use as a car park.

Albert Street is a street of unsophisticated night restaurants and stalls. Singapore guidebooks tell you to head straight for Fatty's – we disobeyed, knowing that the prices at Fatty's would have risen with his fame, though that is not to take credit away from this boisterous, chubby Chinaman in his baggy trousers and singlet. For £1 he would cook you a whole roast duck basted in honey and soy sauce. To us that would be the cost of a week's meals. We contended ourselves by dining at the more infamous stalls with the locals, whilst the richer tourist stuffed themselves at Fatty's. An Indian stallholder cooked for Mike and myself a special Indian Irish stew: it tasted like a thick mulligatawny soup, but we came back for more.

The Satay Club is a group of permanent stalls set out rather like a barbecue pitch, situated in Queen Elizabeth Walk and offering a commanding view of Keppel Harbour. Here the menu is predominantly Malay with the likes of nasi goreng, Roti John, mee and satay. Satay is grilled mutton, beef or chicken served on smoking lances which you dip into a hot sauce. The scintillating aroma of meat and hot spices fills the air, whilst the mesmeric hum of marine motors and the rattle of seed pods among the leaves lullabies one in this exquisite corner of Singapore.

No one should be allowed to leave Singapore without having visited Bugis Street (preferably between midnight and dawn). A normal downtown street by day, at night the traffic gives way to food stalls, tables and stools, beer vendors, hawkers (dirty photos – the lot), drifters, eccentrics, tourists, kids who play noughts and crosses for money (and never loose) and, topping the bill, female impersonators. Mike asked me how I knew they were female impersonators, they all look gorgeous. "Look for the 'Adam's apple'," I said. No, Mike, that's not the 'adam's apple' – ah well, he'll learn. These 'girls' (shims or ladyboys) flit from table to table, moving in on unsuspecting tourists. The majority of shims, being Chinese, are smooth-skinned; they dress exotically in alluring dresses or 'cheongsams'. Their hair (or is it wigs?) is trussed in modern styles. A fine pair of breasts by courtesy of silicon completes the set-up. Occasionally their voices betray them. "Hello, darling, you want good time?" It's not a woman's or a man's, but more like a voice in the process of breaking, like in puberty. It's difficult to tell who's who:

the safest way is to assume all females are males, other than that only the personal touch will reveal what side of the fence he or she is on. Whilst their sexual deviation may be a profitable sideline, the shims are kept at the expense of affluent Chinese restaurant owners who see dollar signs in the wake of the tourist attraction created by these 'girls'.

The tempo of Bugis Street rises as the night wears on, reaching its peak just before dawn. Dawn breaks and the customers start drifting away. A few of the less attractive shims are left behind; they are desperate now, as their prices have reached rock-bottom. Nobody is interested in them, but they will be back in the evening. Peggy, Bo, Mike and I had had an entertaining night: we had spent little and had enjoyed watching the shims fleece the rich tourists.

We caught a trishaw back to Race Course Road. Tiredness caused us to ignore the driver's persistent "like good night out (it was 5 am), like jiggy jig, nice girl, very young, very clean, short time, long time": the patter's always the same.

How true the quote from Singapore's guidebooks: a city that never sleeps. From the time the neon lights relieve the sun, till the day 'watchman' returns, the throb of life goes on, pulsating from the bars, clubs, hotels and street stalls.

Many a day was spent wandering through the city's streets. Trishaws and bicycles swerving and wobbling amongst hooting cars and buses. The sounds of squealing brakes and bicycle bells mingle with the arguments of shoes and sandals on the pavements. The endless patter of bare feet and the stray words babbled in a multitude of lingos. Pop groups emanating from duty-free stereos. Girls in miniskirts, eyes flashing, bottoms rotating, lovely legs – stiff neck! A wispy, bearded old man in threadbare shorts and grubby vest shuffles through the traffic carrying his worldly goods in a bundle slung over his scrawny shoulder.

Perhaps a morning would be spent haggling over the price of some article we had no intention of buying. The traders would reciprocate in the bartering ritual with a gamut of gestures and facial expressions. Experience taught us to halve the original quote, then work down from that. How amusing to see tourists (mainly Americans) pay the first quote that was asked for an article, then no doubt running back to their ship or hotel convinced of having secured a bargain.

For bargains one has to go a long way to better the Pasar Malam, which is a nomadic night market which regularly changes its site. It was at Tanglin Road when I visited it. About a quarter of a mile of stalls set up along the pavements, selling everything and anything at rock-bottom prices, providing you barter.

Near Collyer Quay and leading into Raffles Place and the large Robertson's department store (recently ravaged by fire) is Change Alley, a small, lively shopping arcade, crowded with stalls and people. Stallholders with their persuasive chatter, each offering a better bargain than his neighbour. Playing one against the other seems the best way to obtain a bargain.

A short walk from Raffles Place brought us to the People's Park shopping complex, a massive, high-rise building bulging with merchandise. Nearby similar buildings are mushrooming at an alarming rate, the fast-changing face of modern Singapore.

Much of the labouring on these concrete monsters is done by Samsui women. An excellent advertisement for women's lib, these tough women from Southern China toil from dawn to dusk in their wide-brimmed coolie hats and black pyjama suits, the samfoo.

From People's Park you cross a large, steel-girdered bridge. Below, massed sampans huddle like thousands of frightened bugs. The water is hard to find beneath the carpet of boats and floor of human refuse.

You are now swept into Chinatown: a tidal wave of smells engulfs you. A mixture of smouldering sandalwood, incense, food, stale fruit, rotting fish, bad meat, peppers, spices, stale urine, plus others whose source was unaccounted for. A kaleidoscope of noise: a radio screams out, maybe the wail of a Cantonese love song, but more likely Tom

Jones or The Rolling Stones. The cries of hawkers and the whine of trishaws and bicycles along the tarmac. An argument erupts, shouts, yells, calls, it gets heated – we move on. Was that the sound of someone tearing wet linen? No, it's an old man clearing his throat and spitting.

The narrow street is nearly blocked by a decrepit old man, in singlet and loose baggy trousers, straining like a beast of burden in front of a cart piled high with junk. A man peddles past: he is overloaded with two large wicker baskets and a string of gutted fish. A small girl crouches down and widdles in a gutter choked with garbage. In food shops, scraggy, roasted ducks covered in flies hang by their beaks. A rat joins the queue of customers: it's given a boot and ends up in a box of rotting tomatoes. Metal shops, key makers, gold-beaters, cobblers, tailors and carpenters sweat away in their grubby little cubby holes. Children, their reedy voices chattering like a group of starlings quarrelling over a succulent piece of offal. Old men stand in doorways stroking their thin, attenuated beards whilst heavily laden women totter agonisingly about their endless labours.

A drink seller languidly shakes his bell and spits a bloody blob of betel juice on the pavement. The calligrapher squats in a doorway writing letters and religious texts with Chinese characters. Goats, hens, ducks, dogs and cats fossick amongst the rubbish. Washing, impaled by long bamboo poles, reaches out from windows and balconies as if dressed for some gay and everlasting festival.

Celebrations for the Chinese New Year are reaching a climax as the fifteenth day approaches. Scarlet incense sticks burn from every doorway. A stage is being erected in the street for some performance or other. Trucks are being decorated for the final noisy precession of brass bands with their clashing symbols, drums and firecrackers.

In a fit of physical enthusiasm, Jim, Mike and I walk the five miles to the crocodile farm. Here crocodiles are bred. Pools full of 'snapping logs' await their fate, to be transformed into shoes, handbags and other fancy goods.

On our return from the crocodile farm a pleasant surprise awaited Mike and me. Bo and Peggy had arrived, having just returned from visiting Dick at Changi. Since we had parted in Ceylon they had travelled by train to Calcutta, flown to Bangkok, then by rail to Singapore. Bo and Peggy moved in with us at Race Course Road; they also managed to obtain berths on the *Kota Singapura* sailing for Perth in two weeks' time.

On the west coast of the island at Pasir Panjang are the Tiger Balm Gardens. These gardens house what must be Singapore's most famous tourist attraction, Haw Par Villa, a million-dollar creation by Aw Boon Haw. On lawns and slopes overlooking the sea, Technicolored, life-size figures and groups depict Chinese mythology and folklore. Grottoes, caves and shelves house rats, wolf-like frogs, monkeys, women with long talons and many other ghoulish characters. Marbled Buddhas, mythical animals, mermaids and dogs mingle with sadism, murder and assassination. Each setting presents a story with a moral. Maybe about the dangers that beset a monk on a pilgrimage, or of torture, sadism and murder in a Chinese purgatory. Gory, open wounds, mutilation and liberal splashings of synthetic blood add realism.

Continuing around the island we arrived at the Jurong Bird Park. Fifty acres of natural environs contain over 5,000 birds. Miniature lakes satisfy the marine species, whilst a gigantic net covering a whole tropical hillside, including an impressive waterfall, contains a host of colourful, feathered aeronautics. Mike and I spent over three hours wandering through the maze of large aviaries, and still we did not see it all. An ominous black cloud curtailed our tour, but the sudden downpour miraculously cleared away, being replaced by a blazing sun which produced rising clouds of steam from the streets and monsoon ditches.

From our lofty perch at the bird park we could see Singapore's new industrial complex: steel mills, an oil refinery, shipyards and a host of factories manufacturing furniture, clothing, chemicals and rubber products.

Sampans on waterway in Singapore.

Tiger Balm Gardens, Singapore.   *China Town, Singapore.*

At Tanglin can be found the Botanic Gardens, a vast acreage of natural habitat for the monkeys that roam wild through the tropical foliage and jungle trees hung with lianas. There is a small lake and pavilion and a plant house that contains many rare orchids.

Visits to the National Museum's Japanese Trade Exhibition at the Victoria Memorial Hall and to the Aquarium with its 80 tanks of tropical fish, sharks and octopuses, helped pass the time.

Travelling eastward out of the city you come to the New World Amusement Park. A trade fair was in progress during our visit, adding a touch of sanity to the conglomeration of food stalls with their steaming cauldrons of rice, beanshoots, noodles and fish, merry-go-rounds, dodgem cars and professional ladies with their propositions. I must have received at least four quotes within minutes of arriving. The crowds had thinned, and stallholders and tradesmen were putting up their shutters for the night. The girls that were left were the remnants of the Lord Mayor's Show. Even though their cheongsams gave full appreciation to their padded figures, their facial paintwork deterred all but the most desperate sexual stirrings. We gave them a miss and returned to the comparative safety of our recluse in Race Course Road.

Mike and I visited the Immigration Department and successfully applied for an extension to our two-week allocation to stay in Singapore.

The days rolled by, the novelty of Singapore drifted to monotony, and we were eager to move on again.

After frequent visits to the travel agency, more than was really necessary – but she was an attractive receptionist, and so friendly – we were at last presented with our boat tickets. Trouble with printing and maiden voyage are the usual excuses.

I could not leave Singapore without a nostalgic visit north of the island to Sembawang, where I had been stationed for nigh on eighteen months.

Along with Roamer, Jim and Mike, we travelled by bus through the jungle core of the island. Familiar names returned. Nee Soon, where 'Nellie no nose' once paraded her wares on the rather inaptly named 'Virgins' Corner'. We passed the Royal Naval barracks of HMS *Terror*, through the neatly gardened married quarters and modern C of E church snuggled in their tropical surroundings and on into Sembawang village.

Sembawang in its heyday was a bustling naval base; now, since the virtual withdrawal of British forces from the island, the village is very much a shadow of its former self. The 'cream' from the matelot's pockets no longer swell the coffers of the enterprising girls and shop- and barkeepers who now stand forlornly outside their establishments waiting to pounce on the odd customer or two. I walked past the long line of empty bars, a girl in the doorway of 'Peanuts' bar winked and jerked her head back. "Come inside, Johnny, very good music, nice girls." I showed her my empty pockets, she returned to the dark, air-conditioned interior.

No one stopped us as we strolled through the dockyard gates. A couple of policemen looked uninterestedly at us, then returned to their argument. The graveyard atmosphere of a once bustling dockyard. It had been taken over by civilians. In the place of lines of battleship-grey frigates, destroyers, minesweepers, and the odd aircraft carrier and fleet replenishment boats, were a couple of rusty tankers wallowing in midstream, framed beneath a backcloth of tropical palms from the nearby Malayan mainland.

The sprawling township of dockyard workshops was practically silent. Occasional noises came from minor repairs being carried out on some insignificant harbour craft swallowed up in the vast KGV Dry Dock. There was little consolation from the couple of Commonwealth frigates tucked into obscurity in some distant corner of the dockyard. As Dylan once sang, "The times they are a-changing".

The old families' swimming pool in the dockyard looked inviting. "Let's go for a dip," suggested Roamer. The sun was beating down: it seemed a good idea, though from Mike's point of view his loss of a tooth whilst taking a dive proved an expensive one.

Overlooking the dockyard gates was the modern building of 'Agnes Weston's Sailor Rest'. Built around a pleasant swimming pool, it was the haunt of many a pleasant weekend during my Navy days. Surprisingly it was still in operation, though practically empty. We had a drink beside the pool before moving off to catch the bus back to the city.

The journey back to the city took us past the vast labyrinth of multistorey housing complexes, built to accommodate Singapore's rapidly expanding population and to replace the slums and shanty towns.

The evening prior to our departure from Singapore, Janet, Loxley and Dick entertained Peggy, Bo, Mike and me at their home in Changi. Liberal servings of char-kway-teow, washed down with Tiger beer, ensured a memorable parting.

We had little packing to do. I rolled up my sleeping bag, strapped it to my bulging rucksack and waited at the foot of the rickety staircase to hail a passing taxi. The wait was brief. Peggy, Bo, Mike and I piled in. There was no 'one last look' at our room at Race Course Road: we were glad to be leaving.

The taxi hopscotched through the mob of mobile metal to the docks. Police at the dockyard gates refused to believe there was such a boat as the *Kota Singapura* in port. We presented our tickets: they grunted disbelievingly and allowed us through.

In torrential rain we searched the docks for the elusive boat. As the exasperated taxi driver was about to dump us off, the white hulk of a small passenger boat peeped from behind a large warehouse. Sure enough there was our nautical objective: the *Kota Singapura*.

CHAPTER 17

Kota Singapura

A nest of drunken ants sprayed the dockside, disappearing and reappearing from the bowels of the ship. Piles of baggage, cases and crates stood dejectedly pleading for attention.

Confusion reigned. We tried to get on-board: admission refused. "You must wait until 1800, the ship is not ready yet," said an agitated officer. Back on the dockside we joined other confused faces waiting to board.

The white-coated custodian of the gangway relaxed his guard: we grabbed our bags and smuggled on-board. An overworked purser accepted our intrusion and showed us to our cabin. "I apologise for the confusion, only the ship has just completed a refit and we are rather unprepared." He unlocked the door, I stepped in and nigh on drowned: the cabin was six inches under water. "There must be some mistake, this must be the swimming pool," said Bo. There was no mistake, a water mains had burst. "We are still having teething troubles," spluttered the purser. "I will get it fixed."

We returned to the bar, leaving a trail of soggy footprints on the plush, carpeted passageway. Soft drinks only, still in harbour.

Our sailing had been delayed till 0100 am. Dick arrived on the quayside, along with Loxley's two sisters, to see us off. There being still five hours before the ship was due to leave, we joined him on the jetty. Dick had borrowed Loxley's car. We disappeared to a nearby bar for a final farewell drink.

Back on-board we watched the last-minute confusion. The gangway was removed, put back and removed again. At about 0030, with an almost visible sigh of relief, the *Kota Singapura* slowly drifted from the jetty. There was a cursory wave before Dick finally merged into the background of Singapore's neon night. The adverts relinquished their usefulness as they merged with the light haze of Singapore. The dominant 'National' advertising hoarding offered a farewell wink and the red and yellow Tiger sign managed one more leap as we slipped into the South China Sea.

A game of cat and mouse ensued, with the hordes of fishing junks wallowing in the shimmering fluorescence of the tropical night. Fish traps composed of long poles and complicated fishnets into which the fish were lured by the blinding glare of a kerosene lamp which hovered overhead.

The *Kota Singapura* picked her way through the sea of nautical glow-worms. From a nearby junk the explosion of a firecracker disturbed the peace, probably to ward off evil spirits. Whether we came into that category or not, we carried on unmolested.

An increasing throb from the ship's engine completed our harbour manoeuvres. Our adversaries faded astern, leaving us in the hands of the elements.

I left the moon to do its light fandango on the placid waters and returned to the bar. Petite Asiatic stewardesses in colourful silk gowns fussed around the few faithfuls who kept the bar till ringing until 0400. Familiarity increased with the consumption of Tiger beer. The waitresses, all experiencing their first taste of nautical servitude, had a rough passage, but survived the night with decorum.

Organisation and service on-board were minuscule. An understaffed and inexperienced crew did little to help matters. But, having roughed it for over four months, we relished the comparative luxury of this small, one-class liner.

Two plush bars and a casino (complete with female croupiers) helped the evening pass pleasantly. Days were spent bathing in the hot tropical sun.

A few days out from Singapore the placid waters lost their temper. The bulbous boat rolled its way southwards. Passengers and crew hibernated. The few passengers still mobile served their own meals which, as the days rolled by, degenerated into a continuous salad menu. Our little clique appeared to have the bars to ourselves. Waitresses turned green and disappeared, except for one – Gloria, a cute little slice of India, about four feet nine inches tall with doll-like features.

Passengers and crew came out of hibernation and the ship returned to normal.

Entertainment was supplied by an Asian pop group and a couple of Latin American singers. Fancy dress and talent contests were well patronised. Bar hours were erratic. Occasionally we would stock up with amber liquid to last us through till dawn.

The ship passed close to many tropical islands and atolls. Overpopulated with tall palms and with beautiful sandy beaches, these islands offered an inviting prospect. An announcement by the captain proclaimed we were passing the island of Bali. There were none to dispute him, his guess was as good as ours. A day later he informed us that the land on our port side was in fact the west coast of Australia. Restrained cheers broke out from the Australian passengers. They were pessimistic. Why did the captain walk around with his fingers crossed?

Regardless, the ship ploughed on through fields of flying fish and playful dolphins.

Last night celebrations drifted into the early hours. Tiger beer flowed, glasses and voices were raised. There was good cause for celebration. For Peggy, Bo, Mike and me it was practically the end of almost five months' hard travelling that had taken us nearly 20,000 miles.

It seemed very much an anticlimax. Having almost reached our objective, it was time to think about employment. A gloomy thought, but our meagre monetary resources were fast dwindling. The bottom of our barrel was in sight. Nevertheless, we could feel well satisfied. I had started the journey with only £350. This had been supplemented by the sale of the Land Rover which had paid for the flight from Karachi to Ceylon.

During the evening, I received a telegram: "will meet you at Fremantle". It was from Frank and Anita, a couple who had lived opposite my flat in Bristol and had emigrated to Australia.

By the time I had woken, the ship had berthed in Fremantle. Most of the passengers had already disembarked. I gathered my belongings, threw them in my rucksack, and proceeded bleary-eyed to the upper deck.

CHAPTER 18

Arrive Australia

My attention was drawn to frantic shouts from ashore. Focussing my bloodshot eyes, I could just make out the blurred forms of Frank and Anita and their two children. Also the unmistakable shape (still in his suit) of Ron.

I prepared myself for the battle with the custom and immigration authorities. "How long are you staying?" "Don't know." Thump! And yet another stamp in my passport. "Collect your bags and move on to customs." "Anything to declare?" "No." My honest face got me, though. I was now free to join Frank, Anita and Ron in the visitors' lounge.

Bo, Peggy and Mike were met by Bo's parents who would be accommodating the trio at Marchagee until such time as they returned to Perth in search of employment. I bade Bo, Peggy and Mike farewell and rejoined Frank, Anita and Ron. "You're staying with us," said Frank. I did not argue: at least it was one problem solved. Ron was already staying with Frank. He had travelled from Singapore on a Russian charter ship which had arrived in Perth two weeks previously. As yet he had not found employment apart from a brief introduction on door-to-door selling.

"Before I take you home I shall take you to the 'local' for a couple of good Aussie beers." After the previous night's escapade my stomach squirmed at Frank's suggestion, but soon resigned itself to a further alcoholic dose. The ice-cold Swan beer seemed strange at first but soon acclimatised itself to me.

It was midday by the time we finally reached Frank's house at Balga, fifteen miles north of Perth, a typical Australian suburban area of detached bungalows and neat, open-planned gardens. A stone's

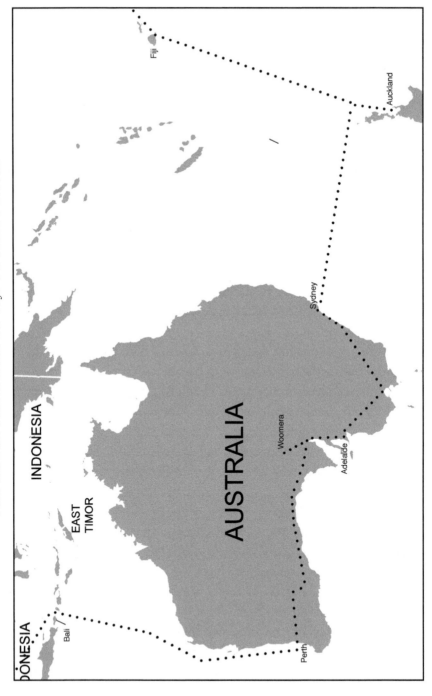

throw from bush country and with it the ever-prevailing threat of bushfires.

My first evening in Perth was spent in typical Australian fashion – a barbecue. 'Snags', steaks and chops plus, of course, a keg of beer which the male contingent clung to as if it were gold.

At the first opportunity I paraded myself at the employment exchange. The interviews still left me unemployed, but at least the wheels were turning for me to receive $17 dole money.

Days passed with negative results. Early morning scans through the 'sits vac' columns, telephone calls and numerous journeys through Perth proved fruitless. There always seemed about 50 people queueing up for one job. I had hit Perth during one of its slack periods.

An off chance phone call to a plastering firm brought a glimmer of hope. "You can have a job providing you have a union card." This I did not have. A visit to the Union office and, with the pretence that I had left my union card in the UK, I was furnished with a temporary card which was sufficient to get me the job.

With practically no plastering experience I did not expect to last long, but at least I was guaranteed one day's pay.

I purchased a second-hand bike to transport me the three miles to and from work. Tools were borrowed from the foreman.

My first assignment was a new high-rise building in St. Georges Terrace. Much of my time was spent trying to ape the other plasterers, though it was becoming increasingly difficult. Bulges appeared in my plasterwork. The more I tried to rid them, the worse they got, until eventually whole sections would sag and collapse in a sloppy heap on the floor. Even advice from experienced plasterers – to pee in the plaster before spreading it on the walls to stop it going off so quickly – failed to work. I think they were just taking the p---!

It came as a relief when the foreman informed me that my services were no longer required. Surprisingly I had survived five weeks.

During these weeks I had managed to see much of Perth. A

delightfully pleasant city with long, wide streets and a charming suburbia. Overlooking much of Perth is Kings Park, an impressive acreage of greenery and tall trees. From here there is an excellent view of the Swan River as it meanders through the city. A recently completed maze of flyovers and bridges cowers below the park's slopes.

Stretching along the horizon are the gentle curves of the Darling Ranges where more often than not can be seen the ashen haze of a minor bushfire somewhere or other. The tang of eucalyptus from the native gums fills the air – the smell of Australia.

On the banks of the Swan I spent many a weekend collecting mussels which we would boil and eat on the beach.

During the Easter period I travelled with Frank and Anita to Lancelin, a small coastal outback town some eighty miles north of Perth.

The road north is rather monotonous, consisting mainly of uninteresting scrub and bush land apart from a pleasant stretch which passes close to the Yanchep National Park, where koalas and other native animals abound.

Being the holiday weekend and the venue for Western Australia's dune buggy championships, Lancelin's campsite was crowded. Fortunately, we managed to acquire a pitch for our two-roomed tent adjacent to Frank's friend, John.

At Lancelin I experienced my first attempt at water-skiing. Using John's boat and skis, I persevered all day, seemingly only succeeding in wrapping the skis around my neck or dragging myself along the seabed. After numerous suicide attempts I suddenly rose ungracefully out of the water. Rather like riding a bike for the first time, I soon overcame my shaky start and quickly gained confidence. Once waterborne I was reluctant to stop, though the arrival of an obese-looking seal dampened my waxing enthusiasm. I did not relish an argument with that whiskery monster.

The weekend was all too short and it was soon time to pack up and return to Perth.

Ron had by now secured employment as a booking clerk at Perth's YMCA. As accommodation was provided, he moved out of Frank's house.

No sooner had Ron left when his place was taken by the arrival of Dick. He had managed to obtain a berth on the *Kota Singapura's* next voyage to Perth. After staying a week, Dick travelled across country to Sydney from where he would make his way following the coast to the north of Australia. Dick obtained temporary work as a jackaroo on a cattle station in Queensland before moving on to Darwin from where he flew home to the UK.

Meanwhile, Bo, Peggy and Mike had returned to Perth in the hope of finding work. They were renting a couple of one-roomed flats, but so far no work.

I, too, was having no luck in regaining my employed status. With the prospect of work brighter in the eastern states, I resigned myself to once again moving on.

I signed up with TravelMates, a firm who for a nominal fee will put you in contact with a driver heading east who requires a passenger to share expenses.

Within three days I was partnered with a chap going to Melbourne. I would get off at Adelaide. Thus I joined up with Ted, the owner of a Holden station wagon, and Bob, another passenger. They, too, were hoping to find work east.

It was almost midday by the time we had left Perth. Taking it in turns at the wheel, we drove steadily through the attractive wooded countryside of the Darling Ranges.

From Northam, on the eastern slopes of the ranges, the terrain is quickly transformed into arid bush land, mile upon mile of scrub broken only by the occasional flourish of trees.

With very little traffic to impede us and an excellent bitumen road, progress was good. Habitation was sparse. Now and then we would pass a small railway settlement or a sheep or cattle station. Apart from Southern Cross, the first real sign of life was at Coolgardie.

Once a prosperous mining town, Coolgardie is now practically a ghost town, in which role it is becoming increasingly popular with tourists, its wide main streets having changed little since its pioneering days. Today most of its hotels, banks, shops and houses are empty. We stayed a while for a look around. A door creaked open and slammed shut in the breeze. I peeked inside: it was empty and smelled of age. Outside, a hitching rail, no longer required, stood in memory of a bygone era.

From Coolgardie the road branches, the left veering off to the more prosperous mining township of Kalgoorlie. We veered southwards towards Norseman.

Dusk came and with it the ever-increasing danger from kangaroos. These endearing but stupid animals become mesmerised by a vehicle's lights and more often than not would jump towards a car rather than away from it, which can have drastic results to both the animal and the vehicle. Fortunately, despite the large amount of 'roos' we saw, we escaped with a slight scrape down the car's side from a large red.

At 11 pm we stopped for the night in a lay-by just past Norseman. We were eager to get some rest before tackling the Nullarbor Plain in the morning.

A dull, red sun struggled through a dusty dawn as we stirred ourselves from our cramped 'bedroom'. It was 6 am: the solar rays had yet to show their force. Little time was wasted in mobilising ourselves and we were soon rolling along the deserted Eyre Highway.

Taking advantage of the early morning coolness, we resisted the temptation to stop at Balladonia Motel for breakfast.

The temperature rose as the day progressed. Even the close proximity to the sea failed to lower the temperature with its cool breezes. What little wind there was came from the north, having travelled one thousand miles over hot desert, and it was in no mood to offer us any relief. Even the scrub seemed to have decided to call it a day. By the time we had reached Eucla on the western/southern

Australia border, most forms of plant life had disappeared, giving way to stony desert – the start of the Nullarbor Plain.

At Eucla we stopped at the motel for 'brunch' and to refuel. From the motel we could see the sea. Below us the small cove of Wilson Bluff, whilst further out the Great Australian Bight shimmered in the sun, looking refreshingly cool.

Once we had left Eucla our driving honeymoon expired. Here the bitumen ends and the dirt road begins – three hundred miles of it. Bulldust, potholes, rocks and stones. A murderous challenge to the best of tyres and suspensions. Added to these hazards was the dust from passing preceding vehicles. Dust for mile upon mile, if one is unfortunate enough to travel behind a vehicle, even it if is a mile or so ahead, you have the prospect of practically travelling blind until such time as you have overtaken the offending vehicle. Another hazard can be from flying stones thrown up from passing vehicles. Broken windscreens are commonplace.

There is little to see whilst crossing the Nullarbor apart from endless miles of flat stony desert and dust. The road shifts inland, though never more than 40 miles from the sea.

Occasionally we would stop to let the car cool down. This would usually be the cue for an invasion of a myriad of flies, black clouds of buzzing insects crawling in eyes, nostrils, mouth and ears. We get out of the car to stretch our legs, the sun pushes down on our heads like a great weight. We talk and the hot dust in our mouths makes us gasp.

At Ivy Tanks we had a meal and refuelled at the motel. With the coming of dusk the sun relaxed its grip, but still the dusty tang lingered. It was a relief to get to Penong and be able to swill our sandpapery mouths with ice-cold beer.

Prior to our arrival at the coastal town of Ceduna we stopped at a checkpoint where officials searched our vehicle for fruit. One is not allowed to contaminate South Australia with Western Australian fruit.

Crossing the Nullabor Desert,
giving the car a cool down.

Me making friends with a
native at Woomera.

Island Lagoon, deep space
tracking station near Woomera.
how to read a map.

Ceduna heralds the end of the dirt road and the Nullarbor. On the outskirts of the town we pulled into a lay-by and retired for the night.

Stirred into action by a refreshing breeze, we made another dawn start. Vegetation increased and scrub returned, making a welcome change from the monotonous relief of the Nullarbor.

In the distance to our left could be seen the low-lying ridges of the Gawler Ranges. To our right loomed the huge, artificial-looking mineral mounds of Iron Knob. Heavy machinery fussed about like ants as they gnawed into the monstrosities.

Tall smokestacks spewing pollution welcomed us to the industrial town of Port Augusta. Here we stopped for a meal and a drink at a bar that was full of Aborigines, all of whom appeared drunk.

From Port Augusta we veered south, running parallel to the Flinders Ranges. We are now in wheat country. Either side of us shimmering fields of yellow ripple in the breeze. Huge concrete silos blot the copybook landscape.

Skirting Port Pirie at the top of the Yorke Peninsula, we followed the railway southwards passing the small townships of Crystal Brook and Snowtown.

Minor engine trouble necessitated us retiring to a garage for repairs. Dusk was falling by the time we were back on the road.

Traffic increased as we neared Adelaide, but the road was good and fast. A glow on the horizon confirmed the proximity of the city. The lights of Salisbury and Elizabeth twinkled on our left, guiding us into South Australia's premier city.

Ted and Bob were continuing on to Melbourne. I was dropped off at Magill, one of Adelaide's eastern suburbs. Here I was made welcome by Cam and Sue, an Australian couple who had befriended my sister during their stay in England.

Being a weekend there was little I could do in my quest for employment. Instead I accepted Cam's offer of a tour of Adelaide. A beautiful and sedate city spreading beneath the Adelaide Hills.

Creeping up the hills are the eastern suburbs. Spacious, detached houses rub shoulders with sprawling vineyards: a pleasant area offering the advantages of city life and the seclusion of the countryside. Barely a stone's throw away is the rambling Belair National Park and Waterfall Gully. These two rambling wooded acreages offer miles of picnic areas and delightful walks.

Nearing the city centre a square belt of rustic parkland provides a recluse from the bustle of the city. Adelaide's centre is a system of wide, symmetrical streets. Large department stores and office blocks are slowly eroding the more colonial-style buildings. Competing with Adelaide's national park are miles of golden beaches.

With the weekend over I set about the unenviable task of job hunting. Luck was with me. A phone call secured an interview that day. It was successful. Tomorrow I would be driven north to Woomera to start work as a painter.

Together with two Aborigines, Ken and Dave, I was driven the 290 miles to the weapons research establishment of Woomera.

From Port Augusta we joined the Sturt Highway. Most of this road is dirt, but intermittent stretches of bitumen have been laid.

It was dark and we could see little, not that there was much to see. Trees gradually became sparser, degenerating into scrub before finally relegating to barren, rocky desert the closer we got to Woomera.

Occasionally a kangaroo would jump into the road, hesitate before bounding off haphazardly in panic-stricken leaps.

We arrived at Pimba, a small settlement of about twelve buildings, two of which are garages. Here the Sturt Highway leaves as it goes its way through the desert to Coober Pedy and on northwards to Alice Springs.

From Pimba the bright lights of Woomera glare eerily in the surrounding desert blackness, looking every bit like the front of some seaside resort.

CHAPTER 19

Woomera

We arrived at Woomera's main gate and were immediately accosted by the Commonwealth Police. There were forms to fill in, 'bona fides' to be checked. "That's just the start," said one of the policemen. "Wait until you do your routine tomorrow." We were handed over to the custody of my new boss who escorted us to our overnight accommodation.

The following morning was spent form-filling. "All necessary in the cause of security," we were told. We were rehoused in one-roomed flatlets, small but adequate.

By the afternoon we were ready to start work. My job was to go from house to house painting air conditioning units. We worked in gangs, I was with Paul, a jovial Swiss man, and Ken, an Aborigine. We got on well together. They were good times. Little work was done: much of the time was spent in me teaching Paul English, and Ken teaching me bushcraft. Much time was spent drinking in the houses and chatting up the wives whilst hubby was at work.

The job lasted six weeks when I was politely told that, because of the end of the tax year, cuts would have to be made. The painting staff were to be axed.

I had little trouble in obtaining another job. For a week I was employed gardening before managing to get more lucrative employment at the space tracking station at Island Lagoon, about eighteen miles from Woomera, American-owned and operated by an Australian company. It was constructed in the 1950s to track the American space probes, during which time Island Lagoon has tracked the moon, Mars, Jupiter and many other interplanetary missions.

Sited on the edge of a large salt lake some 80 miles long, Island

Lagoon's name derives from the stark tors which rise objectionably from amongst the vast expanse of glaring whiteness. Contrasting with the lake, the surrounding areas are a desolate expanse of reddish desert. Stark, stony and sterile. The occasional creek where a few bushes struggle pathetically to survive gives some relief. Kangaroos and emus are plentiful. They shelter from the hot sun in the creeks, but are frequent visitors to the station, especially during droughts. During my first eight months at Island Lagoon we had no rain, with the result that many of the kangaroos and emus would venture onto the site to obtain water and feed off the grass from the well-watered lawn, the only greenery around.

The drought was broken by three days of continual downpour which turned the dry creeks into raging torrents. But they soon dried up, leaving an aftermath of debris. Overnight green shoots appeared, but they stood little chance against the hot sun, and soon withered away.

Between December and April, the heat can become almost unbearable with temperatures reaching 120 degrees Fahrenheit. At times like these the two large, Olympic-sized swimming pools were very popular.

Occasional cold spells, though these are rarely below 80 degrees Fahrenheit, bring some respite, but only temporarily: soon one is again spending sleepless nights in pools of sweat.

From Woomera we would travel daily to and from Island Lagoon, a rather boring half-hour journey which was often brightened by the antics of "k'roos" who most days would position themselves by the side of the road looking everything like a timekeeper clocking us in.

Work was comparatively relaxed. Although the station was busy tracking Mariner, Mars and pioneer Missions, there was a holiday atmosphere about the place. Notice had been given by the American Space Agency that Island Lagoon had lived its life and would commence closing down on completion of the Apollo moon mission.

Staff would be either transferred to other tracking stations or made redundant with three months' pay. Most would be opting for the latter, but as yet there was no firm date and many would be required to stay at Island Lagoon to close the station and pack up. This could take up to five or six months.

Life was not all work. Entertainment in Woomera's isolated community was, although limited, varied. Clubs, theatre, bowling green, swimming pool and facilities for most sports catered for all tastes, with dances most weekends and the occasional live show. There were also opportunities for adult education classes.

Any visitor to Woomera expecting to see launching pads, rockets and other scientific jargon will be very disappointed. The launching pads are tucked away some 30 miles into the desert.

Woomera is, however, a pleasant spot with neatly laid out streets and a surprising amount of greenery. An oasis in the surrounding immensity which seems to dwarf the village by the vastness of its setting. Many thousands of trees have been imported and arranged neatly along the streets and gardens rather as a child would arrange miniature trees on his toy farm. From the air, Woomera must give the impression of having been tossed into the wilderness by a passing giant grown tired of his toys. Trees and lawns are kept alive by regular watering. A few days' neglect in the torrid summer can soon parch the greenery. A pleasant, secluded corner of the village is Breen Park with its zoological perimeter consisting of native animals and birds. Two excellent ovals provide a popular venue for soccer, cricket, softball and Australian rules football.

There are shops, schools, churches and a hospital to facilitate this self-contained community of over 5,000 people, many of whom are American, British and Australian servicemen.

Links with the outside world are provided by a fairly regular air service and railcar which runs three times weekly to Adelaide.

Occasionally I would go to Adelaide for a weekend, but the

nine-hour overnight journey discouraged more frequent excursions. Whenever the urge to get away from my isolated habitat arose there was never any lack of car owners travelling to Adelaide only too pleased for company on the long and arduous journey.

80 miles north of Woomera are the opal fields of Andamooka, a popular spot for Woomera weekenders. Occasionally I would travel up with my South African drinking partner, Jim.

It's an unusual journey northwards: I should imagine rather like driving on the moon, barren and dusty. A few parched shrubs dot the landscape, but they are the exception. Now and then the dazzling glint of the sun on a distant salt lake breaks the monotony.

The going is rough. The road, little more than a potholed, rock-strewn track, plays havoc with tyres and suspension. We had two 'blowouts' on our first trip to Andamooka. Having used up our two spares, we could ill afford a further mishap. To be stranded for long in the outback can be far from pleasant in these extreme climatic conditions, where temperatures well over the century mark are the rule. Fortunately fate decided we had had our fair share of bad luck and allowed us through without further mishap.

About the only signs of habitation between Woomera and Andamooka are a couple of sheep stations. Lonely outposts, indeed, but a welcome sight for the traveller who may have lost hope of seeing civilisation again.

A 'paperchase' across the desert of empty beer cans and mutilated tyres guides us to the opal town. Introducing Andamooka are hundreds of white mounds, the aftermath of opal diggings.

There can be few townships the likes of Andamooka, inhabited by very much a floating population, a cosmopolitan mixture of Yugoslavs, Italians and Greeks. Australians were in the minority.

Homes are primitive: a small tin or stone shack or maybe an underground dugout. The few houses of any luxury or size belong to the opal buyers whose affluent status suggests that the outback can be

Emus in the outback.

*The opal settlements
at Andamooka.*

*The main road
into Andamooka.*

kind to some. For the everyday miner it's a subterranean existence, living in hope of the elusive opal seam. A few do hit the jackpot, a fitting reward for such a nomadic existence. Others are not so lucky, but I still did not see anyone starving, and by the way they downed their beer it cannot be all that bad.

Many visitors come to Andamooka to try their hand at 'fossicking'. Days spent grovelling through the blancoed mounds, which have been thrown up by the miners, in the search for scraps of opal that the 'regulars' had missed.

Jim and I spent many hours searching through the piles of rubble, but found nothing. Still, there was always the off chance, and besides, it was fascinating to wander amongst the 'claims' and see the primitive mining devices still in use.

Heavy machinery is increasingly being used. Bulldozers were gouging huge chunks out of the ground in the hope of finding a short cut to an opal seam. Mechanical boring devices are used to drill the initial hole in which the miner will lower himself before he starts to tunnel his way underground.

Law and order are practically non-existent. Claims are jealously guarded. Only the week previous to my visit, a gelatin bomb had exploded outside a rival's shack.

There seems to be little respect for law and order. Untaxed, near-vintage cars rattle along the potholed dust tracks that masquerade as streets. Why should they bother with officialdom? The nearest police force is some 80 miles away at Woomera. It is said of the opal miners that they refuse to pay tax. For that reason, the government have yet to install electricity or roads.

During Jim's and my stay in Andamooka it was comparatively peaceful, with the exception, understandably, of the bar, which was in the usual Australian uproar. Talk was of opals, claims, finds and prices. Greeks, Yugoslavs and Italians gibbered in their typically excitable manner.

Practically hidden behind scrub we discovered a very interesting shack. A scribbled notice stated that it was a museum. Inside the 'cupboard'-sized room is an assortment of old prospecting relics from the pioneer days. An old wheelbarrow that had been pushed from Adelaide to Coober Pedy in the mid-north, a distance of some 500 miles. Old newspapers and implements told the harshness of a bygone era.

A 'mildewed' swagman shuffled across the dusty main street oblivious to the hordes of dogs yapping at his feet. He disappeared into a hole. Maybe his 'claim', but more likely his home. We did not stay long enough to see if he would reappear. It was time to leave this forsaken town in the outback.

From Andamooka we headed southwards towards the comparative sanity of Woomera.

Dusk was falling as we arrived at Arcoona sheep station. The jackaroo's horses were having a final prance in the large corral before settling down in the deep tangerine glow of the desert twilight. Here at Arcoona is held an annual woolshed dance which takes place in the huge, hangar-sized woolshed, a social event that attracts revellers from all over Australia. Akin with most outback stations, Arcoona's 'spread' covers an area the size of an average English county.

Desert and sky merged as we proceeded in the vacant blackness of the nocturnal outback. Comforting it was to see the homely glow of Woomera's lights as we approached the prohibited area of the rocket range.

The months slipped quickly past. Island Lagoon station had tracked its final space mission. Now it was time to get down to the work of dismantling and packing up, a job that was scheduled to take up to five months. Each week saw the departure of members of staff: our ranks were being depleted. Sad though it was to see familiar faces go, it was not without its jovial side. Farewell parties and barbecues were thrown with increasing gusto. No club or bar escaped our riotousness. Few heads escaped the mornings' thumpings.

We had to contend with not only our own farewell parties, but also the everyday round of coming and going parties of the Woomera establishments. On the rare occasions when there were no parties on, along with my two exuberant mates, Jim and Ron, I would soon make one. Usually in the women's quarters! Where else? On nights when our thirst overran the drinking time, Jim and I would journey 30 miles north to Koolymilka, one of Woomera's outposts, where Ron had the congenial job of barman. Whatever time we arrived, Ron was only too pleased to open the bar, resulting in sessions that often lasted through the night. There is nothing like bending the rules in the lion's den. Koolymilka was the headquarters of the Commonwealth Police.

The road between Woomera and Koolymilka was a favourite spot for kangaroos. Many a time we nearly came to grief at their expense. On one occasion Jim almost wrecked the front of his car when he collided with an oversized roo.

Most weekends there were dances in one club or another. With such a small percentage of females there was plenty of competition. After a while even the plainest of Janes took on the looks of a ravishing Madonna. "Take note, plain Janes, go to Woomera and be an instant beauty." Some of the male fraternity found the competition too fierce and fell into the outback web by sheltering behind an alcoholic haze.

One of my best friends at Woomera was Ken, an Aborigine whose love for the amber liquid was matched by his passion for painting and Aussie rules football. The rivalry in the latter between the four teams at Woomera was fierce, culminating in many scraps, both on and off the field.

I played soccer for a full season and though not of great standards, we did manage to create sufficient interest to raise four teams and make it competitive. If ever we did win, it was always an excuse for celebration. As if we needed any excuse! One evening a week our team would religiously meet in one of the clubs for a training session. Unfortunately, only our right elbow received any exercise.

The summer heat was now upon us, beer sweated out of us. Any hopes of an easy last few months were quashed. Time was running out for us. The deadline set by NASA was drawing nigh. With only a month to go there was still much to be dismantled and crated up. The majority of gear was being shipped back to America, whilst others would be transported to other tracking stations in Australia.

Staff had now dwindled to about ten, too few for the amount of work still to be done. There were few idle moments. We were now paying the price for the relaxation after the final tracking mission over four months ago.

Along with the majority of the staff I accepted a request to stay on an extra week in an attempt to tie up the many loose ends. Company vehicles had to be sold, hired ones returned, offices cleared out, waste to be burnt etc. The list seemed endless, but we ploughed on. What work still needed to be done after our allotted period would be left in the hands of government personnel from Woomera. Vans and artics ferried to and fro, taking away crates as fast as we could pack them. Slowly but surely, rooms and offices were emptied.

An atmosphere of desolation and nostalgia hung around the lagoon. Even the kangaroos appeared to sense the upheaval, peeping inquisitively around buildings as if waiting for us to depart before claiming the station for themselves.

In my opinion a year at Woomera is just about enough. It is so easy to fall into a rut. Even so, I had my misgivings as my 'date' drew nearer. I had had some great times, not undue to the many friendly acquaintances I had made during my stay. These were times for reminiscing. Like the occasion when I was woken up at 4 am and had a bottle of wine thrust down my throat and my bed filled with crisps and biscuits with the compliments of Ron and Jim. My punishment for chickening out on a midnight cheese and wine party – more wine than cheese.

May 4th, my final date, drew nigh. The final fling of farewell parties was behind us, concluding with a rather elite affair given with the compliments of the firm: a six-course meal with champagne. Misty heads, slurred speeches, parting handshakes and exchanged addresses.

Liquid renderings of "We'll meet again" and "Auld Lang Syne" drifted from the bars. A fitting conclusion to an eventful year. I had completed my intended duration in Australia, now it was time for me to start the homeward trek. This I planned to do in a less arduous fashion than the outward journey.

Bookings were made for a berth on a ship travelling to England from Sydney via the US, thus completing my round-the-world trip. My fourteen months' employment had reimbursed my outward journey's expenses and more than paid for my return trip.

From Woomera I got a lift for my final journey down the dirt road to Adelaide where I would be spending the weekend with friends. During this weekend, I spent an evening with Bo and Peggy who were now living in Adelaide. An evening of reminiscing, photographs, slides and lots of "do you remember?"

My friends drove me to Adelaide coach station where I was to catch the overnight Pioneer Express to Melbourne. It was dark by the time the coach left Adelaide, meandering its way over the Adelaide Hills, affording me my final glimpse of the city. A doormat of glow-worms before an aquatic threshold where the occasional light betrays some nautical hulk slinking through the Gulf St Vincent.

Excellent commentary by our driver kept us informed of our progress, though by now most of the passengers were more concerned with settling down for the night. First stop was at Murray Bridge where we crossed the Murray River and on through the Tailem Bend.

A night drive down the Dukes Highway offers little to the sightseer. We had to take the driver's word that we were passing through Coonalpyn, Tintinara or Keith. At 2 am we were woken to be informed that we were stopping for an hour's break at the motel at Bordertown near the Victoria state border. Drowsily I struggled through a coffee and roll before returning to the comfort of the coach, and sleep.

After only faint recollections of having passed through Horsham, Stawell, Ararat and Ballarat, I finally dozed off. Dawn was breaking: the hustle and bustle of an early morning Melbourne greeted me as I peered through hazy eyes out of the window.

I staggered off the coach. "Where do I go from here?" Inspiration seeped into my addled brain. I had an address of an old school friend of mine who was now residing in Melbourne. A phone call confirmed not only his whereabouts, but also an offer of accommodation for the night. As he was working I arranged to meet him at his office later in the day, leaving me the day to explore the city.

After the negative traffic problems of Woomera, the rush of Melbourne left me bemused. Trams rattled to and fro, snaking their way through a congested mob of mobile metal.

Like most Australian cities, you are never far from parklands. I crossed the Yarra by the Princes Bridge and strolled into the Alexandra Gardens. A peaceful refuge from the nearby vehicular madhouse. Nearby, amongst a vast expanse of greenery, is the futuristic structure of Melbourne's 'Bowl' where pop festivals and concerts are held in the open air.

Becalmed by the soothing peace of the parks, I wandered aimlessly past Government House and on into the Botanical Gardens. Ducks and swans glided sedately on the large ponds oblivious to the cackling humans. I got pleasantly lost amongst the maze of shrubs and plants, eventually finding myself on the banks of the Yarra River. Past the rowing club buildings, up over the bridge and back into Melbourne's main streets to be greeted with a medley of traffic noise and the acrid smell of exhaust fumes.

Unfortunately, my stay in Melbourne was brief. An evening of reminiscing over school days with my friend now living in suburban Watsonia, it was time to move on again. The following evening I was once again seated in a Pioneer coach, this time heading along the Hume Highway towards Canberra.

Little can be said of the journey northwards: it was dark and I was tired. I knew by looking at the map that we passed through Benalla, Wodonga and Albury on the New South Wales border. It was here that we stopped for another of those annoying middle of the night one-hour coffee breaks. At times like this I have little interest in the driver's information that we were at "the scenic jewel of the Murray Valley". Combining with Wodonga, Albury forms a thriving industrial complex and is also an important convention and exhibition centre and has many tourist attractions, including nearby Lake Hume. "Thank you, driver, now can I go back to sleep."

Continuing along the Hume Highway we proceeded to Gundagai, a small town put on the map by several popular songs. A lethargic dawn opened up a scene of fertile pastoral grasslands, heavily populated with fluffy lumps of Merino sheep. At Yass we diverted south and started the steady climb towards Australia's capital city, Canberra.

Canberra was living up to its reputation as being one of Australia's cold spots. A frosty mist hung over the modern city giving a refreshingly clean and virginal look about the place. It was a pleasant change from the heat of Woomera to see a white blanket of frost covering the ground. But having come unprepared for such a drop in temperature, I was soon shivering in my thin summer garb. Canberra is a splendid young city of lakes, gardens, trees, modern houses and buildings, home of Australia's parliament and an administration centre. Its elevated site accounts for its frequent chilly periods.

A breakfast and a quick stroll around and it was time to rejoin the coach for the final leg to Sydney. Canberra's mist gave way to beautiful, spring-like weather as we neared Goulburn, a commercial centre for a prosperous pastoral and agricultural district. Here, too, is one of New South Wales's largest prisons, which can be seen from the northern approaches to the town.

The landscape becomes mountainous, though contrasting pleasantly with verdant farms and grassy slopes. Centre of this scenic area is Moss Vale, a town of beautiful homes and gardens, and along with Bowral is a popular tourist and health resort. Razorback Mountain, on the highway between Picton and Camden, affords impressive panoramic views.

All too soon industry and buildings take over, hinting at the approaches to Sydney's outer suburbs: Liverpool, Parramatta and the big city itself.

Sydney, cosmopolitan capital of New South Wales, is Australia's largest and must be its liveliest city.

I walked out of the coach station to be faced with centuries-old Georgian and Victorian architecture boldly punctuated by the towering concrete and glass canyons of the high-rise buildings which have been erected to cope with the city's thriving commercial status.

There was to be no accommodation problems for me whilst in Sydney. I had been invited to stay with a friend at Avalon, a coastal resort about 30 miles north of the city.

A surprise awaited me as I boarded the bus to Avalon. The conductor was one of my old shipmates from my seafaring days. Small world indeed.

Connecting the city area with the north shore suburbs is Australia's best known landmark, the magnificent Sydney Harbour Bridge. An engineering masterpiece and the longest arched bridge in the world. It has an eight-lane highway, two railway lines, foot and cycle paths. A sentinel overlooks the broad, sweeping harbour of Port Jackson which, with its 22 square miles of picturesque inlets and rivers, must rank as one of the world's most beautiful deep-water harbours. A recent addition to the harbour skyline is the Opera House, a unique and awe-inspiring structure looking everything like a conglomeration of concrete sails.

North of the bridge the mood simmers to a more suburban one. Neat, detached dwellings replace the more sombre commercial buildings. The sea was never far away. If it did disappear it was only to wait for us to round a bend. A gleaming chain of golden sandy beaches, playgrounds for surfers, skiers and other leisurely pursuits. Manly, Dee Why, Collaroy, Narrabeen – we must be getting near, but no, we still have Mona Vale and Newport to pass through yet. At last Avalon.

I could not see the sea, but I could hear its thundering applause as it pounded against the sand dunes.

With the help of a taxi I soon found my friend's house. Tucked away amongst thick foliage on a steep incline, barely a stone's throw from the beach. Pat and John were 'mine host' at my 'local' when I left England. They had recently emigrated and were in the throes of settling down to a new life down under. John had not forgotten my lust for the amber liquid and had fortified his beer supply, which by the early hours of the following morning was looking rather depleted.

Two eventful days of drinking, sightseeing, barbecuing and swimming ensued. The golden beaches of Avalon and Palm Beach played host for much of my time in Sydney.

Where is the beauty to surpass that of Sydney's northern coastline of coves and inlets? Uncrowded beaches sandwiched between an opal sea, and an almost tropical greenery which rises steeply from a 'buttered' shoreline.

My last Australian barbecue, only hours before the departure from Australia, was with Pat and John on a near-deserted Whale Beach. Across the dancing water of Pittwater I could see the emerald expanse of the Chase National Park, illuminated by a warm autumn sun, which slowly slipped beyond the headland and into Broken Bay, leaving its embers glowing in a flaming sky.

Reluctantly I gathered my gear and, enticed by a crate of Foster's, drove with Pat and John to Sydney's Circular Quay. From the Harbour Bridge I could look down on the illuminated frame of the *Australis*, the boat that I would be joining for the five-week trip home.

There was little of the elation that I suppose I should be feeling at the prospect of returning to my homeland. The last nineteen months or so had been so carefree, away from all the worries of strikes, unrest, inflation and all the other depressing forecasts that have become commonplace in the British way of life. However, the prospect of five leisurely weeks and friends and relatives to meet at the other end afforded some recompense, and after all I could always return 'down under'.

I was jogged back into this world by celebrating Aussies huddled round crates of beer. Farewells, welcomes, someone's lost, someone's crying. It was chaotic.

Having found my cabin, I rejoined Pat and John on the upper deck to finish off our crate of beer before the impatient hints from the ship's siren and incessant prodding from the tannoy hustled them off the boat.

Eventually the ship parted from the quayside, still secured by thousands of streamers reluctant to release their grip. Unable to hold the 35,000 tons of steel any longer, they parted, limping sadly into the murky dockside waters. I was caught in a crossfire of friendly insults and witticisms "Bugger off, you Pommie bastards." Friendly people, these Aussies: they mean no harm. Shouts and farewells faded away in the night. Faces merged into a rustling line of tearful flesh.

The ship backed its way out of Sydney Cove, showed its stern to the illuminated Harbour Bridge, pirouetted, gathered momentum, and steamed seawards, giving a final blast as it passed the Opera House – my last sight of Australia. The ship shrugged off its harbour attendants and sallied forth to challenge the elements.

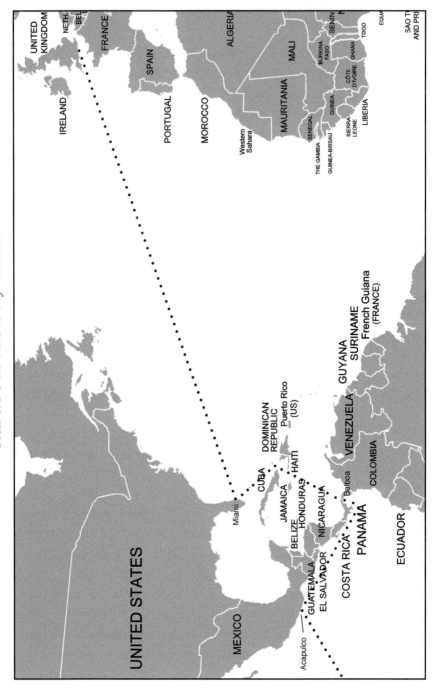

CHAPTER 20

SS *Australis*

The SS *Australis*'s brochure states that it is a compact, floating city where the chores and routine of everyday life are left behind, but the comfort and necessities travel with you. Well, I had nearly five weeks to verify their statement.

With twelve years' sea experience, shipboard life came easy. But what a relaxing change from my Navy days. Dancing every night, shows and cinema, whilst the days were spent sunbathing, swimming or playing deck quoits or volleyball.

Many of the passengers were young Australians whetting their appetite for a first taste of Europe. Any fear of female starvation was soon quashed. There was a welcome surplus helped by a large contingent of Australian nurses.

Three days since leaving Sydney we arrived at our first port of call, Auckland, on New Zealand's North Island.

Typically English weather greeted our arrival: a fine drizzle and a fresh breeze. But this did not dampen my enthusiasm to cram as much sightseeing as possible into the too short a time available.

A visit to the very English-looking university and the colourful Albert Park and thence to the top of Mount Eden. Mount Eden is some 650 feet above sea level and one of the highest of Auckland's many extinct volcanoes. A rustic sentinel that overlooks a beautiful panorama of Auckland and its suburbs. To one side stretched the widespread Waitematā Harbour, whilst on the other paraded Manukau Harbour.

Leaving Auckland's loftiest perch I descended to The Domain, nearly 200 acres of parkland in the heart of the city. A dormant sun stole much of the limelight, but imagination substituted for the solar indifference to display the gardens at their zenith. The nearby Winter Gardens with their lakeside gardens offer an all-weather alternative, a glass dome of steam where tropical plants and visitors indulge in masochistic perspiration. Aged homo sapiens fire away with their instamatics at defenceless orchids.

Our guidebook instructs us to visit Ellerslie Racecourse. This we did, but, like any other racecourse on non-race days, it looked rather naked without the horse and crowds.

In the inclement conditions the beaches of St. Heliers, Kohimarama and Mission Bay looked uninviting. But obviously inviting enough for the owners of the exclusive seafront properties.

In pouring rain I raced through the city's gaily lit shopping centre to the docks in time to beat the 11 pm sailing deadline.

A two-day voyage from Auckland brought us to Suva, capital and chief port of Fiji, the most important island group in the tropical South Pacific. Suva is the administrative, communication and trading centre of the group.

The area is one of the world's greatest regions of growing corals, and the reefs of Fiji are measured in thousands of miles. No doubt the captain was aware of this as he squeezed the *Australis* between the dangerous-looking reefs which surround Suva's harbour. Crystal-clear waters reveal jagged rocks and coral mobilised by hundreds of beautifully coloured fish.

The ship berthed a stone's throw from Suva's main shopping streets: market stalls heaped with a rich variety of tropical fruits, vegetables, fish and a host of other unidentifiable foodstuffs. Smiling Fijians selling baskets of necklaces, local shells, hand-carved boats and other souvenirs. Unlike most street vendors they did not appear offended when I did not make a purchase.

Although very much a bustling little city, Suva has that refreshing air of tranquillity. The Oriental bazaar atmosphere of Cumming Street, a fascinating meeting place of West and East where practically any commodity can be found in the many Chinese or Indian shops.

I boarded a bus for a tour of the island: it had no glass in the windows and wooden seats. Who needs comfort when travelling through such fascinating scenery as Fiji's?

From the beautiful botanical gardens with its tall King palms we drove along the palm-fringed golden beaches of Laucala Bay, where once flying boats ploughed to and fro New Zealand. Moving inland we crossed Fiji's largest river, the Rewa, which is navigable for many miles by small boats and punts.

The terrain becomes more primitive, dense tropical foliage, weeping fig trees, palms and garish displays of tropical flowers and plants. Narrow gravel roads wind through mountainous countryside. From our elevated position we get an occasional glimpse of the sea shimmering in the steamy tropical sun over a canopy of jungle greenery.

We stayed a while at a small Fijian village. Here the Fijians live in traditional thatched 'bures' – single-roomed wooden buildings raised off the ground on short stilts. They live simply enough, many working in the sugar industry which is the background of Fiji's economy. Coconuts, too, play their part. I watched fascinated whilst a Fijian 'fly-walked' up a towering palm to gather the fruit.

Fijians are habitually friendly. Everywhere I went I was greeted with a smile and a wave. There were offers to look around their homes, and they seemed honoured at having their photographs taken. Small children gladly enact a native dance, or was it just another tourist stunt? I do not think so. They seem so genuine, and even though they had willingly accepted a 'copper' or two there was no offence at a refusal.

We drove through forestry departments and native bush country across the Tamavua Heights to the Suva reservoir area where we stopped to admire a fantastic view of Suva Harbour, with the *Australis* looking little more than a toy plaything smoking contentedly alongside the miniature wharfs.

Our antiquated bus slithered cautiously down the mountainous track, its screeching brakes bemoaning its burden. The 20th century returned as we arrived at Suva's outskirts.

Resisting the temptation to bankrupt myself at Suva's duty-free shops, I spent the rest of my time browsing through the local markets, picking up an oddment here and there – not useful bits and pieces, but memories.

The sound of the *Australis's* siren jolted me: my time was running out. I raced back to the dockside and not too soon – the last gangway was about to be removed. A ceremonial police band played as the ship unshackled its tethers and headed once more between the reefs and into the Pacific.

Shortly after leaving Suva we crossed the International Date Line which meant us having to reverse our clocks 24 hours, thus giving us two Thursdays. There were now ten days before our next landfall. Perfect weather helped the days pass pleasantly, days spent sunbathing and admiring bikini-clad passengers. Dancing and riotous upper deck parties helped the nights along. When not suffering from a hangover there was always Zorba's dance lessons, deck quoits, volleyball and swimming to keep us occupied. Shows, beauty contests, fancy dress, bingo and quizzes. Never a dull moment. Being only human, we had to have a complaint. Ours we vented on the chefs whose Greek culinary delights ensured that if the normal shipboard activities did not keep you occupied, running back and forth to the loo would.

It was a gloriously hot, cloudless day as we approached Mexico's playground city of Acapulco. Steep, tree-clad hillsides closed in on us, and ahead the concrete and clay structures of the city. Like moths around a light, small boats flittered around us. A waterskier played in our boats wake, whilst at a safer distance a parachute skier lifted into the sky.

As soon as we had anchored, ship's tenders were ferrying passengers ashore. As we stepped ashore we were bombarded by vendors thrusting puppets, Mexican hats and other topical bric-a-brac. Doing what all good tourists do, I opted for an organised bus tour.

We were driven through Acapulco's crowded streets to the main square with its unique cathedral. Thence to the fort of San Diego: "Sorry, entrance forbidden". Leaving the city limits we continued up the hillside, a drive that offered a fantastic view of Acapulco. Below us, we could look down on a 'horseshoe' of golden beach caressing a brilliant blue sea. Luxurious hotels crammed the waterfront whilst mud huts and shacks cowered behind. From our elevated position we could look further afield to the spacious residences of the affluent. These homes, splattered amongst the tree-clad slopes, are the retreats of many American film stars. John Wayne's house was pointed out to us, but this was probably pure tourist patter.

Acapulco is not all wealth. A few miles outside the city we passed through squalid villages. Whitewashed huts glared in the hot, searing sun. It was siesta time. A wall is propped up by a bundle of colourful cloth crowned by a sombrero – a sleeping Mexican. Ragged, barefooted children kick a deflated football with 'cup final' ferocity.

Before returning to Acapulco we were taken to the Aztec Hotel, a luxurious concrete pyramid where bed and breakfast could cost you up to £100 a night.

Acapulco is the home of the famous cliff divers. From the clifftop balcony of the Hotel El Mirador we shared the suspense as we watched the fearless divers plunge over 136 feet into the sea from the cliff of La Quebrada. The ordeal starts as the divers scale the near-vertical cliff face to the appropriate ledge. The divers offer a prayer at the cliff edge altar before composing themselves for the ordeal. Skilfully judging the ebb and flow of the tides (a miscalculated dive would mean 'curtains' for the diver), they take the breathtaking plunge poised in mid-air for what seems minutes, before hitting the water with a resounding splash to reappear triumphantly to the tumultuous applause from the awed crowd.

Acapulco cliff divers.

'SS Australis' going through the Panama Canal.

The 'mule' trains pulling the 'SS Australis' through the Panama Canal.

Returning to the city, I joined up with friends off the *Australis* for a more informal tour of Acapulco, away from the expensive hotels and tourist traps. There are still many parts of Acapulco unspoilt by rich American tourists.

Backstreets of Acapulco, the Mexico I imagined. Dormant Mexicans in sombreros and ponchos shelter from the hot sun beneath whitewashed walls of a stone 'cubed' house. A rotund woman throws a pail at a disappearing group of ragged children who have just stolen some fruit from her stall. There passes a heavily laden donkey, its saddlebags full of an unknown fruit, plodding sleepily past. Its owner ambles behind as if in a trance. In a cloud of feathers a chicken throws itself out of a window followed closely by a mangy dog who soon gives up the chase and retires to the shade of a giant cactus. A goat fossicks amongst a pile of rubbish and disappears into a dingy bar. A small boy tries to sell us some Mexican jumping beans (they really do jump). We decline, but his woeful look compels us to recompense him with a few cents.

Life, at least in this part of Acapulco, remains Mexican, unaffected by the dollar influx.

Normality returns as we approach the beach. They say the beach is golden, but it was hard to see. It was covered by a field of coloured 'mushrooms' shielding masochistic tourists. Changing huts stand sentry alongside straw-covered shelters. Ice creams, milkshakes, candyfloss, suntan lotions. Just add water and a pinch of sand – instant holidays, eeuch!

There was a last-minute rush to rid ourselves of our 'loose' Mexican currency at the bazaar: gaily lit corridors of overstocked souvenirs sold at inflated prices. But why should the stallholders care? – the tourists will buy. Useless oddments to be taken home, shown off, and then relegated to some insignificant corner to collect dust.

A beautiful moonlit sky guided us out of Acapulco. Neon hoardings flashed abusively on the hillside. The city's lights flickered out, leaving us becalmed with the soothing serenade of a passive Pacific.

Hugging the Central American coast we sailed southwards to our next port of call – Balboa, the terminal port for the Panama Canal. Our first sight of land was a group of small islands known as the Fortified Islands. These islands are connected to the mainland by a long causeway which was built from the rock excavated in the construction of the canal.

Our stay in Balboa was brief, barely eight hours, but long enough. There is hardly anything there to set the tourist brochures alight.

Dawn was breaking as we slipped from our moorings for the ten-hour journey through the canal to the Atlantic. It was humid and overcast with a steady drizzle which dampened my enthusiasm at getting up so early to see the unique operation of lifting the *Australis* 85 feet above sea level.

Still at sea level we followed the canal channel to Miraflores Locks, where we passed through the huge lock gates to be placed on the first step of the giant water stairway.

These huge lock gate 'leaves', 82 feet high and weighing 730 tons, are swung back into recesses along the concrete walls, enabling the *Australis* to enter the first chamber. The initial gate 'leaves' are the tallest in the canal system due to the extra tidal variations encountered from the Pacific Ocean. Most of the other gates are slightly less than 50 feet in length and just under 400 tons in weight. The 'leaves' are compartmental so that they practically float in the water, thus reducing strain on the giant hinges.

With no perceptible notion or disturbances and with uncanny swiftness the *Australis* is lifted the first two steps in the water stairway at Miraflores and is raised the third and final step at Pedro Miguel which is about a mile away at the other side of Miraflores Lake.

We were towed from chamber to chamber by six electric locomotives (mules) which are connected to the ship by wire hawsers and run along a lockside cogged track. No pumps are used to operate the locks, since the flow of water is produced by the force of gravity.

From Pedro Miquel lock we proceeded through the eight-mile Gaillard Cut. This cut represented half the total excavation of the entire canal and opened out into Gatun Lake. Gatun Lake was originally formed by the damming of the Chagres River, with a length of 23 miles the largest man-made body of water in the world.

Either side of us dense tropical undergrowth slipped leisurely past. A steamy emerald mass of jungle.

We were not alone in the canal: a continuous parade of ships filed past for our scrutiny along this maritime jugular vein. Ships of all sizes and nationality. This is no place for faint-hearted navigators. Scattered along the canal banks are numerous hulks of ships that never 'stayed' the course.

During the 50-mile passage through the canal we were given a commentary on the canal's history. The first tangible efforts to build the canal began in 1880 by the French Canal Company under the leadership of Ferdinand de Lesseps, the builder of the Suez Canal. From the outset problems befell the canal. Inadequate machinery, insecure financial arrangements and the scourge of yellow fever, malaria and labour problems contributed to the failure of the venture in 1889. In 1894 a new French canal company was formed and made modest progress until taken over by the US Government in 1904, when the work was entrusted to the control of the US Army Corps of Engineers, with much of the labour being supplied by natives from the West Indies. This purchase followed the negotiations of a treaty with the Republic of Panama, which in the previous year had declared its independence from Colombia. This treaty granted the US full sovereign rights over the 10-mile strip of land now known as the Canal Zone. It covers an area of some 600 square miles.

The canal was unofficially opened on August 15th 1914, but not officially opened until July 20th 1920. At present the canal handles about 12,000 ships annually.

What goes up must come down, and we were no exception. Having been raised 85 feet, we now had to be lowered. This we did at Gatun when in a one-mile stretch we were hustled through three locks which lowered the *Australis* the 85 feel to the level of the Atlantic Ocean. Emerging from the final lock we were confronted by an armada of ships awaiting their turn to take the short cut to the Pacific.

The outstretched arms of the long breakwater of Cristobal Harbour welcomed us to the Atlantic Ocean.

Plucking ourselves from the canal bottleneck, we settled down again to normal shipboard routine after our fascinating ten-hour diversion.

The humid atmosphere of the Central American latitudes cleared as we nosed northwards to the clearer air of America's Florida coastline.

Port Everglades was to play host for our brief stay in America. Only a stone's throw from American's playground city of Miami. Miami's a disappointing city of high-rise hotels and crowded beaches. I preferred the less commercialised Fort Lauderdale.

A short walk from the rambling Everglades docks brought me to Fort Lauderdale's Ocean World. An aquarium of performing porpoises and sea lions, wrestling alligators, turtles, sharks and playful monkeys. So much to see and so little time. I wandered on towards the beach. Six glorious miles of sun-spangled beach front Fort Lauderdale, bordered by tropical palms and an irresistible pounding surf. There is a little conglomeration of offensive buildings to mar the beaches and to cast hulky shadows. Offshore barrier reefs tame heavy seas, leaving inshore waters calm.

The Gulf Stream passes close to Lauderdale's beaches, providing all-year-round central heating. Adding to the city's fascination is a beautiful myriad of waterways, 165 miles of lagoons, rivers and canals meandering through the city. Everybody seems to live on an island, and marinas are as common as car parks. Flamboyant islands accommodating handsome homes, luxurious yachts and big cars.

Just outside Suva, Fiji.

Fort Lauderdale, Florida.   *Beach front, Miami.*

Dollars do not seem in short supply and everyone seems to go out of their way to let you know. Still, with a milkshake at 50p they need it. Expense aside, this corner of America is really beautiful. Tropical yet not uncomfortable. Where wild orchids grow on trees and stilt-legged birds wade in the shallows of this American Venice.

Wide streets and tree-lined boulevards, expensive streets and big cars. This is America.

To the brassy sounds of a shoreside band, the *Australis* gingerly manoeuvred out of Everglades harbour, past shouting well-wishers and a cavalcade of hooting harbour craft. There was a short delay whilst the ship stopped to embark three girls who had missed the boat, saved from a financially embarrassing position by the generosity of the police launch.

The sun, beneath a pelmet of gathering storm clouds, was setting over Florida as we steamed towards the closing curtains of an Atlantic dusk. We were now on our last legs, the final stride before England, a seven-day jaunt across the Atlantic.

It was three weeks since we boarded the *Australis*. Shipboard life was becoming familiar. Friends had been made, alliances sealed and romances blossomed. Parties gathered momentum as if this was the final fling before the big crunch. Some of us were returning to start a fresh life in England. But for most of the young Australians this would be their first visit to Europe.

Apprehension must be creeping in. I know it did with me a few days prior to my arrival in Australia. The step had been taken: there could be no turning back now.

Upper-deck activities were tempered as we headed north. Bikinis disappeared and deckchairs became vacant. The final transformation came when half a dozen icebergs passed closely by. The captain's assurance that they were breakaway flows from the Arctic ice fields melting in the spring temperatures did little to dispel our suspicions that we had overstepped our right-hand turn.

Apart from the weather, which had become foggy, the first hint of our nearness to England came from a cricket commentary from John Arlott on the New Zealand versus England Test match.

There was now little left of the voyage apart from the captain's farewell dinner and cocktail party and the packing, passport checking and form-filling in preparation for British immigration and custom officials.

The day of reckoning arrived. A dawn champagne breakfast where the sadistic crunch of potato crisps did little to quell the hangover from the previous night's celebrations.

Somewhere in my head someone was sparring with a punchbag. I realised that my eyes had been replaced by two peeling red discs that tore into the flesh of my face.

I strained ahead and could see the misty outline of the Isle of Wight. Familiar sights, a hovercraft, the Needles Lighthouse, Cowes yacht marina, Nab Tower and the flaming stacks of the Fawley oil refinery.

Memories flooded back to nearly two years ago when I passed inconspicuously through these waters on the midnight 'milk run' ferry to France.

We arrived at Southampton to face the crowds waiting to welcome long-absent friends. Would anybody be there to greet me? I scanned the never-ending line of gesticulating figures. No, I did not recognise anyone: at least it would give me a chance to slip below for a can of beer. But wait, who's that jumping up and down? It can't be! Yes, it is, it's my sister and brother-in-law and two of my brothers and a nephew. And to think I slipped out of the country unnoticed.

I have been to well over 50 countries at the last count. Even so, there is still plenty left to see as I seem to have missed quite a bit along the way. I do not know why, perhaps lack of imagination, or maybe I did not concentrate on my geography or history whilst at school, which must make me one of the world's worst sightseers. I resent being one of a squad of instant tourists being bossed by guidebooks and under the command of noisy guides. I suppose I must class myself as a slipshod traveller. To me that little statue, bar or coffee house that one unexpectedly discovers down an alleyway means more to me than the temple one has been instructed to admire for erudite and probably incomprehensible reasons. I must be the only person to have visited Athens three times before bothering to pay my respects to the Acropolis.

What have I gained from my experiences? They have provided me with a much broader outlook on life. I had met and lived with people of many nationalities, cultures and beliefs which helped me to understand that there are so many different ways of life and to appreciate the freedom that a British passport makes possible.

Maybe we did keep a tight hold of the purse strings, but we had gained experiences and enjoyed ourselves much more than any G.T. Luxury tour could, and I hope that I have rekindled a spark that smoulders in us all.

Epilogue

Imagine doing that journey now in today's political climate. The roads are certainly a lot better, but the paperwork required would be enormous.

Yugoslavia has had a vicious war that has divided it into several different countries and factions. In Turkey, Istanbul, now just a typical modern city, is suffering from acts of terrorism. Syria has been ripped apart, and Aleppo, where we had been afforded such hospitality and kindness from its lovely inhabitants, has been all but destroyed. The desert that we drove across from Aleppo to Baghdad via Raqqa and Fallujah is now controlled by religious fundamentalists and terrorists. Deir ez-Zor has recently suffered a horrendous massacre of many of its civilian population by ISIS. Iraq has had enormous problems, having been ruled by a ruthless dictator, and suffered two wars by coalition forces, and is now imploding into a land of warring factions, where suicide bombings are part and parcel of everyday life.

Iran is only just starting to open its doors to travellers after years of upheaval and instability since the fall of the Shah. Afghanistan has fostered the Mujahedin and now the Taliban, and has been invaded by Russian, American and coalition forces.

As has been happening for the last two thousand years or so, feudalism is a way of life among the tribesmen and warlords who are still fighting amongst themselves, and will continue to do so with or without outside intervention. The northern parts of Pakistan are now a virtual no-go area for Westerners wanting to travel there. Sri Lanka, where we were treated as honoured guests, is slowly recovering from a bloody civil war with the Tamil Tigers. There is still tension between India and Pakistan, though the conflict thankfully ended quite soon after we had left.

Thailand is now well and truly on the tourist trail. Malaysia's capital, Kuala Lumpur, is now a vast modern city, whilst Singapore is a sterile metropolis; the small fragment of what is left of Chinatown is now just part of Singapore's "must see" tourist agenda. The delightful original Bugis Street, where we spent many a happy night, has long since been replaced, consigned to memory.

If anyone attempted a similar trip now I'm sure they would be armed with sat nav, mobile phones, social media, iPads, Google Maps, TripAdvisor and every other modern aid that's out now to assist them.

I often wonder what happened to Sweaty Betty since I last saw her on that isolated desert road in no man's land between Afghanistan and Pakistan. Was she used to smuggle hashish or opium, or was she used as a toy for some warlord? Maybe her heart gave out in the desert, and that is where she still lies, a long way off from her humble beginnings on a pig farm in Somerset.

I did hear a rumour that has come back with the troops returning from Afghanistan that, whilst on guard duties at night, as dawn arrived they had visions of white Toyota pick-up trucks approaching through the desert mist and sand, and they were always led by a ghostly blue Series 1 Land Rover with a machine gun welded on the back. If only Sweaty Betty could talk, I'm sure she would have an amazing story to tell.

The world has changed so much in such a short time; I'm just so glad I experienced it before that change came about.

As Bob Dylan once sang, "the times they are a-changin'".

Glossary

Bure	Wood and straw hut, or a structure built with anything that comes to hand.
Char-kway-teow	Rice noodles stir-fried with shrimp or chicken, chives and soy sauce.
Dal	Lentils, peas and beans.
Gecko	Small lizard which has the ability to walk up walls and hang from ceilings.
Ghee	Indian type of butter.
Kampong	Malaysian hamlet or village.
Liana	Emerald creeper plant, jade vine.
Mee	Malaysian noodle dish.
Roti John	Malaysian omelette sandwich.
Samsui women	Chinese immigrants who came to Singapore in search of industrial and construction jobs.
Souk	A market stall.
Tongkang	Small, wooden boat used for carrying goods.

History

Ceylon   Now Sri Lanka.
Drachma   Pre-euro Greek currency.
Ivangrad   Now in Montenegro but renamed Berane in 1992.
Madras   Now Chenai.
Malaya   Now Malaysia.
Titograd   Now called Podgorica (since 1992) and is the
              administrative centre of Montenegro.
Singapore   Singapore has got its independence.
Skopje   Now in the Republic of Macedonia and its
              capital, and financial and political centre.
Yugoslavia   Now divided into Bosnia and Herzegovina,
              Croatia, Kosovo, Macedonia, Montenegro, Serbia,
              Slovenia and Vojvodina.

Acknowledgements

My thanks to Margaret Castle for typing my handwritten manuscript and pointing me in the right direction.

To Dave Markham for reading through it and correcting my English and highlighting my PC gaffes.

To Daniel and Lee for their constructive criticism and suggestions.

To Richard Williams for help in jogging my memory and his contribution and input to this story.

To Tim Evans for mothering Sweaty Betty and keeping her rolling.

To Ron Harvey for being Ron and making up the crew at such short notice which enabled this venture to get off the ground.